Android Application Development

Rick Rogers, John Lombardo, Zigurd Mednieks, and Blake Meike

O'REILLY®

Beijing · Cambridge · Farnham · Köln · Sebastopol · Taipei · Tokyo

Android Application Development

by Rick Rogers, John Lombardo, Zigurd Mednieks, and Blake Meike

Published by O'Reilly Media, Inc., 1005 Gravenstein Highway North, Sebastopol, CA 95472.

O'Reilly books may be purchased for educational, business, or sales promotional use. Online editions are also available for most titles (*http://mysafaribooksonline.com*). For more information, contact our corporate/institutional sales department: (800) 998-9938 or *corporate@oreilly.com*.

Editor: Andy Oram
Production Editor: Sumita Mukherji
Copyeditor: Genevieve d'Entremont
Proofreader: Sada Preisch

Indexer: Joe Wizda
Cover Designer: Karen Montgomery
Interior Designer: David Futato
Illustrator: Robert Romano

Printing History:

May 2009:   First Edition.

 This book uses RepKover™, a durable and flexible lay-flat binding.

ISBN: 978-0-596-52147-9

[M]   [11/09]

1257782723

Table of Contents

Part II.   Programming Topics

Preface

When Google announced the development of Android, the field of mobile platforms was already well established. Even in the narrower category of open source platforms, a number of viable alternatives were being pushed by proponents. Yet Android has stimulated not only widespread technical interest but rampant speculation about its potential to completely transform the world of the personal device. Instead of a convenient prop to support a set of familiar functions, such as phone calls, email, and restaurant lookups, the electronic device could become an open-ended window into the whole world—could become, in short, anything that the user and the developer could think to make it.

How much of the cogent analysis and fervid hype will come to pass can be discussed elsewhere; this book is for those who want to get to know the programming environment for Android and learn what they themselves can do to make a difference. We have spent many grueling months investigating the source code over multiple releases and trying out the functions of the library and development kit. We have been working hard to uncover the true Android, going beyond any documentation we could find online or in print.

This book, read carefully, can enable any Java programmer to develop useful and robust applications for Android. It also takes you into the internals in some places, so you know how Android supports what you're doing—and so you can play around with its open source code if you like.

Audience

This book is intended for experienced software developers who want to develop applications in the Android mobile environment. It assumes you have some experience with the Java programming language, with using Java to implement user interfaces, and that you are at least familiar with the technologies Android uses, such as XML, SQL, GTalk(XMPP), OpenGL-ES, and HTTP.

How This Book Is Organized

This book is organized around the core example program introduced in Chapter 2. Later chapters illustrate development techniques by adding to the example through implementing modular extensions, where this is feasible. Some chapters (and the Appendix) cover more advanced topics that are not required for many applications.

Part I, *Development Kit Walk-Through*, gets you started with the basics you'll need to write applications.

Chapter 1, *Getting to Know Android*, explains Android's place in the market and its basic architecture.

Chapter 2, *Setting Up Your Android Development Environment*, tells you how to download the software you need, including Eclipse and the Android plug-in, and how to get started programming.

Chapter 3, *Using the Android Development Environment for Real Applications*, describes the files that make up a typical Android program.

Chapter 4, *Under the Covers: Startup Code and Resources in the MJAndroid Application*, looks at the fundamental Java code and XML resources that every application needs.

Chapter 5, *Debugging Android Applications*, introduces a number of tools for debugging and performance, including Eclipse, logs, the Android Debug Bridge (**adb**), DDMS, and Traceview.

Chapter 6, *The ApiDemos Application*, offers a high-level tour of the sample Android code included in the toolkit, with tips for exploring it yourself.

Chapter 7, *Signing and Publishing Your Application*, shows you how to make your application ready for public use.

Part II, *Programming Topics*, explores in depth the major libraries you'll need, and shows you how to use them effectively.

Chapter 8, *Persistent Data Storage: SQLite Databases and Content Providers*, shows how to use the two most powerful means in Android for storing and serving data.

Chapter 9, *Location and Mapping*, shows how to determine and display the user's location, and how to use Google Maps.

Chapter 10, *Building a View*, introduces graphical programming on Android by explaining how to create and manipulate windows and views.

Chapter 11, *A Widget Bestiary*, covers the most popular and useful graphical interface elements provided by Android.

Chapter 12, *Drawing 2D and 3D Graphics*, shows how to lay out graphics, and delves into drawing, transforming, and animating your own graphics.

Chapter 13, *Inter-Process Communication*, covers Intents and Remote Methods, which allow you to access the functionality of other applications.

Chapter 14, *Simple Phone Calls*, shows how to dial a number from an application, and explains how Android carries out the request.

Chapter 15, *Telephony State Information and Android Telephony Classes*, shows how to get information about telephony service and phone calls, and offers a tour of telephony internals.

Appendix, *Wireless Protocols*, offers some background and history on wireless services.

Conventions Used in This Book

The following typographical conventions are used in this book:

Italic
> Indicates new terms, URLs, email addresses, filenames, and file extensions.

`Constant width`
> Used for program listings, as well as within paragraphs to refer to program elements such as variable or function names, databases, data types, environment variables, statements, and keywords.

`Constant width bold`
> Shows commands or other text that should be typed literally by the user.

`Constant width italic`
> Shows text that should be replaced with user-supplied values or by values determined by context.

 This icon signifies a tip, suggestion, or general note.

 This icon indicates a warning or caution.

Using Code Examples

This book is here to help you get your job done. In general, you may use the code in this book in your programs and documentation. You do not need to contact us for permission unless you're reproducing a significant portion of the code. For example, writing a program that uses several chunks of code from this book does not require permission. Selling or distributing a CD-ROM of examples from O'Reilly books does require permission. Answering a question by citing this book and quoting example code does not require permission. Incorporating a significant amount of example code from this book into your product's documentation does require permission.

We appreciate, but do not require, attribution. An attribution usually includes the title, author, publisher, and ISBN. For example: "*Android Application Development* by Rick Rogers, John Lombardo, Zigurd Mednieks, and Blake Meike. Copyright 2009 Rick Rogers, John Lombardo, Zigurd Mednieks, and Blake Meike, 978-0-596-52147-9."

If you feel your use of code examples falls outside fair use or the permission given here, feel free to contact us at *permissions@oreilly.com*.

Safari® Books Online

When you see a Safari® Books Online icon on the cover of your favorite technology book, that means the book is available online through the O'Reilly Network Safari Bookshelf.

Safari offers a solution that's better than e-books. It's a virtual library that lets you easily search thousands of top tech books, cut and paste code samples, download chapters, and find quick answers when you need the most accurate, current information. Try it for free at *http://my.safaribooksonline.com*.

How to Contact Us

Please address comments and questions concerning this book to the publisher:

O'Reilly Media, Inc.
1005 Gravenstein Highway North
Sebastopol, CA 95472
800-998-9938 (in the United States or Canada)
707-829-0515 (international or local)
707-829-0104 (fax)

We have a web page for this book, where we list errata, examples, and any additional information. You can access this page at:

http://www.oreilly.com/catalog/9780596521479

To comment or ask technical questions about this book, send email to:

bookquestions@oreilly.com

For more information about our books, conferences, Resource Centers, and the O'Reilly Network, see our website at:

http://www.oreilly.com

Acknowledgments

We'd like to thank Bill Dimmick, Brad O'Hearne, and Hycel Taylor for their thoughtful and careful reviews of this book under a high-pressure timeline.

Rick Rogers

Like anything worth doing, I suppose, this book ended up taking more time and effort than any of us planned in the beginning. I'd like to thank my coauthors and the great folks at O'Reilly for sticking with it and bringing the work to fruition, through all the twists and turns. I'd also like to thank my family and friends, who encouraged me all through the process, and lent an ear when I just needed to talk. Most especially, though, I want to dedicate the book to my wife, Susie, whose patience knows no bounds, and whose amazing attitude toward life is an enduring inspiration for me no matter what I'm doing.

John Lombardo

I would like to thank my wonderful wife, Dena, who kept life from interfering when I closed the office door to work on the book. I want to dedicate this book to my mother, Marguerite Megaris, who died suddenly in 2007. I gave her a copy of my first book, *Embedded Linux* (New Riders), back in 2001. She cracked it open to a page with some assembly code, looked at it for about 10 seconds, closed it, and said, "That's nice, dear." We had a good laugh over that. I'd also like to thank all the wonderful people at O'Reilly for all their hard work. I'd especially like to thank Andy Oram, who coddled and prodded us in just the right doses to keep the book humming along at a good clip.

Zigurd Mednieks

Thanks to Terry, Maija, and Charles for putting up with my schedule while I was writing, and to Andy Oram and my coauthors for letting me participate, and hopefully, contribute.

Blake Meike

I am very grateful to have been invited to work with such an amazing group of people. Thanks to Zigurd for suggesting it; Andy Oram for practically holding my pen; and Rick, John, and Isabel Kunkle for making those Thursday morning calls a pleasure. Thanks to Mike Morton for actually reading both the text and the code. Though it may seem obvious, thanks to the Google Android developers. Not bad guys. Not bad at all. Finally, love and thanks to my wife, Catherine, who never let me see any disappointment when I said, yet again, "Can't. Gotta work on the book this weekend." Yes, babe, let's do the bookcase now.

PART I

Development Kit Walk-Through

This book gets you started with Android. We'll explain what's special about Android's features and how its architecture achieves its goals, and show you how to get started programming. You'll learn the tools that let you write programs using Eclipse; run them on the Android emulator; and carry out debugging, tracing, and profiling. The last chapter in Part 1 shows you how to sign your program for public distribution.

CHAPTER 1

Getting to Know Android

Why Android?

Google's Android mobile phone software platform may be the next big opportunity for application software developers.

Google announced the Open Handset Alliance and the Android platform in November of 2007, releasing the first beta version of the Android Software Development Kit (SDK) at the same time. Within a matter of a few months, over 1 million people had downloaded versions of the SDK from Google's website. In the United States, T-Mobile announced the G1 Android mobile phone in October of 2008, and estimates are that several hundred thousand G1s were sold before the end of that year. There are already several competing mobile phone software stacks in the market, so why is there such interest in Android?

Android has the potential for removing the barriers to success in the development and sale of a new generation of mobile phone application software. Just as the the standardized PC and Macintosh platforms created markets for desktop and server software, Android, by providing a standard mobile phone application environment, will create a market for mobile applications—and the opportunity for applications developers to profit from those applications.

Why hasn't it been profitable to develop mobile applications for smartphones until now? And what are the problems that Android alleviates?

Fragmentation
> About 70 million smartphones were sold in 2007, so there are a lot of phones available to run applications, but each brand has a different application environment. This is particularly true of Linux-based phones, where each handset vendor has had to assemble scores of pieces of third-party software to create a viable mobile phone platform. There is no chance that they would all choose the same components to build a mobile smartphone.

Java was supposed to help this situation, with J2ME and the wireless Java recommendations (CDC, CLDC, MIDP, JTWI, MSA, etc.) providing a common applications environment across handsets. Unfortunately, almost every handset that supports J2ME also support vendor-proprietary extensions that limit the portability of applications.

Proprietary software stacks

Most existing smartphones use proprietary, relatively closed software stacks, such as Nokia's Series 60 with the Symbian operating system, or Microsoft's Windows Mobile. Modifications to these stacks (adding a driver, for example) have to be done either by the stack owner or by the handset manufacturer. The stacks are not open source, so changing anything in the stack is difficult at best. Most Linux-based phones to date have an open source kernel (as required by the GPL license), but keep other details of the software stack (application framework, multimedia framework, applications) proprietary.

Closed networks

Series 60 and Windows Mobile do allow the addition of third-party applications, but mobile operators often lock the handsets so applications cannot be added. The operators claim this is needed to preserve the integrity of their mobile networks, making sure that viruses and spam are not inadvertently installed by end users. It also suits the operator's business model, because their mobile phone customers are confined to the operators' "walled garden" of applications, both on the phone and in the network. Android includes an open catalog of applications, Android Market, that users can download over the air to their Android phones. It also allows direct loading of applications via USB connection.

Android gives developers a way to develop unique, creative applications and get those applications in the hands of customers. Hundreds of thousands of Android mobile phone users are already there, looking for the next clever or useful application, and that application could be yours.

The Open Handset Alliance

Google and 33 other companies announced the formation of the Open Handset Alliance on November 5, 2007. According to the joint press release from that day:

> This alliance shares a common goal of fostering innovation on mobile devices and giving consumers a far better user experience than much of what is available on today's mobile platforms. By providing developers a new level of openness that enables them to work more collaboratively, Android will accelerate the pace at which new and compelling mobile services are made available to consumers.

For us as mobile application developers, that means we are free to develop whatever creative mobile applications we can think of, free to market them (or give them, at our option) to Android mobile phone owners, and free to profit from that effort any way we can. Each member of the Open Handset Alliance has its own reasons for participating and contributing its intellectual property, and we are free to benefit.

The Open Handset Alliance integrates contributed software and other intellectual property from its member companies and makes it available to developers through the open source community. Software is licensed through the Apache V2 license, which you can see at *http://www.apache.org/licenses/LICENSE-2.0.txt*. Use of the Apache license is critical, because it allows handset manufacturers to take Android code, modify it as necessary, and then either keep it proprietary or release it back to the open source community, at their option. The original Alliance members include handset manufacturers (HTC, LG, Motorola, Samsung), mobile operators (China Mobile Communications, KDDI, DoCoMo, Sprint/Nextel, T-Mobile, Telecom Italia, Telefonica), semiconductor companies (Audience, Broadcom, Intel, Marvell, NVidia Qualcomm, SiRF, Synaptics), software companies (Ascender, eBay, esmertec, Google, LivingImage, LiveWire, Nuance, Packet Video, SkyPop, SONiVOX), and commercialization companies (Aplix, Noser, TAT, Wind River). The Alliance includes the major partners needed to deliver a platform for mobile phone applications in all of the major geographies.

The Alliance releases software through Google's developer website (*http://developer .android.com*). The Android SDK for use by application software developers can be downloaded directly from that website. (The Android Platform Porting Kit for use by handset manufacturers who want to port the Android platform to a handset design is not covered in this book.)

The Android Execution Environment

Applications in Android are a bit different from what you may be used to in the desktop and server environments. The differences are driven by a few key concepts unique to the mobile phone environment and unique to Google's intentions for Android. As you write applications for an Android handset, you will use these concepts to guide the design and implementation of the application:

Limited resources
> Mobile phones today are very powerful handheld computers, but they are still limited. The fundamental limitation of a mobile device is battery capacity. Every clock tick of the processor, every refresh of memory, every backlit pixel on the user's screen takes energy from the battery. Battery size is limited, and users don't like frequent battery charging. As a result, the computing resources are limited—clock rates are in the hundreds of MHz, memory is at best a few gigabytes, data storage is at best a few tens of gigabytes. Throughout this book we will talk about the mechanisms included in Android to optimize for these limited resources.

Mobile mashups

In the desktop Internet world, mashups make it very easy to create new applications by reusing the data and user interface elements provided by existing applications. Google Maps is a great example: you can easily create a web-based application that incorporates maps, satellite imagery, and traffic updates using just a few lines of JavaScript on your own web page. Android extends that concept to the mobile phone. In other mobile environments, applications are separate, and with the exception of browser-based applications, you are expected to code your applications separately from the other applications that are running on the handset. In Android you can easily create new applications that incorporate existing applications. Chapter 13 focuses on these mobile mashups.

Interchangeable applications

In other mobile software environments, applications are coded to access data from specific data providers. If you need to send an email from a Windows Mobile application, for example, you code explicit references to Pocket Outlook's email interface, and send the email that way. But what if the user wants to use another email client?

Android incorporates a fundamental mechanism (Intents) that is independent of specific application implementations. In an Android application, you don't say you want to send email through a specific application; instead, you say you want to send an email through whatever application is available. The operating system takes care of figuring out what application can send emails, starts that application if needed, and connects your request so the email can be sent. The user can substitute different browsers, different MP3 players, or different email clients at will, and Android adapts automatically.

Components of an Android Application

Your Android applications will be built from four basic component types that are defined by the Android architecture:

Activities

These are comparable to standalone utilities on desktop systems, such as office applications. Activities are pieces of executable code that come and go in time, instantiated by either the user or the operating system and running as long as they are needed. They can interact with the user and request data or services from other activities or services via queries or Intents (discussed in a moment).

Most of the executable code you write for Android will execute in the context of an Activity. Activities usually correspond to display screens: each Activity shows one screen to the user. When it is not actively running, an Activity can be killed by the operating system to conserve memory.

Services

These are analogous to services or daemons in desktop and server operating systems. They are executable pieces of code that usually run in the background from the time of their instantiation until the mobile handset is shut down. They generally don't expose a user interface.

The classic example of a Service is an MP3 player that needs to keep playing queued files, even while the user has gone on to use other applications. Your application may need to implement Services to perform background tasks that persist without a user interface.

Broadcast and Intent Receivers

These respond to requests for service from another application. A *Broadcast Receiver* responds to a system-wide announcement of an event. These announcements can come from Android itself (e.g., battery low) or from any program running on the system. An Activity or Service provides other applications with access to its functionality by executing an *Intent Receiver*, a small piece of executable code that responds to requests for data or services from other activities. The requesting (client) activity issues an Intent, leaving it up to the Android framework to figure out which application should receive and act on it.

Intents are one of the key architectural elements in Android that facilitate the creation of new applications from existing applications (mobile mashups). You will use Intents in your application to interact with other applications and services that provide information needed by your application. Intents and Intent Receivers are covered in more detail in Chapter 13.

Content providers

These are created to share data with other activities or services. A content provider uses a standard interface in the form of a URI to fulfill requests for data from other applications that may not even know which content provider they are using. For example, when an application issues a query for Contact data, it addresses the query to a URI of the form:

```
content://contacts/people
```

The operating system looks to see which applications have registered themselves as content providers for the given URI, and sends the request to the appropriate application (starting the application if it is not already running). If there is more than one content provider registered for the requested URI, the operating system asks the user which one he wants to use.

An application doesn't have to use all of the Android components, but a well-written application will make use of the mechanisms provided, rather than reinventing functionality or hardcoding references to other applications. URIs and Intents together allow Android to provide a very flexible user environment. Applications can be easily added, deleted, and substituted, and the loose coupling of intents and URIs keeps everything working together.

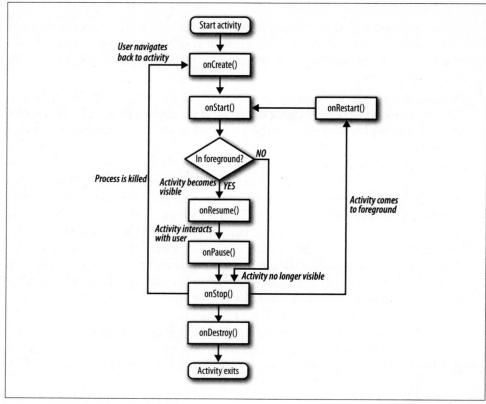

Figure 1-1. Android Activity lifecycle

Android Activity Lifecycle

Android is designed around the unique requirements of mobile applications. In particular, Android recognizes that resources (memory and battery, for example) are limited on most mobile devices, and provides mechanisms to conserve those resources. The mechanisms are evident in the Android Activity Lifecycle, which defines the states or events that an activity goes through from the time it is created until it finishes running. The lifecycle is shown diagrammatically in Figure 1-1.

Your activity monitors and reacts to these events by instantiating methods that override the Activity class methods for each event:

onCreate
> Called when your activity is first created. This is the place you normally create your views, open any persistent datafiles your activity needs to use, and in general initialize your activity. When calling onCreate, the Android framework is passed a Bundle object that contains any activity state saved from when the activity ran before.

onStart

Called just before your activity becomes visible on the screen. Once onStart completes, if your activity can become the foreground activity on the screen, control will transfer to onResume. If the activity cannot become the foreground activity for some reason, control transfers to the onStop method.

onResume

Called right after onStart if your activity is the foreground activity on the screen. At this point your activity is running and interacting with the user. You are receiving keyboard and touch inputs, and the screen is displaying your user interface. onResume is also called if your activity loses the foreground to another activity, and that activity eventually exits, popping your activity back to the foreground. This is where your activity would start (or resume) doing things that are needed to update the user interface (receiving location updates or running an animation, for example).

onPause

Called when Android is just about to resume a different activity, giving that activity the foreground. At this point your activity will no longer have access to the screen, so you should stop doing things that consume battery and CPU cycles unnecessarily. If you are running an animation, no one is going to be able to see it, so you might as well suspend it until you get the screen back. Your activity needs to take advantage of this method to store any state that you will need in case your activity gains the foreground again—and it is not guaranteed that your activity will resume. If the mobile device you are running on runs out of memory, there is no virtual memory on disk to use for expansion, so your activity may have to make way for a system process that needs memory. Once you exit this method, Android may kill your activity at any time without returning control to you.

onStop

Called when your activity is no longer visible, either because another activity has taken the foreground or because your activity is being destroyed.

onDestroy

The last chance for your activity to do any processing before it is destroyed. Normally you'd get to this point because the activity is done and the framework called its finish method. But as mentioned earlier, the method might be called because Android has decided it needs the resources your activity is consuming.

It is important to take advantage of these methods to provide the best user experience possible. This is the first place in this book we've discussed how programming for mobile devices is different from programming for desktop devices, and there will be many more such places as you go through later chapters. Your users will appreciate it if you write your activities with the activity lifecycle in mind, and you will ultimately benefit.

Android Service Lifecycle

The lifecycle for a service is similar to that for an activity, but different in a few important details:

onCreate and onStart differences
> Services can be started when a client calls the `Context.startService(Intent)` method. If the service isn't already running, Android starts it and calls its `onCreate` method followed by the `onStart` method. If the service is already running, its `onStart` method is invoked again with the new intent. So it's quite possible and normal for a service's `onStart` method to be called repeatedly in a single run of the service.

onResume, onPause, and onStop are not needed
> Recall that a service generally has no user interface, so there isn't any need for the `onPause`, `onResume`, or `onStop` methods. Whenever a service is running, it is always in the background.

onBind
> If a client needs a persistent connection to a service, it can call the `Context.bind Service` method. This creates the service if it is not running, and calls `onCreate` but not `onStart`. Instead, the `onBind` method is called with the client's intent, and it returns an `IBind` object that the client can use to make further calls to the service. It's quite normal for a service to have clients starting it and clients bound to it at the same time.

onDestroy
> As with an activity, the `onDestroy` method is called when the service is about to be terminated. Android will terminate a service when there are no more clients starting or bound to it. As with activities, Android may also terminate a service when memory is getting low. If that happens, Android will attempt to restart the service when the memory pressure passes, so if your service needs to store persistent information for that restart, it's best to do so in the `onStart` method.

How This Book Fits Together

Android is a sophisticated platform whose parts all work together: drawing and layout, inter-process communication and data storage, search and location. Introducing it in pieces is a challenge, but we've entertained the conceit of introducing the complexities of the platform in a linear order.

The platform is also so rich that we can't hope to show you how to use everything you want, or even a large subset of its capabilities. We expect you to consult the official documentation while reading this book and trying the examples. You should also use other online resources—but be careful about web pages or forum postings that have been around a while, because interfaces change. There is also a substantial amount of misinformation out on the Web; we discovered scads of it while writing the book.

This book is written for experienced developers who want to quickly learn what they need to know to build Android applications. The book is written with references to an example application (MJAndroid, discussed in much more detail in the next chapter) that you can freely download and reuse. The major topics covered in the book include:

New Android concepts

> Android builds upon a lot of legacy technology (Java, Linux, and the Internet, just to name a few), but it also introduces some new concepts needed to enable the application environment.

Android development environment

> We'll show how to install the free, open source Android development environment on your own system, and how to use that environment to develop, test, and debug your own applications. You'll not only learn the mechanics of using the system, but also what's going on behind the scenes, so you'll have a better understanding of how the whole system fits together.

Android user interface

> The Android user interface elements are similar to things you've seen before, but also different. We'll show you what the principal elements are, how they're used, and what they look like on the screen. We'll also show you the basic layout types available for the Android screen.

Intents

> Android makes it easy to leverage existing applications through the use of Intents. For example, if you want to dial a phone number, you don't have to do all the work in your application, or even know what applications are available that know how to dial. You can just ask Android to find you an installed application that knows how to dial out, and pass it the string of numbers.

Location-based services and mapping

> As you'd expect from a Google-sponsored environment, mapping and location are major features of Android. You'll see how easy it is to create sophisticated mapping and location-based applications.

Persistent data

> Android includes the `SQLite` database libraries and tools, which your application can use to store persistent data. Content providers, which we've already introduced, provide data to other applications. Using the libraries can be a little tricky, but in Chapter 8 we'll guide you through the creation of a database, and reading, writing, and deleting data records.

Graphics

> Your application has access to 2D and 3D graphics capabilities in Android. Animation and various advanced effects are also provided. This book will show you

how to use those libraries so you can build a compelling user interface for your application.

Communications

Android, even more than most smartphone operating systems, places great emphasis on communication—by voice, by text messaging, by instant messaging, and by Internet. You'll see how your application can take advantage of these capabilities so your users can become part of a larger community of data and users.

The next three chapters, Chapters 2 through 4, set you up with a working application, and will give you a sense of how the files and basic classes fit together. Chapter 5 empowers you to better understand what you're doing and helps you debug your first efforts.

The Android toolkit naturally comes with an enormous number of working code examples in its ApiDemos application. Unfortunately, its very size and sophistication make it a formidable castle for novices to enter. Chapter 6 guides you through it.

A bit of experience with ApiDemos will convince you that you need some more background and tutorial help. In Chapter 7, we'll show you how to sign and publish your application, which you need to do in order to test it with Google Maps, even before you're ready to go public.

Chapter 8 presents tutorials on two data storage systems.

Chapter 9 presents location and mapping, which are key features that draw people to mobile devices and which you'll surely want to incorporate into your application.

We then turn to a critical part of any end-user application, graphics, in three information-packed chapters, Chapters 10 through 12.

Chapter 13 takes another step into the complexity and unique power of Android, by discussing how applications can offer functionality to other applications. This allows for powerful mashups, which involve one program standing on the shoulders of other programs.

Let's not forget that Android runs on telephones. Chapters 14 and 15 wrap up the book by showing you how to place and track phone calls.

There's even more to Android than these features, of course, but programmers of all stripes will find in this book what they need to create useful and efficient programs for the Android platform.

CHAPTER 2

Setting Up Your Android Development Environment

Setting Up Your Development Environment

Android applications, like most mobile phone applications, are developed in a host-target development environment. In other words, you develop your application on a host computer (where resources are abundant) and download it to a target mobile phone for testing and ultimate use. Applications can be tested and debugged either on a real Android device or on an emulator. For most developers, using an emulator is easier for initial development and debugging, followed by final testing on real devices.

To write your own Android mobile phone applications, you'll first need to collect the required tools and set up an appropriate development environment on your PC or Mac. In this chapter we'll collect the tools you need, download them and install them on your computer, and write a sample application that will let you get the feel of writing and running Android applications on an emulator. Linux, Windows, and OS X are all supported development environments, and we'll show you how to install the latest set of tools on each. Then, we'll show you any configuration you need to do after installing the tools (setting PATH environment variables and the like), again for each of the three operating systems. Finally, we'll write a short little "Hello, Android" application that demonstrates what needs to be done in order to get a generic application running.

The Android SDK supports several different integrated development environments (IDEs). For this book we will focus on Eclipse because it is the IDE that is best integrated with the SDK, and, hey, it's free. No matter which operating system you are using, you will need essentially the same set of tools:

- The Eclipse IDE
- Sun's Java Development Kit (JDK)
- The Android Software Developer's Kit (SDK)
- The Android Developer Tool (ADT), a special Eclipse plug-in

Since you're probably going to develop on only one of the host operating systems, skip to the appropriate section that pertains to your selected operating system.

Creating an Android Development Environment

The Android Software Development Kit supports Windows (XP and Vista), Linux (tested on Ubuntu Dapper Drake, but any recent Linux distro should work), and Mac OS X (10.4.8 or later, Intel platform only) as host development environments. Installation of the SDK is substantially the same for any of the operating systems, and most of this description applies equally to all of them. Where the procedure differs, we will clearly tell you what to do for each environment:

1. **Install JDK:** The Android SDK requires JDK version 5 or version 6. If you already have one of those installed, skip to the next step. In particular, Mac OS X comes with the JDK version 5 already installed, and many Linux distributions include a JDK. If the JDK is not installed, go to *http://java.sun.com/javase/downloads* and you'll see a list of Java products to download. You want JDK 6 Update *n* for your operating system, where *n* is 6 at the time of this writing.

   Windows (XP and Vista)
   - Select the distribution for "Windows Offline Installation, Multi-language."
   - Read, review, and accept Sun's license for the JDK. (The license has become very permissive, but if you have a problem with it, alternative free JDKs exist.)
   - Once the download is complete, a dialog box will ask you whether you want to run the downloaded executable. When you select "Run," the Windows Installer will start up and lead you through a dialog to install the JDK on your PC.

   Linux
   - Select the distribution for "Linux self-extracting file."
   - Read, review, and accept Sun's license for the JDK. (The license has become very permissive, but if you have a problem with it, alternative free JDKs exist.)
   - You will need to download the self-extracting binary to the location in which you want to install the JDK on your filesystem. If that is a system-wide directory (such as */usr/local*), you will need root access. After the file is downloaded, make it executable (`chmod +x jdk-6`*version*`-linux-i586.bin`), and execute it. It will self-extract to create a tree of directories.

   Mac OS X
   Mac OS X comes with JDK version 5 already loaded.

2. **Install Eclipse:** The Android SDK requires Eclipse version 3.3 or later. If you do not have that version of Eclipse installed yet, you will need to go to *http://www .eclipse.org/downloads* to get it, and you might as well get version 3.4 (also known as Ganymede), since that package includes the required plug-ins mentioned in the next step. You want the version of the Eclipse IDE labeled "Eclipse IDE for Java Developers," and obviously you want the version for your operating system. Eclipse will ask you to select a mirror site, and will then start the download.

   Windows (XP or Vista)
   > The Eclipse download comes as a big ZIP file that you install by extracting the files to your favorite directory. For this book, we'll assume that you extracted to *C:/eclipse*. Eclipse is now installed, but it will not show up in your Start menu of applications. You may want to create a Windows shortcut for *C:/eclipse/ eclipse.exe* and place it on your desktop, in your Start menu, or someplace else where you can easily find it.

   Linux and Mac OS X
   > Note that, as of this writing, the version of Eclipse installed if you request it on Ubuntu Hardy Heron is 3.2.2, which does not contain all the plug-ins needed for Android. The Eclipse download comes as a big tarball (*.gz* file) that you install by extracting the files to your favorite directory. For this book, we'll assume that you extracted to */usr/lib/eclipse*. The executable itself is located in that directory and is named *eclipse*.

3. **Check for required plug-ins:** You can skip this step if you just downloaded a current version of Eclipse as we recommended. If you are using a preinstalled version of Eclipse, you need to make sure you have the Java Development Tool (JDT) and Web Standard Tools (WST) plug-ins. You can easily check to see whether they are installed by starting Eclipse and selecting menu options "Windows → Preferences...". The list of preferences should include one for "Java" and one for either "XML" or "Web and XML." If they aren't on the list, the easiest thing to do is reinstall Eclipse, as described in the previous step. Installing "Eclipse IDE for Java Developers" will automatically get the needed plug-ins.

4. **Install Android SDK:** This is where you should start if you already have the right versions of Eclipse and the JDK loaded. The Android SDK is distributed through Google's Android site, *http://developer.android.com/sdk/1.1_r1/index.html*. You will need to read, review, and accept the terms of the license to proceed. When you get to the list of downloads, you will see a table of distributions. Select the one for your operating system (XP and Vista use the same distribution). The package (file) names include the release number. For example, as this is written, the latest version of the SDK is 1.1_r1, so the filename for Windows is *android-sdk-windows-1.1_r1.zip*.

For versions 3.3 and later of Eclipse, the Android download site provides directions about how to install the plug-in through Eclipse's software updates utility. If you're using Eclipse 3.2 or the software update technique doesn't work for you, download the SDK from the Android site and install it using instructions in the next paragraph.

The file you download is another archive file, as with Eclipse: a ZIP file on Windows, a tar-zipped file for Linux and MacOS X. Do the same thing as for Eclipse: extract the archive file to a directory where you want to install Android, and make a note of the directory name (you'll need it in step 6). The extraction will create a directory tree containing a bunch of subdirectories, including one called *tools*.

5. **Update the environment variables:** To make it easier to launch the Android tools, add the *tools* directory to your path.

- On Windows XP, click on Start, then right-click on My Computer. In the pop-up menu, click on Properties. In the resulting System Properties dialog box, select the Advanced tab. Near the bottom of the Advanced tab is a button, "Environment Variables," that takes you to an Environment Variables dialog. User environment variables are listed in the top half of the box, and System environment variables in the bottom half. Scroll down the list of System environment variables until you find "Path"; select it, and click the "Edit" button. Now you will be in an Edit System Variable dialog that allows you to change the environment variable "Path." Add the full path of the *tools* directory to the end of the existing Path variable and click "OK." You should now see the new version of the variable in the displayed list. Click "OK" and then "OK" again to exit the dialog boxes.

- On Windows Vista, click on the Microsoft "flag" in the lower left of the desktop, then right-click on Computer. At the top of the resulting display, just below the menu bar, click on "System Properties." In the column on the left of the resulting box, click on "Advanced system settings." Vista will warn you with a dialog box that says "Windows needs your permission to continue"; click "Continue." Near the bottom of the System Properties box is a button labeled "Environment Variables" that takes you to an Environment Variables dialog. User environment variables are listed in the top half of the box, and System environment variables in the bottom half. Scroll down the list of System environment variables until you find "Path"; select it, and click the "Edit" button. Now you will be in an Edit System Variable dialog that allows you to change the environment variable "Path." Add the full path of the *tools* directory to the end of the existing Path variable, and click "OK." You should now see the new version of the variable in the displayed list. Click "OK" and then "OK" again to exit the dialog boxes.

- On Linux, the PATH environment variable can be defined in your *~/.bashrc ~/.bash_profile* file. If you have either of those files, use a text editor such as *gedit*, *vi*, or Emacs to open the file and look for a line that exports the PATH variable. If you find such a line, edit it to add the full path of the *tools* directory to the path. If there is no such line, you can add a line like this:

```
export PATH=${PATH}:your_sdk_dir/tools
```

where you put the full path in place of ***your_sdk_dir***.

- On Mac OS X, look for a file named *.bash_profile* in your home directory (note the initial dot in the filename). If there is one, use an editor to open the file and look for a line that exports the PATH variable. If you find such a line, edit it to add the full path of the *tools* directory to the path. If there is no such line, you can add a line like this:

```
export PATH=${PATH}:your_sdk_dir/tools
```

where you put the full path in place of ***your_sdk_dir***.

6. **Install the Android plug-in (ADT):** Throughout this book, we will make use of the Android Development Tool plug-in that Google supplies for use in building Android applications. The plug-in is installed in much the same way as any other Eclipse plug-in:

   a. Start Eclipse, if it's not already running.

   b. From the menu bar, select "Help → Software Updates → Find and Install...".

   c. In the Install/Update dialog, select "Search for new features to install" and click on "Next."

   d. In the Install dialog, click on "New Remote Site." A "New Update Site" dialog pops up. Enter a name for the plug-in ("Android Plugin" will do), and the URL for updates: *https://dl-ssl.google.com/android/eclipse*. Click "OK."

   e. The new site should now appear in the list of sites on the Install dialog. Click "Finish."

   f. In the Search Results dialog, select the checkbox for "Android Plugin → Developer Tools" and click "Next."

   g. The license agreement for the plug-in appears. Read it, and if you agree, select "Accept terms of the license agreement" and click "Next." Click "Finish."

   h. You will get a warning that the plug-in is not signed. Choose to install it anyway by clicking "Install All."

   i. Restart Eclipse.

   j. After Eclipse restarts, you need to tell it where the SDK is located. From the menu bar, select "Window → Preferences." In the Preferences dialog, select "Android" in the left column.

   k. Use the "Browse" button to navigate to the place you installed the Android SDK, and click on "Apply," then on "OK."

Congratulations—you have installed a complete Android development environment without spending a penny. As you'll see in this and subsequent chapters, the environment includes a very sophisticated set of tools to make Android programming easier, including:

- An Integrated Development Environment based on Eclipse, arguably the premier IDE for Java development. Eclipse itself brings many valuable development features. Google and OHA have taken advantage of Eclipse's extensibility to provide features customized for Android, including debugging capabilities that are tuned to the needs of mobile application developers like you.

- A Java development environment and Dalvik virtual machine that build on Sun's JDK foundation to provide a very sophisticated programming environment for your applications.

- A complete mobile phone emulator that allows you to test your applications without having to download them to a target mobile phone. The emulator includes features for testing your application under different mobile phone communication conditions (fading, dropped connections, etc.).

- Test tools, such as Traceview, which allow you to tune your application to take best advantage of the limited resources available on a mobile phone.

Hello, Android

So enough downloading; let's write a program. A "Hello World!" program is traditional, and we will start with something similar to demonstrate what you need to do to create, build, and test an Android application. We won't explore much of the Android API for this program—that's left for the following chapters—but here we'll get a taste for the development environment and the steps you go through to create an application for Android.

Where We're Going

There isn't much functionality in this program. We just want to display some text on the Android emulator window that says "Hello Android!" (see Figure 2-1).

Starting a New Android Application: HelloWorld

Several components are needed to build an Android application. Fortunately, the Eclipse IDE with the Android plug-in automates a lot of the work needed to create and maintain these components. We will start by using the IDE to create a project for our application. Start up Eclipse and select "File → New → Project..." from the menu bar (be sure to select "Project...", not "Java Project"). You'll see a list of project types, similar to the menu in Figure 2-2.

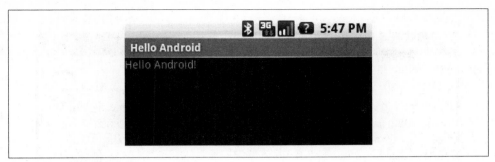

Figure 2-1. "Hello Android" screenshot

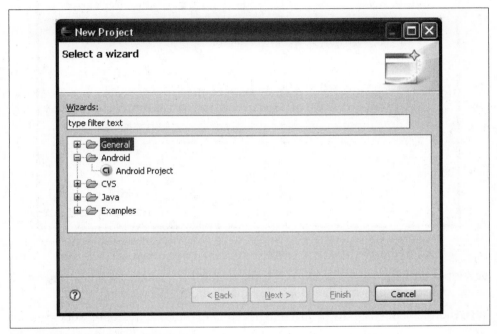

Figure 2-2. Eclipse New Project menu

Select "Android Project" and click "Next" to get the "New Android Project" dialog box (Figure 2-3).

We'll use "HelloWorld" as the name for both the Project and the Application. You don't need to change the button or checkbox selections, and we'll use the package name `com.oreilly.helloworld` as shown.

Every Android application has to have at least one Activity (an executable that usually has a user interface), so let's say we're going to include an Activity called `Hello WorldActivity`, as shown in the dialog box. Click "Finish," and the Android Software Development Kit does a number of things for you, to make your life easier as a

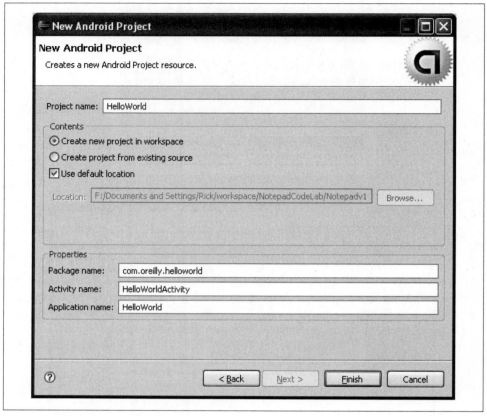

Figure 2-3. Eclipse New Android Project dialog

developer. In Figure 2-4, I've expanded the tree in the Package Explorer window to show some of the files and directories that the Android SDK created.

The Android SDK created a *HelloWorld* directory in the default Eclipse workspace for your project. It also created subdirectories for your source files (*.src*), references to the Android Library, assets, resources (*.res*), and a manifest file (*AndroidManifest.xml*). In each of the subdirectories it created another level of subdirectories as appropriate. Let's take a quick look at them:

Sources (under src)

- Contains a directory structure that corresponds to the package name you gave for your application: in this case, *com.android.helloworld*.

- Contains a Java template for the Activity you indicated was in the application (`HelloWorldActivity`) and may contain a directory of resource references (*R.java*). *R.java* is actually generated by the Android SDK the first time you compile your application; it contains the Java version of all the resources you define in the *res* directory (covered later). We'll come back to *R.java* later.

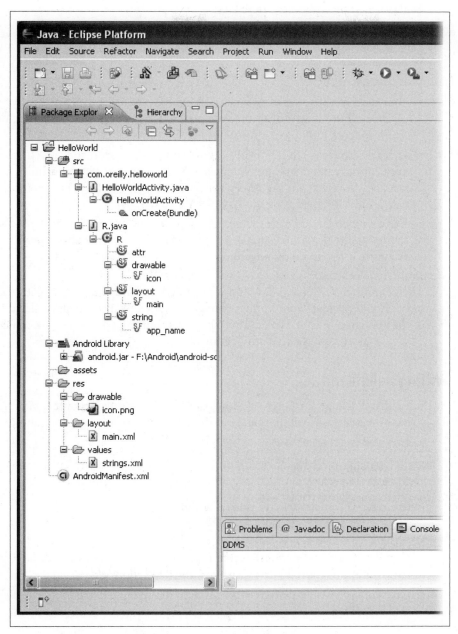

Figure 2-4. Eclipse project listing after creation of the HelloWorld project

Android Library

This is just what it says. If you like, you can expand the *android.jar* tree and see the names of the modules included in the library. This is where your application will go for Android library references.

assets

Files you want to bundle with your application. We won't have any for HelloWorld.

Resources (under res)

- Drawable resources are any images, bitmaps, etc., that you need for your application. For HelloWorld, the Android SDK has supplied us with the default Android icon, and that's all we'll need.

- Layout resources tell Android how to arrange items on the screen when the application runs. These resources are XML files that give you quite a bit of freedom in laying out the screen for different purposes. For HelloWorld, we'll just use the defaults generated by the Android SDK.

- Values are constants, strings, etc., available for use by your application. Keeping them outside the sources makes it easier to customize the application, such as adapting it for different languages.

Manifest (AndroidManifest.xml)

This is another XML file that tells the Android build system what it needs to know to build and package your application so it can be installed on an Android phone or the emulator. This file has its own specialized editor, which we'll describe when we get to more complicated applications.

Writing HelloWorld

In the Eclipse Package Explorer window, double-click on `HelloWorldActivity.java`. This opens the source file of that name in the center window, ready for editing:

```
package com.oreilly.helloworld;

import android.app.Activity;
import android.os.Bundle;

public class HelloWorldActivity extends Activity {
    /** Called when the activity is first created. */
    @Override
    public void onCreate(Bundle savedInstanceState) {
        super.onCreate(savedInstanceState);
        setContentView(R.layout.main);
    }
}
```

Looking quickly at the template code that the Android SDK has provided for us, we can note several things:

- The Android SDK has included the package reference we asked for, which is consistent with the directory structure it created.

- It has also created a (collapsed) set of imports for the library references it knows we need.

- It created a class definition for the Activity we said we wanted (`Hello WorldActivity`), including a method called `OnCreate`.

  For the moment, don't worry about the parameter passed into `OnCreate`. The `savedInstanceState` Bundle is a way of passing data between activities and storing data between instantiations of the same Activity. We won't need to use this for HelloWorld.

- One special line of code has been included in `OnCreate`:

  ```
  setContentView (R.layout.main);
  ```

  Remember that Android uses layouts to define screen layouts on the target, and that *main.xml* was the name of the default layout file that the Android SDK created for us under *.res/layout*. The *R.java* file is generated automatically and contains Java references for each of the resources under *.res*. You will never need to edit the *R.java* file by hand; the Android SDK takes care of it as you add, change, or delete resources.

Again in the Eclipse Package Explorer window, double-click on *main.xml* and you will see the default layout screen in the center window. There are two tabs at the bottom of the panel that say "Layout" and "main.xml". Click on the one that says "main.xml" to bring up the code version:

```xml
<?xml version="1.0" encoding="utf-8"?>
<LinearLayout xmlns:android="http://schemas.android.com/apk/res/android"
    android:orientation="vertical"
    android:layout_width="fill_parent"
    android:layout_height="fill_parent"
    >
<TextView
    android:layout_width="fill_parent"
    android:layout_height="wrap_content"
    android:text="@string/hello"
    />
</LinearLayout>
```

Again, let's look at the key features of this template code:

- Like any other XML file, this one starts with a reference to the XML version and encoding used.

- LinearLayout is one of the screen layout formats provided by the Android SDK. There are several others, which can be combined hierarchically to create very complex screen layouts. For our purposes, a simple linear layout is fine. More Layout types are covered later in the book in Chapter 11.

—The LinearLayout definition:

```
xmlns:android="http://schemas.android.com/apk/res/android"
```

identifies the XML schema being used.

—This code:

```
android:orientation="vertical"
android:layout_width="fill_parent"
android:layout_height="fill_parent"
```

defines an orientation, width, and height for the entire scope of the layout.

- TextView describes an area where text can be displayed and edited. It resembles the text boxes you may have encountered when programming in other graphical environments.

—Within the TextView definition:

```
android:layout_width="fill_parent"
android:layout_height="wrap_content"
```

define a width and height for the TextView box.

—This code:

```
android:text="@string/hello"
```

provides some text to display in the TextView. The actual string is defined in a separate file, *res/values/strings.xml*. If we open that file (again by clicking on it in the Package Explorer), we see a specialized string editor added by ADT. If you select "hello (String)" by clicking on it, you'll see the current value for that string. By a stroke of luck, the Android SDK has already included text that is close to what we wanted to display anyway. Just to show them who's boss, change the value of the String hello to say "Hello Android!", or something else equally clever.

Save the Project either from the Eclipse File menu (File → Save) or by clicking on the disk icon in the menu bar.

Believe it or not, we're done. We don't have to write a single line of Java to create this application.

Running HelloWorld

From the Eclipse menu bar, select Run → Run. A "Run As" dialog box will pop up. Select "Android Application" from the list, which displays the dialog shown in Figure 2-5.

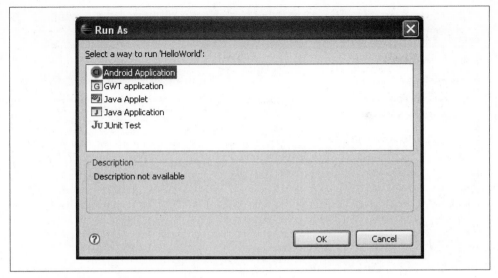

Figure 2-5. Eclipse Application Type selection

A command window will pop up, followed quickly by an emulator window that looks just like a mobile phone. The emulated phone will then go through its boot sequence, which takes a few minutes (relax; if anything goes wrong, it will tell you). After a few minutes you should see the screen shown in Figure 2-6.

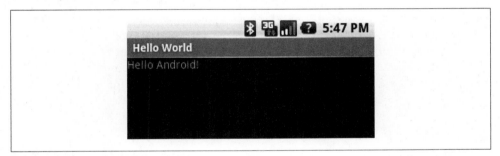

Figure 2-6. First try at HelloAndroid

Notice anything different between that screen image and the one we showed in Figure 2-1? The application prints out "Hello Android!", or whatever you wrote into the `android:text` line earlier, but it also displays the title of the application as "Hello World". Let's change the title to match our creative change to the application text.

In the Package Explorer in the left panel of the Eclipse workbench, reopen the *strings.xml* file (the one where we found the String `hello` before). This will open the file in the editing window. The intent of this file is to give you a place to define strings that will be used by your application, without actually embedding them in the Java source code. The other string that's defined here is `app_name`. To make things consistent, change the definition of `app_name` to `HelloAndroid`, as shown in Figure 2-7.

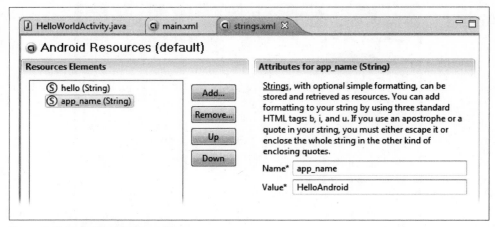

Figure 2-7. HelloWorld String editing

Now when we run the application, we get a screen that looks just like what we set out to do, as shown previously in Figure 2-1.

Congratulations! You've just created your first Android program by doing nothing more than changing the text in one line of code. There are much greater challenges ahead.

CHAPTER 3

Using the Android Development Environment for Real Applications

MicroJobs: This Book's Main Sample Application

We want to take a look at applications that are more complex than "Hello, Android," and that's what we'll do in this chapter. Based on the theory that it's often easiest to explain things through an example, we'll take an in-depth look at a more complex application, called MicroJobs. Some of the application's code modules are named MJAndroid, so we'll also use that name for the code associated with MicroJobs.

We'll first take a look at what we want the MicroJobs application to do, then we'll quickly get into the code itself. After looking at the structure of the application, we'll describe in detail how to build the application and how to get it running on the emulator. Finally, we'll take a look at some helpful debug hints in case you're developing a similar application and it doesn't start up. The reasons are not always obvious in the Android environment.

Android and Social Networking

One of the great promises of Android mobile phones is their ability to run applications that enhance opportunities for social networking between users. This promise echoes the reality of the Internet. The first generation of Internet applications were about user access to information, and many of those applications have been very popular. The second wave of Internet applications has been about connecting users to each other. Applications such as Facebook, YouTube, and many others enhance our ability to connect with people of similar interests, and allow the application's users to provide some or all of the content that makes the application what it is. Android has the potential to take that concept and add a new dimension: mobility. It's expected that a whole new generation of applications will be built for users of mobile devices: social networking applications that are easy to use while walking down the street; applications that are aware of the user's location; applications that allow the easy sharing of content-rich information, such as pictures and videos.

As mentioned in the previous chapter, we are going to study just such an application as an example of Android application development. The code is available for you to download from the book's website (*http://www.oreilly.com/catalog/9780596521479*), and is based on an actual entry in the first round of the Android Developer Challenge, sponsored by Google. The application is an example of a class of applications known as "friend finders" because that's the central idea.

In the case of the MicroJobs application, instead of finding friends, the user is trying to locate a temporary job in the vicinity, so she can work for a few hours and make some money. The premise is that employers looking for temporary help have entered available jobs, descriptions, hours, and offered wages in a web-based database that is accessible from Android mobile phones. Anyone looking for a few hours' work can use the MicroJobs application to access that database, look for jobs in the immediate area, communicate with friends about potential employers and potential jobs, and call the employer directly if she is interested in the position. For our purposes here, we won't create an online service; we'll just have some canned data on the phone. The application has a number of features that extend that central idea in ways that are unique to mobile handsets:

Mapping
> The Android mobile phone environment provides very rich support for dynamic, interactive maps, and we're going to take full advantage of its capabilities. You'll see that with very little code, we'll be able to show dynamic maps of our local neighborhood, getting location updates from the internal GPS to automatically scroll the map as we move. We'll be able to scroll the map in two directions, zoom in and out, and even switch to satellite views.

Finding friends and events
> A graphic overlay on the map will show us where jobs are placed in the area, and will allow us to get more information about a job by just touching its symbol on the map. We will access Android's Contact Manager application to get address information for our friends (telephone numbers, instant messaging addresses, etc.), and access the `MicroJobs` database to get more information about posted jobs.

Instant messaging
> When we find friends we want to chat with, we will be able to contact them via instant messages (IMs), by trading SMS messages with our friends' mobile phones.

Talking with friends or employers
> If IMing is too slow or cumbersome, we'll be able to easily place a cellular call to our friends, or call the employer offering a job.

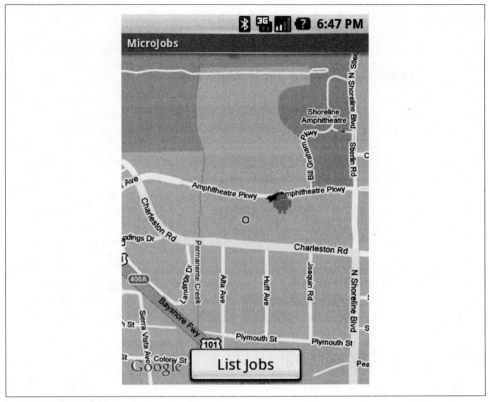

Figure 3-1. MJAndroid opening screenshot

Browsing the Web

Most employers have an associated website that provides more detailed information. We'll be able to select an employer off a list or off the map and quickly zero in on their website to find out, for example, what the place looks like.

This is a fun application that could easily be developed further into a full-blown service, but our intent in this book is to show you just how easy it is to develop and combine these powerful capabilities in your own application. The complete source code for the application is available to you on the book's website, and we will refer to it frequently throughout this book. Although it's not absolutely required in order to understand the material in the book, you are strongly encouraged to download the source to your own computer. That way, you'll have it readily available for reference, and it will be easy to copy sections of code and paste them into your own applications as you move on.

Figure 3-1 shows the screen displayed by MJAndroid when you first run it. It's a map of your local area, overlaid with a few buttons and pins.

Downloading the MJAndroid Code

The MJAndroid application source code and project files are available from the O'Reilly website, at *http://www.oreilly.com/catalog/9780596521479*. To download it to your development system, use a browser to navigate to the link given, and select "Download MJAndroid." Your operating system (Windows, Linux, or OS X) will ask you to confirm that you want the download to happen, and ask you where to put the downloaded files. It doesn't matter where you put the downloaded, compressed files, but you want to extract the uncompressed files into the directory that Eclipse uses as your default workspace, to make it easy to load the project. The default place is a folder called *workspace* under the *eclipse* directory that you created when you installed Eclipse. If you can't remember where that is, start Eclipse, go to File → Switch Workspace, and it will display the location of the current workspace directory. Expand the compressed files into that directory, and be sure "use directories" is checked in the decompression dialog, so the correct folders will be created and the files written to them.

To import the MJAndroid project into Eclipse, go to File → Import..., and you'll see a Select dialog list of possible import types. Click on "Existing Projects into Workspace," and use the Browse button to find the directory where you just expanded MJAndroid. Eclipse will import the project, and it should appear in the Project Explorer pane.

A Brief Tour of the MJAndroid Code

MJAndroid is a relatively simple application, despite the capabilities it gives its users. This section will give you an overview of the code and resource modules, tell you where they are located in the directory structure, and provide a glimpse of what each component does. You may want to refer to this section in the future when you're trying to find example code for a particular function and want to locate it in the MJAndroid code tree. MJAndroid uses a directory structure that is derived directly from the standard Android application directory structure, so this will also serve as a guide to finding code in other application source trees.

The Project Root Folder (MJAndroid)

If you use Eclipse's Package Explorer to look at the MJAndroid project, you will see a set of folders and files. It turns out all of these were originally created by Eclipse and the Android Development Tool, and similar folders and files are created for any Android application. Let's see what they do:

src folder
> *src* is short for Source, and this is where Eclipse and ADT expect to find all of the Java source files in your application. Almost all of the work you do to create an Android application is done in this folder and the *res* folder. In the next section, we will take a more detailed look at how the *src* folder is structured for MJAndroid.

Android Library

This is just what it says: a pointer to the library of Android class files that Eclipse links to in order to provide the Android APIs. You don't need to do anything with this entry, but if you ever need to confirm that a particular Android class is (still) there, this is where you would look.

assets folder

This folder is useful for holding assets that are used by the application: fonts, external JAR files, and so on. For this book and MJAndroid, we don't have any assets, so we will not be using the *assets* folder.

doc folder

Short for documentation, this is where you can put documentation for a project. For MJAndroid, web pages that describe the Loco project are stored in this folder.

res folder

res is short for resources, and this is where Eclipse and ADT expect to find the resources for your application. Resources include most of the XML files that define the layout of your application, any image files (icons, pictures that are used in your layout, sprites, etc.)—just about everything that isn't part of a Java source file.

AndroidManifest.xml file

This file is created by ADT when you create a new Android project. As the extension suggests, it is an XML file, and it contains a wealth of information about your application: what the activities, services, and intents are, which one starts first, which permissions your application needs from the operating system (for restricted functions such as getting location or making a phone call), and a lot of other information. This file is so important that ADT provides a special editor to maintain it. It's just an XML file, so you could always edit it with a text editor, but you will see later that the specialized editor makes everything a lot easier.

Eclipse also creates two other files and another directory at the same directory level (the root directory of the MJAndroid project) that are not shown by Package Explorer. The *.classpath* file is used by Eclipse to keep track of the location of standard Java classes and libraries. Eclipse uses the *.project* file to store information about the project. You will never need to touch either of these files directly, so Eclipse doesn't bother you with them in Package Explorer. The *bin* directory is where Eclipse puts the compiled class files for each of your Java source files (the ones in *src*). You can see all of these files if you list the directory of the root folder, but you don't really need to pay any attention to them, because Eclipse will do it all for you.

The Source Folder (src)

The package name for MJAndroid is `com.microjobsinc.mjandroid`. Eclipse lays out the equivalent directory structure, just as it would for any Java project, and shows you the whole thing when you open *src*. In addition to these package folders, there is a folder named for the package that contains all the Java files for the project. These include:

MicroJobs.java

The main source file for the application. It designates the Activity that starts first, displays the map that is the centerpiece of the application, and calls other Activities or Services as necessary to implement different features in the user interface.

MicroJobsDatabase.java

A database helper that provides easy access to the local MJAndroid database. This is where all the employer, user, and job information is stored, using SQLite.

AddJob.java and EditJob.java

Part of the database portion of MJAndroid. These provide screens through which the user can add or edit job entries in the database.

MicroJobsDetail.java

The Activity that displays all of the detail information about a particular job opportunity.

MicroJobsEmpDetail.java

The Activity that displays information about an employer, including name, address, reputation, email address, phone number, etc.

MicroJobsList.java

The Activity that displays a list of jobs (as opposed to the map view in *MicroJobs.java*). It shows a simple list containing Employer and Job entries, and allows the user to sort the list by either field and call up specifics of the job or employer by touching the name on the list.

R.java

This file is created automatically by Eclipse and the ADT to contain Java references for all the resources that are defined in the *res* folder (see the next section). You should never have to edit this file by hand, as it is maintained for you as you add or edit resources. Take a look, though, just to see how resources are defined for later use in the other Java source files.

The Resource Folder (res)

The *res* folder contains three folders, and another pointer to the same *Android Manifest.xml* file that shows up in the root directory:

drawable

As you might suspect, this contains all the drawable images that MJAndroid will use: any JPEG or PNG or GIF files or bitmaps.

layout

As with many modern application environments, Android allows you to separate what is displayed by an Activity from how it is displayed. This directory contains XML files that describe the "how"; in other words, they are the layout files for each Activity in the application. When a program runs, Android applies the rules in these files to create the visible layout, a process known as "inflating."

values

Good programming practice calls for the separation of data that does not directly affect the operation of an application, making it a lot easier to do things like translation to foreign languages, theming, etc. We aren't going to be super strict about this in MJAndroid, but we will at least put all of the obvious user-visible text into a file called *strings.xml*. You'll see how easy it is to retrieve these for use in the actual Android Activity source code.

First Steps: Building and Running the MicroJobs Application

So now that we know a bit about which files are located in which folders, what happens when we ask Android to run the MJAndroid application? And for that matter, how do we ask Android to run the application? Let's take a closer look at the Android SDK environment and the views and commands available to us for running and debugging any application.

A Very Short Tour of the Android SDK/Eclipse IDE

The Android SDK provides three "perspectives" for working with Android projects and applications. If you're new to Eclipse, a perspective is a collection of Eclipse views that provides a particular viewpoint of an application. Eclipse and the Android SDK have preassembled sets of views that developers have found useful, and you can switch between those views, either by selecting one from the Window menu or by using the icons in the upper-right corner of the Eclipse window. You are also free to customize the perspectives, but in this book we will assume you use the standard ones provided:

Java

This is the default perspective, launched by Eclipse when you first say that you want to view the workspace. It includes:

Package Explorer

Used for viewing folders and selecting files

Source Editor

Used for editing Java and XML source files

Tabbed Views

Contains a set of useful views, accessed by tabs:

- Problems, which lists errors that Eclipse and the Android SDK find in the application

- Javadoc, which extracts and displays Javadoc documentation from the application

- Declaration, which makes it easy to find the declaration for any variable in the code

- Console, which shows the console terminal output from either the emulator or the Android phone
- Search, which is used to search for results
- Progress, which displays progress as an application is launched and runs

Debug

This perspective is primarily for debugging the application, obviously. If you select Debug from the Run menu, Eclipse switches automatically to this perspective, providing you with views that are useful for debugging:

Debug

A view of the application call stack, showing you how you got to the current debug point

Source View

This shows you the current source location in the running (or stopped) application

Console and Tasks Views

This contains the console terminal (as in the Java perspective), and a window where development tasks can be recorded and tracked

Variables, Breakpoints, and Expressions

This is where you can view current variable values, view breakpoints, and evaluate expressions while debugging

Outline

This shows you an outline of the current activity being executed: the classes declared, and the instances and methods defined

DDMS

This perspective, which stands for Dalvik Debug Monitor Service, is unique to Android. It provides Android-specific debug information, including:

Devices

This shows you what devices (emulated or hardware) are available to run your applications.

Emulator Control

This is where you can adjust parameters that define how the telephony and location emulators work. When running on the emulator, we'll use this to manually send location updates to the location provider.

LogCat

This is a view of the very powerful logging facility available under Android, which allows you to see everything going on in the target system, and to filter out the information you really care about.

Threads, Heap, and File Explorer

This is a tabbed set of views where you can follow the running threads in the application, see how the heap is being used, and select files from the folder hierarchy.

Loading and Starting the Application

Running MJAndroid from the SDK is complicated by the fact that the application uses a MapView. Android requires a special Map API Keywhenever you use a MapView, and the key is tied to your particular development machine. You'll learn all about this in Chapter 7, but right now the easiest way for you to run MJAndroid is simply to install the *.apk* file in the emulator.

Running the MJAndroid Code

If you downloaded the MJAndroid code and tried to use the Android SDK to compile it and run it, it probably didn't work. The most likely reason is that you didn't change the Map API Key to match the key needed by your installation of the SDK. To run an application such as MJAndroid that uses the MapView, you need a Map API Key. The easiest way to run the application is to install the binary we provided from the *.apk* file in the book's examples: *MJAndroid-1.0.0.apk*. You can install the file into the emulator by simply starting the emulator (if it's not already running) from a terminal window:

```
$ emulator
```

You'll then need to open another terminal window to enter the installation command:

```
$ adb install MJAndroid-1.0.0.apk
```

Once MJAndroid is installed on your emulator, you can launch it from the Application Launcher, just like any other application.

If you want to be able to make modifications to the code and build and run under the SDK, read Chapter 7 to learn how to get the Map API Key you need.

You are probably already in the Java perspective, but if not, select it now. If you loaded the MJAndroid application into your Eclipse workspace folder as described earlier, you should see it in the Package Explorer. If you now right-click on the MJAndroid entry, you get a long menu of options. Select Open Project, a little over halfway down the list, and Eclipse will open the MJAndroid project and allow you to see its contents.

If we didn't have to deal with the Map API Key issue, starting the application would be as easy as selecting Run from the menu of the same name. Eclipse shows a dialog box (labeled "Run As") that asks how you want to run the application. You will always select Android Application from the top of the list.

At this point, the Android SDK will either select the target hardware you identified or start the emulator as the target. It will automatically load your application on the target and attempt to start it. In the case of MJAndroid, you should see the opening screen, shown earlier in Figure 3-1.

Digging a Little Deeper: What Can Go Wrong?

As you are developing your application, at some point you will try to run it, as just described, and it won't work. You'll either get an unexpected result or you'll get an error on the target screen that may be less than informative. Let's spend a little time looking at what the Android SDK does to get an application running, and what might go wrong.

As you know, Android applications run under a virtual machine called Dalvik. When you selected "Run" in the previous section, tools in the Android SDK saw that there was not a compiled version of MJAndroid available to run. They first took all the layout and variable information that was coded into XML files and converted it into Java source code (in the *R.java* folder), and then compiled all the Java source code into Java bytecode files (*.class* files). A translator converted the Java bytecodes into Dalvik byte-code files (*.dex* files). The Dalvik modules were combined with other information about the application, including the manifest file *AndroidManifest.xml*, and packaged into an Android package (or *.apk*) file. In the case of the MJAndroid application, this file is *MJAndroid.apk*, located in *.../MJAndroid/bin*. An Android package is what the target receives to load and start the application running. A lot of the startup information is in the *AndroidManifest.xml* file, so let's take a closer look at it.

When you double-click the *AndroidManifest.xml* listing in the Package Explorer, the Android SDK starts the Android Manifest editor in the middle pane of the Java perspective, and loads the file, as shown in Figure 3-2.

As you see, there are five tabs at the bottom of the editor pane, which give you five different views of the manifest file:

Overview
> This is the view presented by default (if the file hasn't been opened before). It shows the package name for the application and shared user ID information (for use when multiple applications have to share a common user ID), presents some options for exporting and signing your application, and provides links to each of the tabs described next.

Application
> This view provides access to a lot of the parameters that can be set for an application. Most of these are either self-explanatory or are not used in an application like MJAndroid. Two areas of interest are:
> - Icon, which tells Android where to find a drawable icon to use for the application on the target.

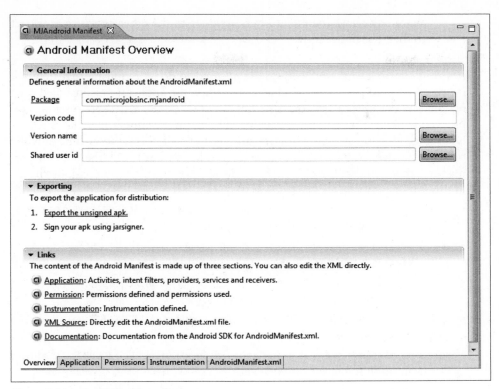

Figure 3-2. Android Manifest editor

- Application Nodes, which identifies the activities, services, and providers in the application. There are a number of things worth noting in this section.

  Uses Library

  For MJAndroid, we will use the MapActivity to display maps. That class is not part of the core Android libraries, so we call out here that we need access to the additional library `com.google.android.maps`.

  Activity Attributes

  Click on the little triangle to the left of MicroJobs (Activity) to see the intent filters attached to that activity. If you recall, activities in Android are run when their intent filters satisfy an intent that was expressed by some already running application. In this case we see two filters for MicroJobs:

  `<action android:name="android.intent.action.MAIN" />`

  This tells the Android application launcher that this activity is the one to be started first for MJAndroid.

  `<category android:name="android.intent.category.LAUNCHER" />`

  This tells Android that the icon for this activity and application is to be displayed on the menu of launchable applications.

We'll talk about the intent filters assigned to the other activities as we get to their use in the code.

Permissions

Android controls what applications are allowed to do by requiring that they ask for permission to perform critical actions. When the application is installed on a real device, the user can choose whether to allow the requested permissions and proceed with installation, or to reject installation (in the emulator environment, it is assumed all permission requests are granted). It is important to include only the permissions needed by your application; you don't want to ask the user for permissions that you don't need. For MJAndroid, we'll need the permissions shown in this tab:

- `<uses-permission android:name="android.permission.ACCESS_FINE_LOCATION" />` allows us to use fine-grained location providers, such as GPS.

- `<uses-permission android:name="android.permission.ACCESS_LOCATION_EXTRA_COMMANDS" />` allows us to access additional location commands.

- `<uses-permission android:name="android.permission.ACCESS_MOCK_LOCATION" />` allows the creation of mock location providers.

- `<uses-permission android:name="android.permission.INTERNET" />` allows us to access the Internet.

- `<uses-permission android:name="android.permission.CALL_PHONE" />` allows the application to place telephone calls.

Instrumentation

Android allows developers to replace Dalvik classes with substitute classes when running in the emulator environment. The intent is to allow one to better instrument particularly tricky code. We won't be using this feature in this book, but you can search for "Instrumentation" in the Android documentation to find out more.

AndroidManifest.xml

This view shows the actual XML file that results from all the choices made in the other views. If you are already comfortable with XML, you may prefer to edit the file directly in this view, rather than using the others. Be careful, though, because Android is very choosy about seeing the right tags in the right places, and doesn't always give you an error message indicating what, exactly, is wrong. The editor used in this view does XML syntax checking for you, but it doesn't know anything about the semantics of the various XML tags defined by Android. It's interesting to make changes in the other views and see their effect on the actual XML file by looking at this view.

So there is a lot of information in the *AndroidManifest.xml* file, and the system uses that information when launching the application. In the next chapter, we'll see what actually goes on inside the application as it starts up.

Running an Application on the T-Mobile Phone

Emulators are great development timesavers, and the QEMU emulator used by Android runs particularly well. You can probably debug 95% of your application just using the emulator. But an Android application doesn't have much *raison d'être* until it gets the chance to run on real phones. Luckily, Android makes it easy for you to try your application on one. As this is written, the T-Mobile G1 phone is the only Android phone on the market, so we'll give instructions for using it with the Android SDK. Future Android phones should be similar.

Enable USB debugging on your phone

Before you connect your T-Mobile G1 to the host, go to the Desktop screen on the phone, and push the Menu button. One of the menu options is Settings. Touch it to select, and you will be taken to the Settings dialog for the phone, which consists of a list of things you can set. The list is bigger than the screen, so scroll up and down until you find Applications, and touch that entry. You're taken to a sublist related to applications, and one of the entries is Development. Touch that, and you're shown two options:

USB Debugging
> You want to enable this option by touching it. A green checkmark should appear in the adjacent checkbox.

Stay awake
> This option will keep the screen on as long as the USB cable is connected. It can be annoying when the screen goes off, taking you back to the opening screen, so you might as well enable this too.

Your T-Mobile G1 now expects to receive debug information through the USB port, but don't plug it in just yet, because we may need to load a special driver on the host.

Load the USB driver for ADB

Depending on which host operating system you are using, you will need to install a driver for the USB port, or configure the existing driver:

Windows (either Vista or XP)
> You will need to install a USB driver that is included with the Android SDK. The driver is located in *<SDK>/usb_driver*, where *<SDK>* is the location in which you installed the Android SDK.
>
> Once you've extracted the driver, plug in the USB cable connecting the phone to the host. A Found New Hardware dialog will pop up that gives you a chance to load the new driver. The details will vary slightly, but in general:

1. Windows will ask if you want to search for a driver, which you don't. Instead, you want to tell it where you put the driver directory, so select the option that is something like "Install from a list or specified location."

2. Ignore any dire warnings from Windows about the driver not being certified. This just means that no one paid Microsoft to perform the certification tests.

3. When asked for the driver's location, browse to the USB driver directory, *<SDK>usb_driver*. The extraction should have created a subdirectory called *android_usb_windows*. Select that subdirectory and click OK.

Windows will load the driver and tell you that the hardware is ready to use.

Mac OS X

You're all set without doing anything.

Ubuntu Linux

For Ubuntu, you need to configure the USB connection with a rules file, located at */etc/udev/rules.d/50-android.rules*. The contents of the rules file are slightly different depending on which version of Ubuntu you are using. If you are using a different Linux distribution, you'll need to look at its documentation to understand how USB rules files are configured.

Ubuntu Dapper Drake

Create a file at */etc/udev/rules.d/50-android.rules* with one line in it:

```
SUBSYSTEM=="usb_device", SYSFS{idVendor}=="0bb4", MODE="0666"
```

Ubuntu Gutsy Gibbon or Hardy Heron

Create a file at */etc/udev/rules.d/50-android.rules* with one line it it:

```
SUBSYSTEM=="usb", SYSFS{idVendor}=="0bb4", MODE="0666"
```

In all cases (Dapper, Gutsy, or Hardy), make the rules file readable and executable by executing from the shell as root:

```
chmod a+rx /etc/udev/rules.d/50-android.rules
```

Connecting the phone

Now that you have the driver loaded, you are ready to plug in the USB cable that connects the T-Mobile G1 to the host. The phone will beep, and Eclipse will update itself as it learns of the new target. If you go to a terminal (Linux or OS X) or Command window (Windows) and type **adb devices**, you should see something like this:

```
>adb devices
List of devices attached
emulator-5554    device
HT840GZ12968     device
```

Running MicroJobs on the phone

Now when you select Run from the Eclipse menu, you will still get the dialog that asks what kind of application you want to run (Android Application, Java Applet, Java Application, etc.), but now you will get a second dialog that asks which target you want to run on. The available targets will be listed, and you can click on either the emulator or the phone, depending on which you'd prefer. Select the phone, and the application is downloaded (using the debug signature; more about application signatures in Chapter 7), and started on the phone. Most of the debug features available on the emulator (covered in detail in Chapter 5) are also available when running in debug mode on the phone.

Summary

We've looked at this more realistic application in some detail to understand the procedures you'll need to follow when developing your own application. Your application is likely to differ in the details, but it will inherit a similar structure, and you will use similar procedures to build and run your application, both on the emulator and on a live phone. You now know all the basics you need to start building your application, but as you'll see, there is a lot more to learn about Android and the features you can build into your application.

CHAPTER 4

Under the Covers: Startup Code and Resources in the MJAndroid Application

Chapter 3 introduced the major application we use in this book to illustrate basic Android concepts. That chapter explained which files make up the source code, but it didn't actually cover any source code in the application. We'll start looking at source code in this chapter. And to allow you to get started developing an application quickly, we'll begin with the first task every standalone application has to perform: initialization.

The events covered in this chapter occur between your selecting "Run As Android Application" from the Eclipse menu and seeing the map that MJAndroid displays at startup. This chapter shows how Android makes it easy to create relatively complex applications. In just 80 lines of code and some associated XML resource files, MJAndroid manages to:

- Display an interactive map
- Track the current location of the Android phone and update the map
- Create a local database of information and load user preferences into it
- Provide a dynamically changing menu
- Display user interface elements such as labels, buttons, and spinners
- Run a new Activity to display a supporting screen

The Java code in an Android application interacts tightly with XML resource files, so we'll bounce back and forth between them in this chapter. As we point out repeatedly, XML files are easier to tweak during development and maintain over the life of an application. The design of Android encourages you to specify the look and behavior of the application in the resource files.

Initialization Parameters in AndroidManifest.xml

As Chapter 3 explained, we told Android to launch *Microjobs.java* as the first Activity for MJAndroid. We defined that on the Application tab of the *AndroidManifest.xml* editor. The first part of the XML code that results from that choice is shown here:

```xml
<?xml version="1.0" encoding="utf-8"?>
<manifest xmlns:android="http://schemas.android.com/apk/res/android"
    package="com.microjobsinc.mjandroid" android:versionCode="1"
      android:versionName="1.0">
    <uses-permission android:name="android.permission.ACCESS_FINE_LOCATION" />
    <uses-permission android:name=
      "android.permission.ACCESS_LOCATION_EXTRA_COMMANDS" />
    <uses-permission android:name="android.permission.CALL_PHONE" />
    <uses-permission android:name="android.permission.ACCESS_MOCK_LOCATION" />
    <uses-permission android:name="android.permission.INTERNET" />

    <application android:icon="@drawable/icon2">
    <uses-library android:name="com.google.android.maps" />
        <activity android:name=".MicroJobs" android:label="@string/app_name">
            <intent-filter>
                <action android:name="android.intent.action.MAIN" />
                <category android:name="android.intent.category.LAUNCHER" />
            </intent-filter>
        </activity>
```

This section of the chapter focuses on the XML in this file. The MicroJobs Activity is identified in the manifest at the beginning of the file. This part of the file is normally created in Eclipse when you first create the Project that you use to write your application.

Like all good XML files, line 1 has the standard declaration of the XML version and the character encoding used. Before we get into the Activities that make up the MJAndroid application, we define a few parameters and declare needed permissions for the whole application:

package="com.microjobsinc.mjandroid"
> This is just the package name we gave when we created the application in Eclipse. It's also the default package for all the modules in the application.

android:versionCode
> This is an integer that should always increment with each new version of the application. Every application should include a version code, and it should always be a monotonically increasing integer from version to version. This lets other programs (such as Android Market, installers, and launchers) easily figure out which is the latest version of an application. The filename of your *.apk* file should include this same version number, so it is obvious which version it contains.

android:versionName
> This version identifier is a string, and it is intended to be more like the version numbers you usually see for applications. The naming convention is up to you, but

generally the idea is to use a scheme like m.n.o (for as many numbers as you want to use), to identify successive levels of change to the application. The idea is that this is the version identifier that would be displayed to a user (either by your application or another application).

`<uses-permission android:name=...`
>There are four of these in MJAndroid, and they declare that the application intends to use features of Android that require explicit permission from the user of the mobile device running the application. The permission is requested when the application is installed, and from then on Android remembers that the user said it was OK (or not) to run this application and access the secure features. There are many permissions already defined in Android, all described in the Android documentation (search for `android.Manifest.permission`). You can also define your own permissions and use them to restrict other applications' access to functions in your application, unless the user grants the other application that permission. The permissions requested here are:
>
>- `ACCESS_FINE_LOCATION`, which is required to obtain location information from a GPS sensor.
>- `ACCESS_LOCATION_EXTRA_COMMANDS`. The Android documentation doesn't tell us which location commands are "extra," so we'll ask for all of them.
>- `CALL_PHONE`. This allows MJAndroid to request that the Dialer place a mobile phone call on its behalf.
>- `ACCESS_MOCK_LOCATION`, so we can get fake location information when we're running under the emulator.
>- `INTERNET`, so we can retrieve map tiles over an Internet connection.

`android:icon="@drawable/icon2"`
>This is the filename for a PNG file that contains the icon you'd like to use for your application. In this case we're telling the Android SDK to look for the icon file in the *drawable* subdirectory of the *res* (resources) directory under MJAndroid. Android will use this icon for your application in the Android Desktop.

Turning our attention to the definition for the first (and main) Activity, MicroJobs, we first define a few attributes for the Activity:

`android:name`
>The name of the Activity. The full name of the Activity includes the package name (which in our application is "com.microjobsinc.mjandroid.MicroJobs"), but since this file is always used in the package's namespace, we don't need to include the leading package names. The Android SDK strips the package name down to ".MicroJobs" when it creates this part of *AndroidManifest.xml*, and even the leading period is optional.

`android:label`

>The label that we want to appear at the top of the Android screen when the Activity is on the screen. We saw this before in HelloWorld, where we changed the string in *strings.xml* to match our application.

We then declare an intent filter that tells Android when this Activity should be run. We talked briefly about Intents in Chapter 1, and now we see them in use. As you'll recall, when Android encounters an Intent to fulfill, it looks among the available Activities and Services to find something that can service the Intent. We set two attributes:

`action`

>Right now Android is trying to launch this application, so it's looking for an Activity that declares itself ready to resolve the MAIN action. Any application that is going to be launched by the Launcher needs to have exactly one Activity or Service that makes this assertion.

`category`

>The Intent resolver in Android uses this attribute to further qualify the Intent that it's looking for. In this case, the qualification is that we'd like for this Activity to be displayed in the User Menu so the user can select it to start this application. Specifying the LAUNCHER category accomplishes this. You can have a perfectly valid application without this attribute—you just won't be able to launch it from the Android user interface. Normally, again, you'll have exactly one LAUNCHER per application, and it will appear in the same intent filter as the opening Activity of your application.

Initialization in MicroJobs.java

Having seen the XML resources that Android uses to launch the application, we can turn to some Java code that initializes the application. Use Eclipse to open *MicroJobs.java* in the Java editor.

After the package declaration and the import statements, the `MicroJobs` class is defined. Most Activities (and the other activities in this application) extend the Activity class. Because we want to display a map in this application, and we want to take advantage of the powerful mapping features built into Android, we declare that MicroJobs will extend MapActivity, as shown in the following code segment. If you look in the Android documentation for MapActivity, you will see that it is a subclass of Activity, and so inherits all the Activity methods and variables:

```
/**
 * MicroJobs
 */
public class MicroJobs extends MapActivity {
```

Skip over the first few variables and the definition of the `MJOverlay` class for the moment, to get to the definition of the `onCreate` method, as shown in the code block that follows.

This is the method called by Android when it first launches an application, so that's where we'll put our initialization code. Let's take a look at it, section by section:

```
MapView mvMap;
MicroJobsDatabase db;
MyLocationOverlay mMyLocationOverlay;
double latitude, longitude;

/**
 * Called when the activity is first created.
 *
 * @see com.google.android.maps.MapActivity#onCreate(android.os.Bundle)
 */
@Override
public void onCreate(Bundle savedInstanceState) {
    super.onCreate(savedInstanceState);

    setContentView(R.layout.main);
```

The first thing to note is that onCreate receives an argument when it runs: a *Bundle* that will be referred to as savedInstanceStte. Note also that the first thing onCreate does is call the onCreate method of its superclass. That makes sense because we want the chain of superclasses to initialize themselves appropriately. But what is this Bundle thing?

A Bundle is one of the mechanisms used by Android to pass structured data between Activities. It's just a parcel of key/object pairs, and you'll see later when we start another Activity that we have the option of passing that Activity a Bundle. In the case of MicroJobs, we aren't going to make use of any of the resources in the savedInstanceState Bundle, but we faithfully pass it on to the onCreate method of our superclass.

The very last line in this section of code sets our Content View. A view, as we explained in Chapter 1, describes how an application window appears and interacts with the user. So the setContentView call tells Android that we want to use the layout information in *R.layout.main.java* to lay out the screen for the Activity. As Chapter 2 explained, the *R.** resource files are generated by the Android SDK from your own XML resource files when you compile your application (as a result of selecting Run); in this case, the parameters come from our *res/layout/main.xml* file. Android "inflates" these parameters when layouts are created, using them to determine how the layout looks.

So let's digress for a minute and take a look at the first part of the XML version of that file:

```
<?xml version="1.0" encoding="utf-8"?>
<RelativeLayout xmlns:android="http://schemas.android.com/apk/res/android"
    android:orientation="vertical"
    android:layout_width="fill_parent"
    android:layout_height="fill_parent"
    android:background="#ffc5d1d4"
    >
  <com.google.android.maps.MapView
```

```
    android:id="@+id/mapmain"
       android:layout_width="fill_parent"
       android:layout_height="fill_parent"
       android:clickable="true"
       android:apiKey="0P18K0TAE0d02GifdtbuScgEGLWe3p4CYUQngMg"
    />
  <TextView
       android:id="@+id/lblMicroJobsToday"
     android:layout_width="wrap_content"
     android:layout_height="wrap_content"
     android:text="MicroJobs for You Today Near:"
     android:textSize="20dp"
     android:textColor="#FF000000"
     android:layout_centerHorizontal="true"
     android:gravity="top"
     />
  <Spinner
     android:id="@+id/spnLocations"
     android:layout_width="250dp"
     android:layout_height="wrap_content"
     android:layout_centerHorizontal="true"
     android:layout_marginTop="2dp"
     android:layout_below="@+id/lblMicroJobsToday"
    />
    <Button
     android:id="@+id/btnShowList"
     android:layout_width="150dp"
     android:layout_height="wrap_content"
     android:text="List Jobs"
     android:textSize="20sp"
     android:gravity="center_vertical"
     android:layout_centerInParent="true"
     android:layout_alignParentBottom="true"
    />
 </RelativeLayout>
```

First, we say that we are going to use a Relative Layout for this screen. Android offers a variety of Layout types, and though it's beyond the scope of this book, you can even define your own Layout types. A Relative Layout says that we are going to define the positions of the different user interface elements by relating their positions to each other and to the overall screen. That may sound a little vague right now, but it will be clear when we go into some of the attributes in detail. We go into much more depth on the process of screen layout later in this book in Chapter 12.

The first few lines of code define overall attributes for the screen layout:

android:orientation

> This tells Android which way we want "gravity" to work in determining the screen layout.

android:layout_width *and* android:layout_height

> These tell Android that we want to make use of the whole screen; we aren't trying to leave room for other Activities to be partially visible.

`android:background`

> This defines the color of the background for the application (which isn't really visible in our case, since the map covers the whole screen).

Colors in Android

This is a good time to talk briefly about defining colors in Android; we'll discuss it further when we talk about graphics in Chapter 12. The color specification will be familiar to you if you've worked with web pages (although on a web page, the Alpha value is the last item instead of the first). Colors in Android are defined by a pound sign (#) followed by four 8-bit integers in hexadecimal:

Alpha
> The transparency of the resulting color, FF being completely opaque and 0 being completely transparent.

Red
> Red's contribution to the resulting color, FF being fully on and 0 meaning no red.

Green
> Green's contribution to the resulting color, FF being fully on and 0 meaning no green.

Blue
> Blue's contribution to the resulting color, FF being fully on and 0 meaning no blue.

Common colors are also defined as global constants for use in Java.

The rest of the file defines each of the visual elements of the screen, and tells Android where we'd like it placed.

The following elements of the application are defined in the file:

Section starting `<com.google.android.maps.MapView`

> This is the main View for this Activity:a Map that consumes most of the screen and shows the locations of jobs that might be of interest to the user. You'll see that most Views can be described in a layout file by just writing the name of the View, but this holds only for Views that are part of Android's default libraries. MapViews are not included, so we create an XML element for it. The MapView View is defined in the maps library, so the full pathname is `com.google.android.maps.MapView`. We assign it the following attributes:

`android:id`
> This defines an identifier that we can use to refer to this View, either from other places in this XML file or from our Java code. You'll see later in the Java initialization code that we connect the Java source code with this XML source through these IDs.

`android:layout_width` *and* `android:layout_height`
> These are the same attributes defined earlier for the application, but here they apply to the MapView alone, not the whole application. The `fill_parent`

value, as its name suggests, asks for permission to fill all the space within the parent. In this case the parent happens to be the whole screen, but it is important to keep in mind that this attribute affects only the relationship between the MapView and its parent.

android:clickable

This tells Android that we want an interactive MapView that the user can click on using the touchscreen on the Android phone (simulated by mouse clicks on the emulated Android phone).

android:apiKey

This is an attribute unique to MapViews. You need an API Key from Google to use a Map View, just as you do when you add a Google map to your web page. You'll see how to obtain and use Map API Keys in Chapters 7 and 9.

Section starting <TextView

This will display a Label telling the user what he's looking at. The attributes defined here are typical of what needs to be defined for a TextView. In addition to attributes we already saw under MapView, this element has:

android:text

This contains the text we'd like to display in the TextView.

android:textSize

This says how big Android should display the text—in this case, 20 scaled pixels high (see the upcoming sidebar for a description of Android dimensions).

android:textColor

This defines the color of the text.

android:layout_centerHorizontal

This tells Android that we want it to center the displayed text horizontally.

android:gravity

This tells the Android layout manager where to position the element vertically relative to its container, when the element is smaller. Gravity can be defined as top, center_vertical, or bottom. Note that gravity and attributes like layout_centerHorizontal are layout hints that the layout manager uses to lay out the children of a container. There is no guarantee that the hints will be followed, but the layout manager attempts to satisfy the combined requests from the container, the children it contains, and any global layout hints from the user interface.

There are many other attributes we could define for our TextView, and they are all described in the Android documentation that accompanies the SDK.

Section starting <Spinner

This is a standard Android control that allows the user to select from the current location or any of several "favorite" locations that are recorded in the user's profile. In addition to the attributes we've seen already, the android:layout_below attribute controls the placement of the Spinner. This is the first attribute we've seen that applies specifically to the Relative Layout we chose at the top of the file. It tells Android that it should position this Spinner just below the interface element whose id is `lblMicroJobsToday`.

Section starting `<Button`

The final segment of *main.xml* defines a Button widget, which is just what it sounds like—a button that the user can press to initiate some action. In this case, we want a button that takes us to the listing of jobs.

`android:layout_width` *and* `android:layout_height`

These are the same attributes used for the other views, but we don't want the Button to take up the whole width of the screen, so we give it a defined width. Vertically, we just tell it to wrap the text that it is displaying.

`android:text`

This places a label on the Button.

`android:textSize`

This tells Android how large we'd like that text drawn—in this case, 20 scaled pixels.

`android:layout_centerInParent`

Since the button is not as wide as the parent (the screen), we need to tell the layout manager where to put the Button horizontally. This says "put it in the middle."

`android:layout_alignParentBottom`

The Button is only tall enough to wrap the label that it displays, so we also need to tell the layout manager where to place it vertically on the screen. This says "put it at the bottom." Note that we could also have said `android:gravity=bottom`. Android provides multiple ways of expressing our layout requests.

Dimensions in Android

Often you will need to specify a dimension for some element of the user interface. In the example here we generally used scaled pixels (abbreviated "sp"), but Android actually offers a rich set of dimensions to choose from:

px (pixels)

If a dimension is set at 10px, it will be exactly 10 pixels long, no matter what the physical size (and physical density) of the pixels on the display. 10px will therefore be different sizes on handset displays with different pixel densities. On a QVGA display, for example (320×240 pixels), it will be 1/24th of the height of the display. The same 10px running on a VGA display (640×480 pixels) will be 1/64th of the height of the display.

dip or dp (device-independent pixels)

In an effort to make it easier to adapt applications to different pixel densities, dimensions can be expressed in device-independent pixels (sometimes also called

---

"density-independent pixels"). When you specify a dimension of 10dpi, Android will scale the resulting object so it appears the same size it would appear on a 160dpi screen. For example, if a 640×480 display is 4"×3", its pixel density is 160 dots per inch (640/4, or 480/3). On that screen, dp's are the same as px's. But if we run the same application on a tablet-size VGA screen—say, 8"×6"—the pixel density is 80dpi, and a dimension given as 10dp will be twice as large as a dimension given as 10px. The scaling factor for dp's is approximate—Android doesn't try to make dp's come out exactly right.

sp *(scaled pixels)*
Scaled pixels are a lot like dp's, but they are intended for elements that need finer control over the density scaling factor, such as text.

pts *(points)*
This is used to express text size in points, just as you would in any text editor. Points are a fixed dimension (roughly 1/72nd of an inch), so the text will appear the same size on any display.

in *(inches)*
This is just what it says: the dimension in inches.

mm *(millimeters)*
This is also just what it says, only metric this time.

More Initialization of MicroJobs.java

The previous section was a rather long digression into XML Layout files, but as you can see, that is where a lot of the initialization of the application's user interface takes place: where views are defined, named, and given attributes; where the screen is layed out; and where hints are given to the layout manager describing the way we would like the screen to look. Let's get back to the Java code that brings up the application, starting where we left off in *MicroJobs.java*:

```
db = new MicroJobsDatabase(this);

// Get current position
final Location myLocation
    = getCurrentLocation((LocationManager) getSystemService(Context.LOCATION_SERVICE));

Spinner spnLocations = (Spinner) findViewById(R.id.spnLocations);
mvMap = (MapView) findViewById(R.id.mapmain);

// get the map controller
final MapController mc = mvMap.getController();

mMyLocationOverlay = new MyLocationOverlay(this, mvMap);
mMyLocationOverlay.runOnFirstFix(
    new Runnable() {
        public void run() {
            mc.animateTo(mMyLocationOverlay.getMyLocation());
            mc.setZoom(16);
```

```
        }
    });
```

Create the database object

We said before that we are going to use a small `SQLite` database to hold the job, worker, and employer information. The first line initializes that database by asking Android to create a new `MicroJobsDatabase` object (and initialize it). The Java code for this is in the file *MicroJobsDatabase.java*, and we'll look at it in detail later in Chapter 8.

Get our location

We'll need to know our current location to do things like finding jobs that are close by, so we get it here by calling `getCurrentLocation`, which is a method defined later and that accepts the name of our `LocationManager` as its argument. The `Location Manager` is a special class that Android instantiates for you, and you can retrieve the instance for your application through the call to `getSystemService`.

Initialize the Spinner

As explained in the previous section, we place a Spinner widget at the top of the screen to help users quickly go to one of their favorite locations and look for jobs. This is the first time we encounter the `findViewById` method, which is the way we access the IDs we defined in the XML layout file. If you recall, we identified the Spinner in *main.xml* as `spnLocations`. When we built the application, Android compiled that XML into a Java identifier that it placed in *R.layout.main.java* and linked it into the application. So now we can use `findViewById` to connect our Java Spinner to the XML attributes we defined.

Initialize the `MapView` *and* `MapController`

Similarly, we connect the Java MapView to the attributes defined for it in *main.xml*, and then attach a MapController to it. You'll see much more about the controller in Chapter 9, but for now think of it as a handle to get to all the methods you need to control the MapView.

Initialize the `LocationOverlay`

We want to create a `LocationOverlay` that will build and draw the Map in our `MapView` when we want to view a map of our local area. Again, Maps are covered in much more detail later, but you can see here that we use the constructor to create a new overlay and tell it to run when it gets its first fix from the LocationManager, so that it displays our current location. We also set the zoom level so it's about right for a metropolitan area.

We'll skip over the map overlay initialization, because that will be covered in more detail in Chapter 9, where we talk about mapping. We still need to initialize the remaining Views on this screen: the `Button` and the `Spinner`. The code for these follows:

```
// Create a button click listener for the List Jobs button.
Button btnList = (Button) findViewById(R.id.btnShowList);
btnList.setOnClickListener(new Button.OnClickListener() {
    public void onClick(View v) {
```

```
            Intent intent = new Intent(MicroJobs.this.getApplication(),
              MicroJobsList.class);
            startActivity(intent);
        }
    });

    // Load a HashMap with locations and positions
    List<String> lsLocations = new ArrayList<String>();
    final HashMap<String, GeoPoint> hmLocations = new HashMap<String, GeoPoint>();
    hmLocations.put("Current Location", new GeoPoint((int) latitude, (int) longitude));
    lsLocations.add("Current Location");

    // Add favorite locations from this user's record in workers table
    worker = db.getWorker();
    hmLocations.put(worker.getColLoc1Name(), new GeoPoint((int)worker.getColLoc1Lat(),
      (int)worker.getColLoc1Long()));
    lsLocations.add(worker.getColLoc1Name());
    hmLocations.put(worker.getColLoc2Name(), new GeoPoint((int)worker.getColLoc2Lat(),
      (int)worker.getColLoc2Long()));
    lsLocations.add(worker.getColLoc2Name());
    hmLocations.put(worker.getColLoc3Name(), new GeoPoint((int)worker.getColLoc3Lat(),
      (int)worker.getColLoc3Long()));
    lsLocations.add(worker.getColLoc3Name());

    ArrayAdapter<String> aspnLocations
        = new ArrayAdapter<String>(this, android.R.layout.simple_spinner_item,
          lsLocations);
    aspnLocations.setDropDownViewResource(android.R.layout.simple_spinner_dropdown_item);
    spnLocations.setAdapter(aspnLocations);
```

Create a callback for the btnList Button View

We first get a handle on the Button View by doing a lookup on its ID, just as we did before for the Spinner and MapView. We then set the behavior of the Button, which uses a construct known as a *listener* to respond to external events.

When a user clicks a button, Android sends an event to its OnClickListener listener. In this code, we set the Button's behavior by setting its OnClickListener to the method that we immediately define, onClick.

When the user clicks on btnList, we want to display a list of available MicroJobs. To do that, we have to launch a new Activity, MicroJobsList.java, which contains the screen that displays the list. We can do that by calling the startActivity method with an Intent that describes the new Activity. The first statement in onClick() creates the Intent, using the constructor for Intents that allows us to explicitly name the Activity. This constructor takes two arguments: a pointer to the context of the current application, and the name of the Class to start. The next statement in onClick() then uses that Intent to start an instantiation of MicroJobsList.

Initialize the list of entries in the Spinner View

We need two data structures to pass to our Spinner: a list of favorite locations that the Spinner will display (and the user can select), and a hash map connecting location names to geographical locations (latitude and longitude). Don't confuse the HashMap with a geographical Map; the HashMap uses the term "map" in the way many programmers use it, to mean an associative array.

We first create the list of location names (lsLocations), and then the HashMap that we'll use to map names to GeoPoints (hmLocations). We then put the first entry, Current Location, into the list and the HashMap. This entry will always return the user to the current location. This item is special because it can be a moving target. For example, the user may be consulting our application on a fast-moving train or an airplane, so we have to dynamically retrieve the location of the device whenever the current location is selected.

We then add three entries for the user's "favorite locations," recorded in the user's record in the workers table in the MJAndroid database. We'll dive into the details of how the database works and how it's set up later. For now, we'll just say that the code immediately following worker = db.getWorker(); loads the location names and positions (latitudes and longitudes) into the lsLocations and hmLocations lists.

Spinner Views require an ArrayAdapter to feed them the list, so we create one named aspnLocations, attaching it to the list of location names in its constructor. Then, we attach the adapter to the Spinner by calling setAdapter. The statement "aspnLocations.setDropDownViewResource(android.R.layout.simple_spinner_dropdown_item);" provides the Spinner with the drop-down layout necessary for the user to display the whole list of locations.

Now that we have initialized the lists, we can add the following code, which enables the appropriate action when the user clicks on an item with the Spinner:

```
// Set up a callback for the spinner
spnLocations.setOnItemSelectedListener(
    new OnItemSelectedListener() {
        public void onNothingSelected(AdapterView<?> arg0) { }

        public void onItemSelected(AdapterView<?> parent, View v, int position,
          long id) {
            TextView vt = (TextView) v;
            if ("Current Location".equals(vt.getText())) {
                latitude = myLocation.getLatitude();
                longitude = myLocation.getLongitude();
                mc.animateTo(new GeoPoint((int) latitude, (int) longitude));
            } else {
                mc.animateTo(hmLocations.get(vt.getText()));
            }
            mvMap.invalidate();
        }
    });
}
```

Initialize the Spinner callback

Just as we did with the Button View, we create a method named `onItemSelected` and set it to be called when the user selects an item using the Spinner. The `onNothingSelected` method is also required, but we leave it empty (not used).

As mentioned earlier, `Current Location` is a special case because we retrieve the device's location dynamically when the user selects that item. The `if` block handles that case: we look to see whether the selection is `Current Location` and if it is, we get the current location and go there. Otherwise, we go to the selected location.

Then, in the final statement, we invalidate the map so it will redraw itself.

Summary

With these explanations (skipping over a few advanced features covered later in the book), we've finished initializing the application—at least as far as the main Activity, MicroJobs, is concerned. We've seen how the Activity gets started, how it gets its layout information from its associated layout XML file (*main.xml*), how it initializes the Views it contains, and how it causes the initialization of other Activities or Services (either by invoking a constructor, as when creating the SQL database instance, or by asking Android to start another Activity, as with MicroJobsList).

CHAPTER 5

Debugging Android Applications

Unless you're really good or really lucky, the applications you write for Android will not be perfect the first time you run them. Fortunately, Eclipse and the Android Software Development Kit provide a rich set of tools for debugging, and even some features that make it easier to write correct code. We'll take a look at the set of available tools in this chapter, and provide some pointers to other places you can look for even more information on some of the tools.

The Tools

Throughout the development lifecycle of writing, building, and running the application, the primary tools Android developers use are:

Eclipse Java Editor
> A specific text editor for Java that Android SDK has informed about the Android programming environment. The editor not only warns you about code the compiler can't parse, but also gives you a wealth of information about what it can.

Java and Dalvik Build System
> Recall that Android converts your Java application to run on the Dalvik virtual machine under Android. The Java compiler and the Dalvik translator both provide error information if they can't build your application.

Eclipse Debugger
> Eclipse provides a source-level debugger that the Android SDK connects with the running Dalvik bytecode, so you have all the debug capability you'd normally expect from a Java program running under Eclipse.

Logcat
> Android also provides a general-purpose logging package that you can take advantage of to log informational or error messages from your running application. Perhaps of more importance, Android uses this facility extensively to tell you what is going on as it starts up, initiates your application, and tries to run it. There is also a special logcat log for telephony-related messages.

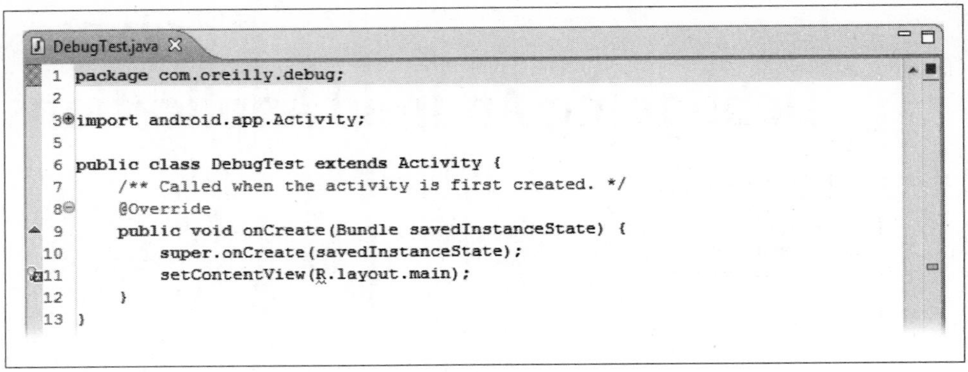

```
DebugTest.java ⊠
  1  package com.oreilly.debug;
  2
  3⊕ import android.app.Activity;
  5
  6  public class DebugTest extends Activity {
  7      /** Called when the activity is first created. */
  8⊖     @Override
▲ 9      public void onCreate(Bundle savedInstanceState) {
 10          super.onCreate(savedInstanceState);
⬚11          setContentView(R.layout.main);
 12      }
 13  }
```

Figure 5-1. Eclipse debug window upon startup

Android Debug Bridge (**adb**)
> This provides a command-line debugging interface to a running Android phone or emulator.

DDMS
> Android also provides a special window-oriented debugging environment custom tailored for Android and the Dalvik VM.

Traceview
> An Android-specific utility that tracks all the method calls your application executed and the time spent in each method.

Eclipse Java Editor

The Android SDK takes full advantage of the features built into the Eclipse IDE, including those in the Eclipse text editor, which is customized for Java source code development. Let's use a simple application as an example of some of that editor's features. If you're already an expert on using Eclipse for Java development, you can skip this section. If you're new to Eclipse (or new to Java), there are some hints here that will speed up your development of Android applications.

Java Errors

We've created a new Android project called DebugTest, using Eclipse and the Android SDK (File → New → Project → Android Project). When you do that, and open the Java source file the SDK created for you, you get a central pane that looks like Figure 5-1. This is the Eclipse Java text editor, and it is already doing its job to point out errors in the nascent application.

In this case, the error indication is in the left margin: the little lightbulb and red X on line 11. Within that line, the editor has underlined the R in R.layout.main to tell you specifically where there's a problem. Editors in Eclipse are smart enough to understand

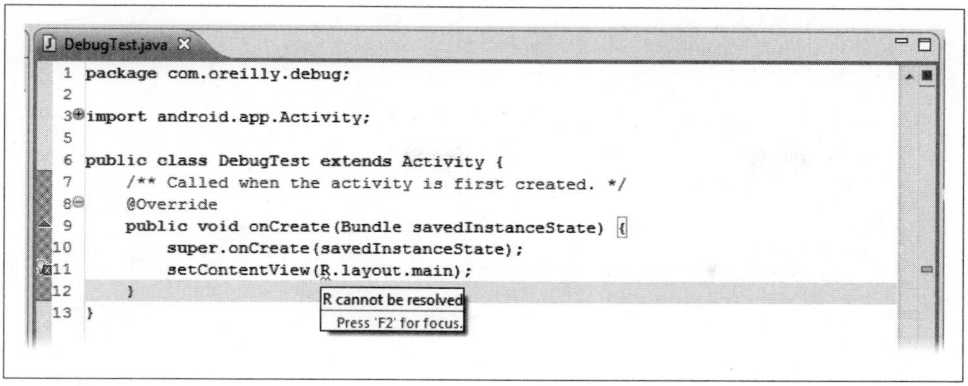

Figure 5-2. Eclipse error detail

the syntax of the language they are editing, and in this case, the error flag is telling us there's a problem with this part of the code. If we use the mouse to hover over the R, we get a pop up that gives us more information, as shown in Figure 5-2. If you hover your mouse over the symbols in the left margin, you get the same pop up.

Notice also that there's a little red indicator in the upper-right area of the pane, indicating there is an error somewhere in this file, and a little red open rectangle in the right margin. If this file were big enough to need the vertical scroll bar, you could easily see the locations of the errors in the file, and you could scroll to them by dragging the scroll segment to the red rectangle. Eclipse makes it very easy to see where it has found errors in your code.

A quick check of the Package Explorer pane shows that there's no *R.java* file. Of course not! It doesn't exist, because we haven't built the project yet, and that's why resources under R can't be resolved. After we build DebugTest (Project → Build All), the error goes away (both the red underline and the symbols in the margin).

So let's add some code for a simple application and see some of Eclipse's debug features. We'll edit *DebugTest.java* and *main.xml* to add a label, a text box, a WebView (we want some Internet action to give us more to look at), and a button. The application will be a trivial browser, with the box being the URL and the button being the trigger to go load the URL into the WebView. We'll throw in some intentional errors to see how Eclipse handles them.

Our altered *main.xml* file now looks like this:

```
<?xml version="1.0" encoding="utf-8"?>
<LinearLayout xmlns:android="http://schemas.android.com/apk/res/android"
    android:orientation="vertical"
    android:layout_width="fill_parent"
    android:layout_height="fill_parent"
    >
<TextView
    android:layout_width="fill_parent"
    android:layout_height="wrap_content"
```

```
        android:text="Enter URL:"
        />
    <EditText
        android:id="@+id/URL"
        android:layout_width="fill_parent"
        android:layout_height="60.0dip"
        android:maxLines="1"

    <Button
        android:id="@+id/btnGo"
        android:layout_width="wrap_content"
        android:layout_height="60.0dip"
        android:text="Go"
        />
    <WebView
        android:id="@+id/wvBrowser"
        android:layout_width="fill_parent"
        android:layout_height="wrap_content"
        />
    <LinearLayout>
```

and *DebugTest.java* looks like this:

```
package com.oreilly.debug;

import android.app.Activity;
import android.os.Bundle;

public class DebugTest extends Activity {
    private EditText txtURL;
    private Button btnGo;
    private WebView wvBrowser;

    // Set up an onClick routine to gather URLs entered by the user
    private final Button.OnClickListener btnGoOnClick = new Button.OnClickListener() {
        public void onClick(View v) {
            try {
                wvBrowser.loadURL();
            }
            catch (Exception e) {}
        }
    };

    /** Called when the activity is first created. */
    @Override
    public void onCreate(Bundle savedInstanceState) {
        super.onCreate(savedInstanceState);
        setContentView(R.layout.main);

        // Find the Views in the layout file
        txtURL = (EditText) findViewById(R.id.txtURL);
        btnGo = (Button) findViewById(R.id.btnGo);
        btnGo.setOnClickListener(btnGoOnClick);
        wvBrowser = (WebView) findViewById(R.id.wvBrowser);
    }
}
```

If you type in these lines (instead of copying and pasting), you'll see that the editor tries to anticipate what you might type given the context of where you are in the code. As you type "wvBrowser.", for example (including the final dot), the editor knows that **wvBrowser** is a WebView, so it gives you a list of methods and variables that WebViews have. This is a great feature that really helps cut down on mistyped method and variable names. Once you've typed or selected the method, the editor shows you the parameters for that method, so you don't have to look those up either.

Since we need to access the Internet to get web pages, we ask for that permission in *AndroidManifest.xml*:

```xml
<?xml version="1.0" encoding="utf-8"?>
<manifest xmlns:android="http://schemas.android.com/apk/res/android"
    package="com.oreilly.debug"
    android:versionCode="1"
    android:versionName="1.0.0">
    <application android:icon="@drawable/icon" android:label="@string/app_name">
        <activity android:name=".DebugTest"
                android:label="@string/app_name">
            <intent-filter>
                <action android:name="android.intent.action.MAIN" />
                <category android:name="android.intent.category.LAUNCHER" />
            </intent-filter>
        </activity>
    </application>
<uses-permission android:name="android.permission.INTERNET"></uses-permission>
</manifest>
```

Looking at *main.xml* in the Eclipse editor pane (now an XML editor, but with many of the same features we saw in the Java editor), we see some errors (Figure 5-3).

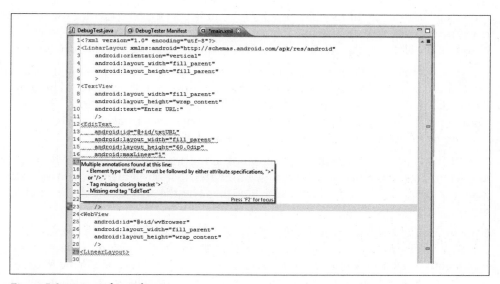

Figure 5-3. main.xml in Eclipse

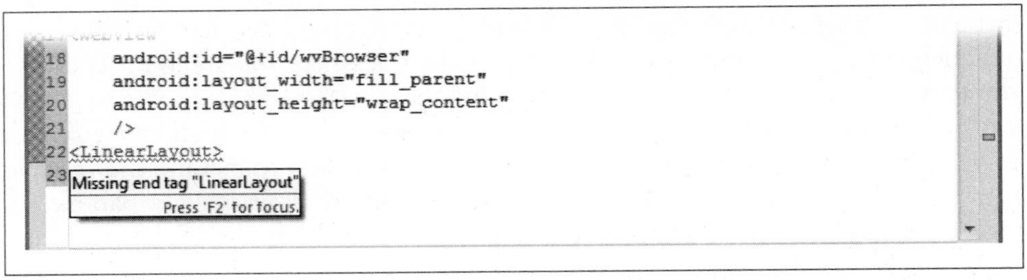

Figure 5-4. Additional main.xml error

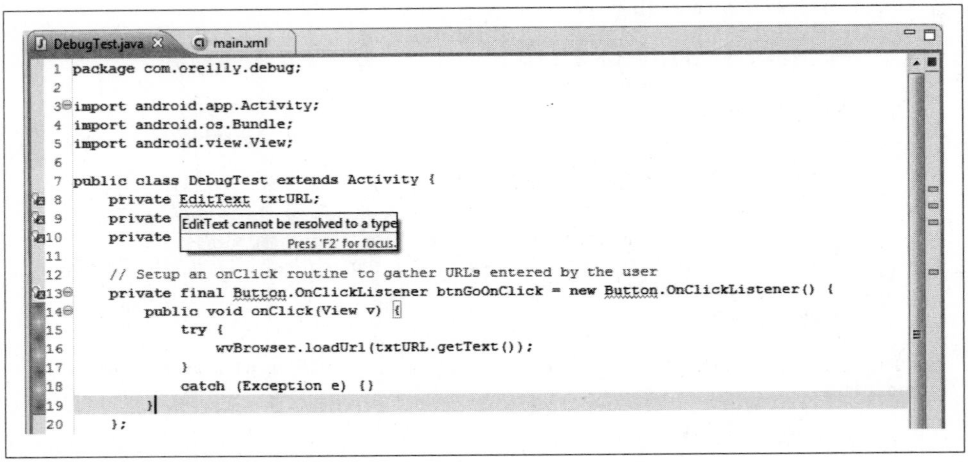

Figure 5-5. DebugTest.java with errors, screen 1

A quick inspection confirms what the editor is telling us—that there's no close tag for the EditText. We type /> into line 17, and the red underlines immediately go away. Now that the EditText tag is fixed, we're left with one more error, shown in Figure 5-4.

It says we're missing the end tag for LinearLayout, but we're really missing the slash that should start the end tag </LinearLayout>. From the editor's syntactical point of view, it knows only that it expected to find a </LinearLayout> before the next <Linear Layout> tag or the end of the file, and it didn't find one. The error message is enough to cause us to look in the right place and figure out what is really wrong.

Now that we have *main.xml* fixed up, let's look at the first part of *DebugTest.java* as it appears in Eclipse (Figure 5-5). We can see from the right scroll margin that there are a total of seven errors, and our mouse is hovering over the error in the declaration of btnGo.

Now for one of my favorite features of Eclipse. The source of the error displayed in Figure 5-5, it turns out, is that EditText can't be resolved in the example, because we haven't imported the package that defines EditTexts. You could go look in the Android documentation and find the right name for the library, but Eclipse has a labor-saving

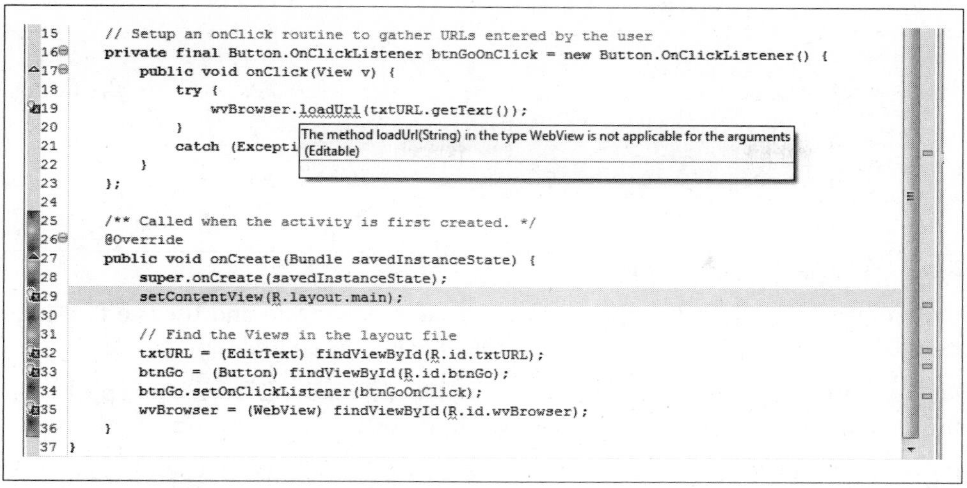

```
 15      // Setup an onClick routine to gather URLs entered by the user
 16⊖    private final Button.OnClickListener btnGoOnClick = new Button.OnClickListener() {
▲17⊖        public void onClick(View v) {
 18            try {
●19                wvBrowser.loadUrl(txtURL.getText());
 20            }
 21            catch (Excepti┌─────────────────────────────────────────────────────────┐
 22        }            │The method loadUrl(String) in the type WebView is not applicable for the arguments│
 23    };               │(Editable)                                               │
 24                     └─────────────────────────────────────────────────────────┘
 25    /** Called when the activity is first created. */
 26⊖    @Override
▲27    public void onCreate(Bundle savedInstanceState) {
 28        super.onCreate(savedInstanceState);
●29        setContentView(R.layout.main);
 30
 31        // Find the Views in the layout file
 32        txtURL = (EditText) findViewById(R.id.txtURL);
 33        btnGo = (Button) findViewById(R.id.btnGo);
 34        btnGo.setOnClickListener(btnGoOnClick);
 35        wvBrowser = (WebView) findViewById(R.id.wvBrowser);
 36    }
 37 }
```

Figure 5-6. DebugTest.java with errors, screen 2

feature that will find it for you. Just type Ctrl-Shift-O (that's the letter O) while the editor has focus, and Eclipse will attempt to resolve all the unresolved references in the file by finding appropriate libraries. With that one stroke, the appropriate packages get imported for EditText, Button, and WebView (you can't see them in Figure 5-5, because they're hidden by the pop up), and those errors disappear from the editing pane as well.

That leaves us with five more errors, so we scroll down as shown in the Eclipse screenshot in Figure 5-6.

The four errors in lines 29, 32, 33, and 35 have the same source as the one in Figure 5-2 and will go away the first time we build the project with the new *main.xml*. Let's fix the remaining error using Eclipse's help.

We currently have the mouse hovering over the error in line 19, and the pop up says we're trying to pass an Editable instead of a String to the loadURL(String) method. That's easy to fix: Editables have a toString method, like most objects, so we can change onClick to look like this:

```
public void onClick(View v) {
    try {
        wvBrowser.loadUrl(txtURL.getText().toString());
    }
    catch (Exception e) {}
}
```

Now we try to build and run the project (Run → Run → Android Application), but Eclipse tells us we still have errors. It helpfully lists all the problems found in the Problems tab, located in the pane at the bottom of the Eclipse window. Figure 5-7 shows that tab.

Clicking on an error in the Problems tab takes us directly to the corresponding line of source code in the Editing pane for *DebugTest.java*. A quick look at *main.xml* reveals

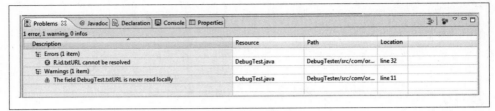

Figure 5-7. DebugTest compile problems

the problem: we referred to the text box as URL in *main.xml*, and tried to find it as txtURL in the Java code. A quick fix to *main.xml*, and the compile completes.

Eclipse starts the Android emulator for us and loads our application so it appears on the screen. The application runs—now to see whether it produces correct results.

If you type in a URL like www.oreilly.com and click the Go button, you get...an error. Instead of the web page you asked for, you see a page that says "Web Page not Available." Let's try http://www.oreilly.com...ah, that works. So let's add code that checks whether the URL starts with http://, and if not, adds it:

```
public void onClick(View v) {
    try {
        String sURL = txtURL.getText().toString();
        if(sURL.substring(0,6).equals("http://")) {
            wvBrowser.loadUrl(sURL);
        }else{
            sURL = "http://" + sURL;
            wvBrowser.loadUrl(sURL);
        }
    }
    catch (Exception e) {}
}
```

Now when we run the program using www.oreilly.com as the URL, it works—but http://www.oreilly.com doesn't! Let's use the debugger to figure out why.

The Debugger

The Android SDK makes the use of the Eclipse debugger completely transparent, so let's use it to see what's going wrong with our program. We'll put a breakpoint at the line we just entered, so the debugger will break there when we run the program. Eclipse gives us three ways to toggle a breakpoint:

- Use the menus. Select the line you want to toggle and choose Run → Toggle Breakpoint.
- Use the keyboard. Select the line you want to toggle and key Ctrl-Shift-B.
- Double-click in the left margin of the editor window at the line you want to toggle (my favorite method).

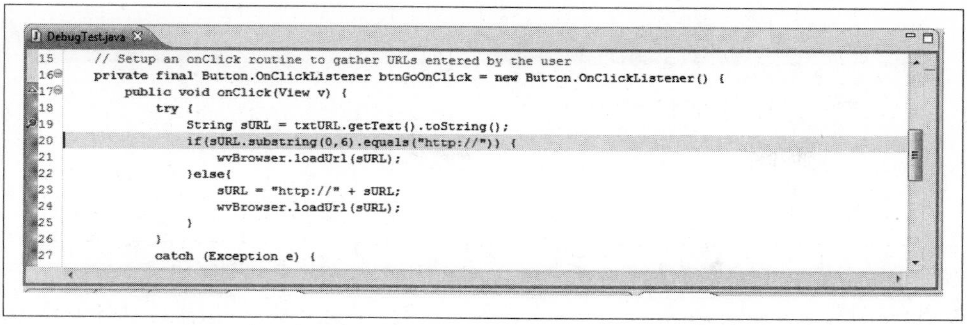

Figure 5-8. Editor pane showing breakpoint

Whatever way you choose, you end up with a breakpoint mark in the left margin of the editor window, as shown in Figure 5-8.

To invoke the Debugger, choose Run → Debug → Android Application from the Eclipse menu. Eclipse and the Android SDK do what they did before (build the program if necessary, convert to Dalvik, invoke the emulator, load your program, and start it running). You may get a window in the Emulator that says "Waiting for Debugger: Application DebugTest is waiting for the Debugger to connect." If you do, just wait a few seconds and the Debugger should finish initializing, the window will disappear, and you'll see the DebugTest screen.

Now enter `http://www.oreilly.com` and click the Go button. DebugTest starts executing and breaks at the breakpoint. Eclipse automatically changes to the Debug Perspective, showing you panes that apply to debugging your application. Starting from the upper left and moving down the window, left to right, these are:

Debug
> The Debug pane has a single tab (Debug) that shows a trace of recent execution. It should show that you are at a breakpoint in a Dalvik thread running DebugTest, at Java line 19. In its toolbar, this pane also contains the buttons for Resume, Suspend, Terminate, Step Into, Step Over, Step Return, etc.

Variables and Breakpoints
> This pane has two tabs, the most useful of which is Variables, where you can see the current value of variables that are in scope. So far it's showing values for `this` and `v`.

Editor
> This contains a tab for each of the source files that you had open in the Java Perspective. The currently displayed tab should show *DebugTest.java*, highlighting the current breakpoint (line 19).

Outline
> This shows the structure of your application. DebugTest is simple, so it shows only one method, `OnCreate`.

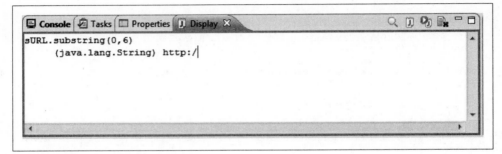

Figure 5-9. Eclipse debugger display pane

Console/Tasks/Properties

This pane has tabs for each of these views, which don't contain much that's interesting at the moment. The Console is the most useful, and in some debug situations can have important information telling you what is (or isn't) happening.

Logcat

This is the subject of the next section: the contents of the Android logcat log, with buttons to filter the content.

Focusing on the Editor pane, which shows us stopped at line 19, let's use the Step Over button (in the Debug toolbar in the pane above) to step the program one line, to line 20. Now sURL appears in the Variables Pane, and it has the right value, http://www.oreilly.com. Step once more and you can tell something's wrong: we expected the program to take the first branch of the if, and it took the second instead. That's why http:// is appearing twice in the URL string. If we step once more we can see that, as the value of sURL changes in the Variables Pane.

To find out why, let's use another debug feature of Eclipse. From the menu, choose Window → Show View → Display. A new Display tab is added to the lower-left pane, and comes to the front. As long as the Debugger is running, you can type any variable or expression that's in scope into this window to display the variable's value or execute the expression. We should be curious about the expression we're comparing the user's URL to, sURL.substring(0,6). So cut and paste this method call from the Editor pane into the Display tab, select the expression, right-click, and choose Display from the pop-up menu. Eclipse evaluates the expression and displays the result in the pane—and what do you know, it's http:/, with the last / missing, as shown in Figure 5-9. This problem may be typical of errors that programmers encounter with the use of Java's substring method, because its second parameter represents the location of the last character, not the count of characters, as in some other languages. We change the 6 to 7, and the program works fine.

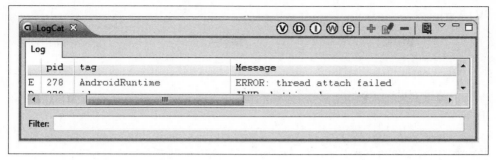

Figure 5-10. Logcat pane, minimized

Logcat

Granted, the errors we debugged in the last section were pretty straightforward—no different from debugging in any other environment. But most applications are not as simple as DebugTest, and many problems are much harder to isolate and solve. Android provides a general-purpose logging facility that can help with many of those more difficult problems.

As mentioned before, there's a logcat pane on the Debug perspective (it's also in the DDMS perspective, which we'll talk about in the next section and in "DDMS: Dalvik Debug Monitor Service" on page 74). The log for DebugTest isn't very interesting, so instead start MJAndroid in Debug mode and we'll take a look at its log.

After the application comes up in the emulator, Eclipse switches to the Debug Perspective and shows the logcat pane on the lower right, as it looks in Figure 5-10.

To make the pane large enough to be useful for reading the log, click on the "full screen" symbol at the upper right of the pane, and it will expand to fill the Eclipse window. You will then see that there are hundreds of log messages in the file, going back to when Eclipse first started the instantiation of the emulator that you are using, continuing through the boot process for Android, loading all the applications, and finally loading and executing MJAndroid. How are you supposed to find anything useful in all of that?

Luckily, Android provides you with some handy filters to apply to the logfile. See the V, D, I, W, and E symbols in the toolbar? These filters successively narrow the scope of messages displayed, as follows:

V (Verbose)
> Show everything

D (Debug)
> Show Debug, Information, Warning, and Error messages (equivalent to V for now)

I (Information)
> Show Information, Warning, and Error messages

W (Warning)
> Show Warning and Error messages

E (Error)
> Show only Error messages

The columns displayed for the log are:

Time
> The time the log entry was made

Priority (the column is not actually labeled)
> One of the log entry types from the previous list (D, I, W, or E)

pid
> The Linux process ID of the process making the entry

tag
> A short tag describing the source of the entry

Message
> The log entry itself

About two-thirds of the way through the log (if you started a new emulator when you brought up MJAndroid), you'll see a message entry something like:

```
11-28 12:10:31.475: INFO/ActivityManager(52): Start proc com.microjobsinc.mjandroid
    for activity com.microjobsinc.mjandroid/.MicroJobs:
                    pid=163 uid=10017 gids={3003}
```

which actually appears all on one line; we've broken it here so it will fit on a printed page.

This is a log message from the Activity Manager telling us that it started MicroJobs with process ID 163 (it will probably be different as you run it). If you click on the green cross at the top of the logcat pane, it will let you define a custom filter. Fill in a random name and the pid number that you saw in the log. Now the log is filtered to show only the messages that apply to this instance of MicroJobs. There are likely still a lot of messages, which you can filter further (using the D, I, W, and E buttons) or just scan.

 If you ask other people for help debugging an error in your own program, one of the first things you'll likely be asked for is a copy of the logcat output. You can easily extract the content of the logfile to a text file by selecting what you'd like to preserve and clicking on the little down arrow at the upper right of the logcat pane, which brings down a pull-down menu. One of the selections on the menu is "Export Selection as Text…", which takes you to a dialog where you can name an output file for the log text.

Figure 5-11. "Stopped unexpectedly" message

Looking at logcat to solve runtime errors

Logcat gives you a lot of information about what happened as Android tried to run your program. It is very useful when you get a generic error message from Android that doesn't tell you much. Let's demonstrate one of my (least) favorites.

In Eclipse, go to *main.xml* for MJAndroid and remove the *apiKey* line under the MapView declaration (save it in a text file or somewhere, so you can restore it; we're doing this just to generate an error). The *apiKey* is needed to access mapping information, so removing it brings the program to a screeching halt. When you run the program, the emulator screen looks like Figure 5-11.

Although it's good to know that the application stopped, the message tells us very little about why. If you now look at the logcat output in the Debug perspective (or the DDMS perspective), you'll find something like this after MicroJobs starts up, all in red type (we've left off the first few columns so it will fit):

```
java.lang.RuntimeException: Unable to start activity
   ComponentInfo{com.microjobsinc.mjandroid/com.microjobsinc.mjandroid.MicroJobs}:
                android.view.InflateException: Binary XML file line #8: Error
                    inflating class java.lang.reflect.Constructor
```

```
        at android.app.ActivityThread.performLaunchActivity(ActivityThread.java:2140)
        at android.app.ActivityThread.handleLaunchActivity(ActivityThread.java:2156)
        at android.app.ActivityThread.access$1800(ActivityThread.java:112)
        at android.app.ActivityThread$H.handleMessage(ActivityThread.java:1580)
        at android.os.Handler.dispatchMessage(Handler.java:88)
        at android.os.Looper.loop(Looper.java:123)
        at android.app.ActivityThread.main(ActivityThread.java:3742)
        at java.lang.reflect.Method.invokeNative(Native Method)
        at java.lang.reflect.Method.invoke(Method.java:515)
        at com.android.internal.os.ZygoteInit$MethodAndArgsCaller.run(ZygoteInit.java:739)
        at com.android.internal.os.ZygoteInit.main(ZygoteInit.java:497)
        at dalvik.system.NativeStart.main(Native Method)
Caused by: android.view.InflateException: Binary XML file line #8: Error
 inflating class
  java.lang.reflect.Constructor
        at android.view.LayoutInflater.createView(LayoutInflater.java:512)
        at android.view.LayoutInflater.createViewFromTag(LayoutInflater.java:564)
        at android.view.LayoutInflater.rInflate(LayoutInflater.java:617)
        at android.view.LayoutInflater.inflate(LayoutInflater.java:407)
        at android.view.LayoutInflater.inflate(LayoutInflater.java:320)
        at android.view.LayoutInflater.inflate(LayoutInflater.java:276)
        at
         com.android.internal.policy.impl.PhoneWindow.setContentView(PhoneWindow.java:227)
        at android.app.Activity.setContentView(Activity.java:1569)
        at com.microjobsinc.mjandroid.MicroJobs.onCreate(MicroJobs.java:132)
        at android.app.Instrumentation.callActivityOnCreate(Instrumentation.java:1122)
        at android.app.ActivityThread.performLaunchActivity(ActivityThread.java:2103)
        ... 11 more
Caused by: java.lang.reflect.InvocationTargetException
        at com.google.android.maps.MapView.<init>(MapView.java:227)
        at java.lang.reflect.Constructor.constructNative(Native Method)
        at java.lang.reflect.Constructor.newInstance(Constructor.java:424)
        at android.view.LayoutInflater.createView(LayoutInflater.java:499)
        ... 21 more
Caused by: java.lang.IllegalArgumentException: You need to specify an API Key for
  each MapView.
  See the MapView documentation
                    for details.
        at com.google.android.maps.MapView.<init>(MapView.java:263)
        at com.google.android.maps.MapView.<init>(MapView.java:244)
        ... 25 more
```

The first three errors basically tell us that Android could not start our application because it could not inflate the Views it found in our layout file. The last error block we showed in the output clearly tells us we need an API Key for each MapView. Logcat is often the best way to get insight into errors where there isn't specific information otherwise.

Writing your own logcat entries

To write your own entries from your application into logcat, Android provides methods corresponding to the different entry priorities. The methods are all of the form:

```
Log.x(String tag, String message, [Throwable exception])
```

where *x* can be v, d, i, w, or e, and the optional exception makes it easy to report exceptions that you didn't anticipate in your code but encounter within a try/catch block. For example, look at the onItemSelected method for the Spinner in *Micro Jobs.java*:

```
try {
    mc.animateTo(mMyLocationOverlay.getMyLocation());
}
catch (Exception e) {
    Log.i("MicroJobs", "Unable to animate map", e);
}
mvMap.invalidate();
```

Android Debug Bridge (adb)

Android comes with a specialized command-line debug utility called adb. It lets you control a device or emulator from your host, offering the kind of remote terminal or remote shell service that embedded programmers have come to expect when working with their target systems. Invoke the **adb** client from a command prompt on the host (Start → Run → cmd.exe on Windows, or open a terminal window on Linux or OS X). The client talks to an adb server that runs in background on the host and processes requests. If the server isn't running when you start the client, it starts the server for you. The server in turn communicates with adb daemons that run on either a device or an emulator. All of this communication is through TCP/IP ports. A single client/server can deal with multiple devices and emulators, but to simplify things for our discussion, we'll assume there's only one.

If you just type **adb** at the command prompt, you get the help information for **adb**:

```
Android Debug Bridge version 1.0.20

 -d                            - directs command to the only connected USB device
                                 returns an error if more than one USB device
                                   is present.
 -e                            - directs command to the only running emulator.
                                 returns an error if more than one emulator
                                   is running.
 -s <serial number>           - directs command to the USB device or emulator with
                                 the given serial number
 -p <product name or path>    - simple product name like 'sooner', or
                                 a relative/absolute path to a product
                                 out directory like 'out/target/product/sooner'.
                                 If -p is not specified, the ANDROID_PRODUCT_OUT
                                 environment variable is used, which must
                                 be an absolute path.
 devices                       - list all connected devices

device commands:
  adb push <local> <remote>   - copy file/dir to device
  adb pull <remote> <local>   - copy file/dir from device
  adb sync [ <directory> ]    - copy host -> device only if changed
                                 (see 'adb help all')
```

```
    adb shell                          - run remote shell interactively
    adb shell <command>                - run remote shell command
    adb emu <command>                  - run emulator console command
    adb logcat [ <filter-spec> ]       - View device log
    adb forward <local> <remote>       - forward socket connections
                                         forward specs are one of:
                                           tcp:<port>
                                           localabstract:<unix domain socket name>
                                           localreserved:<unix domain socket name>
                                           localfilesystem:<unix domain socket name>
                                           dev:<character device name>
                                           jdwp:<process pid> (remote only)
    adb jdwp                           - list PIDs of processes hosting a JDWP transport
    adb install [-l] [-r] <file>       - push this package file to the device and install it
                                         ('-l' means forward-lock the app)
                                         ('-r' means reinstall the app, keeping its data)
    adb uninstall [-k] <package>       - remove this app package from the device
                                         ('-k' means keep the data and cache directories)
    adb bugreport                      - return all information from the device
                                         that should be included in a bug report.

    adb help                           - show this help message
    adb version                        - show version num

DATAOPTS:
 (no option)                           - don't touch the data partition
    -w                                 - wipe the data partition
    -d                                 - flash the data partition

scripting:
    adb wait-for-device                - block until device is online
    adb start-server                   - ensure that there is a server running
    adb kill-server                    - kill the server if it is running
    adb get-state                      - prints: offline | bootloader | device
    adb get-product                    - prints: <product-id>
    adb get-serialno                   - prints: <serial-number>
    adb status-window                  - continuously print device status for a specified
                                         device
    adb remount                        - remounts the /system partition on the device
                                         read-write

networking:
    adb ppp <tty> [parameters]         - Run PPP over USB.
 Note: you should not automatically start a PDP connection.
 <tty> refers to the tty for PPP stream. Eg. dev:/dev/omap_csmi_tty1
 [parameters] - Eg. defaultroute debug dump local notty usepeerdns

adb sync notes: adb sync [ <directory> ]
    <localdir> can be interpreted in several ways:

  - If <directory> is not specified, both /system and /data partitions will be
      updated.

  - If it is "system" or "data", only the corresponding partition
      is updated.
```

Here are a few of the more useful **adb** commands. There is much more information about these and other **adb** commands in the Android documentation and online.

adb devices
Displays a list of devices and emulators that the adb server knows about. This is a good way to find the TCP/IP port for an emulator or device if you don't already know it. The port number is also displayed in the title of each emulator at the top of its window. If there's only one device or emulator running (the normal case, unless you're debugging a multidevice application), any **adb** commands you issue automatically go to that target. The -s and -e options are provided for multidevice applications to let you specify a device or emulator.

adb shell
This connects you with a shell running on the target and gives you a # prompt. The shell is a simplified Unix-like shell, so you can use the usual shell commands (**ls**, **cat**, **rm**, **ps**, etc.) to explore the target and make changes as appropriate. Ctrl-D or **exit** will get you out of the shell and back to your environment on the host.

sqlite3 *[path_to_database]*
A particularly useful shell command (you have to get into the shell with **adb shell** first) for manipulating SQLite database files. The *sqlite3* program is further described in Chapter 8, and on the SQLite website (*http://www.sqlite.org*). You can optionally include the path to the database file you want to manipulate (the MJAndroid database, for example, would be in data/data/com.micro jobsinc.mjandroid/databases/MJAndroid).

adb logcat *[filter_spec]*
This is another way of looking at the logcat log on the target. When you run it, it dumps the existing log to your virtual terminal and continues to send additional log entries as they are generated in the running system. The command is normally entered with a trailing &, the Unix parameter for "run this in a separate process," so that you can go on and use the terminal for other commands (including, eventually, to kill the logcat process). The filter specs are of the form *tag:priority*, where *tag* and *priority* were described in "Logcat" on page 67. So the command to see all AndroidRuntime log entries of priority E would be:

> **adb logcat** AndroidRuntime:E &

This is also useful for reading the "other" logs, of which there are two: radio and events. The radio log is accessed through a command like:

> **adb -b** radio &

Similarly, to read the events log, enter:

> **adb -b** events &

adb install *[-1] [-r] file_spec*
This can be used to install or reinstall an application. The -1 option forward-locks the installation (preventing the application from being copied later to another

device), and the -r option reinstalls the application without overwriting the existing application data. The *file_spec* must be a valid, signed *.apk* file for the application to be installed.

adb uninstall *[-k] package*

This uninstalls the application with the given package name. The *package* parameter needs to be the full name of the package, without the ".*apk*" extension. So to uninstall MicroJobs, for example, you'd type:

```
adb uninstall com.microjobsinc.mjandroid
```

If you want to keep the application's associated data, you include the -k option.

adb push *local remote*

This command copies a file from the *local* name on the host to the *remote* name on the target.

adb pull *remote local*

This is the counterpart to the previous command, and copies a file from the target to the host.

DDMS: Dalvik Debug Monitor Service

Installing the Android Software Development Kit adds DDMS to the Eclipse integrated development environment, providing a window-oriented interface to Android-specific debug information on the target. The most frequently used perspectives are displayed in the upper-right corner of the Eclipse window. If there's a DDMS button there, you can just click on it to switch to DDMS. If not, in that same area there is a little window symbol with a + sign in its upper-right corner. Clicking on this window will open a menu of Perspectives, including DDMS.

The DDMS perspective has four panes by default. Starting from the upper left and going left to right down the screen, these are:

Devices

This lists the available target devices connected to Eclipse, and the processes running on each device. The default emulator device is labeled with its port number (5554). There are also some toolbar buttons in this pane, described later in this section.

Threads/Heap/File Explorer

This provides three different views of what is going on in the target. The Threads tab shows the currently active threads in the selected "client," which is the application selected in the Devices pane. To see the Threads information, you have to click the "Update Threads" button at the top of the Devices pane. The Heap tab shows the state of the VM's heap memory, and is updated at each garbage collect. Again, in order to see the Heap information, you need to enable it by clicking the "Update Heap" button at the top of the Devices pane, and you may need to exercise the application for a while until the VM decides a garbage collect is required before the information will be updated. You can also force a garbage collect by clicking on the "Cause GC" button in the Heap view.

Emulator Control

This gives you control of the Telephony and Location emulation functions:

Telephony Emulator

You can simulate voice and data operation in a variety of network states (unregistered, home, roaming, searching, denied) and at a variety of network speeds and latencies. It's useful to vary these parameters during application testing to be sure that your application responds appropriately in all typical situations. You can also simulate incoming voice and SMS calls from a specific number (to test Caller ID), and create the SMS message to be received.

Location Emulator

Here you can send a specific location fix to the Location Provider by entering a latitude and longitude. You can alternatively load a GPX or KML file of locations to be played back to the Location Provider in a continuous sequence, as though the target was moving around.

Logcat/Console/Outline/Properties

This is similar to the "catchall" pane in the Debug perspective, providing a collection of useful tabs that display the indicated information.

Screen Capture

This isn't a pane, but one of the toolbar buttons in the Display pane. It looks like a very small Android screen, and when you click it, it captures and displays what is currently showing on the target screen. It gives you the opportunity to save the capture to a PNG file, which you can then use as you would any other image.

Traceview

Maybe the problem you're trying to debug isn't about functionality. Maybe your application does exactly what it's supposed to do, but takes too long to do it. Wouldn't it be nice to have a way of seeing how the methods within your classes are interacting, and even to keep track of the relative time spent executing in each method? Traceview is a utility that allow you just that kind of visibility. It consists of two parts, one that you enable before running your program and one that you work with after the run in order to diagnose your findings:

Runtime data collection

You can enable and disable logging for your application. While enabled, routines are linked into your application that create a binary trace file on the target. The trace file records every method instantiation and the time spent in each method.

Trace analysis

If you then copy the binary trace file from the target to your host, you can run a trace analysis program that displays all the information from the file in graphical form. You can easily observe which methods are consuming most of the runtime, and drill down into those methods to find out which methods they in turn call and which of them consume the most time.

Trace data collection

The routines to perform trace data collection are provided in the Android Software Development Kit. All you have to do is:

1. Import the Debug package (*android.os.Debug*) into your application.
2. Call `startMethodTracing` when you want to start collecting trace information.
3. Call `stopMethodTracing` when you're done.

The tracing routines always write their trace information to a file on the target's SD card. If you're running on a real device, you need to plug in an SD card. If you're debugging on the emulator, you need to create a virtual SD card and tell the emulator to use it:

1. Create a virtual SD card with **mksdcard**.

   From the host command prompt, use the **mksdcard** utility to create a file that the emulator can use as a virtual SD card:

   ```
   $ mksdcard -l ANDROID 1024M filename
   ```

   You can create the file anywhere you like, but the root directory for your project is a good place. The utility will allocate a file as big as the size you've given in the **mksdcard** command (1 GB in the example shown).

2. Tell the emulator to use the virtual SD card.

   In Eclipse, choose Window → Preferences → Android → Launch. You'll see a box there for emulator options. Add the following option:

   ```
   -sdcard filename
   ```

   Use the complete path to the file, so the emulator can always find it, no matter where it's running from.

As an example of the code needed, let's add tracing to MicroJobs and collect some data. We add tracing to *MicroJobs.java* as follows:

```
...

import android.os.Debug;

...

    public void onCreate(Bundle savedInstanceState) {
        super.onCreate(savedInstanceState);

        // start trace
        Debug.startMethodTracing("x");
```

...

```
    // stop tracing when application ends
    @Override
    public void onDestroy() {
        super.onDestroy();
        Debug.stopMethodTracing();
    }
```

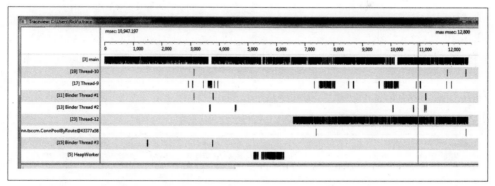

Figure 5-12. Traceview Timeline Panel

Running MJAndroid now creates a file named *x.trace* on the virtual SD card on the target. When tracing is enabled, the Dalvik virtual machine is noticeably slower to start up and slower to run, because it is mapping the virtual SD card into memory, and collecting all the method call and timing data for you as it runs. For this example we went through a few UI operations and then closed the application.

To analyze *x.trace*, move it back to the host:

```
$ adb pull sdcard/x.trace x.trace
```

and start the Traceview program:

```
$ traceview pathnamex.trace
```

For the moment at least, Traceview expects the full pathname of the trace file.

You are rewarded with a display of all the methods that were called between the time you started and stopped the trace—not just the methods in your application, but *all* the methods that were called. The top part of the display is the Timeline Panel, which looks something like Figure 5-12. The numbered line across the top is a timeline (in milliseconds), with each application thread listed as a separate row. Within each row, each method invocation is shown as a little colored block (a little hard to see at the startup resolution). The colors map to a list of methods shown in Figure 5-12.

You can zoom in on a region of interest by moving the mouse into the timeline area, clicking the left mouse button at the start time of interest, dragging to the stop time, and releasing the button. The timeline then zooms in, as shown in Figure 5-13. As you

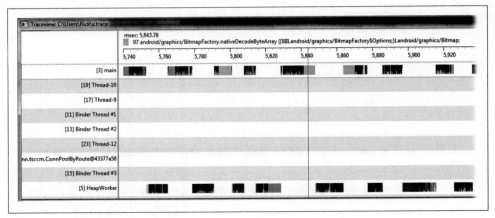

Figure 5-13. Traceview zoom into Timeline Panel

Name	Incl %	Inclusive	Exc...	Exclu...	Calls+...	Tim...
0 (toplevel)	100.0%	12685.140	0.8%	99.003	14+0	906.081
1 android/os/Handler.dispatchMessage (Landroid/os/Message;)V	42.8%	5431.843	0.0%	4.289	23+0	236.167
2 android/view/ViewRoot.handleMessage (Landroid/os/Message;)V	37.0%	4694.532	0.0%	1.116	10+0	469.453
3 android/view/ViewRoot.performTraversals ()V	36.7%	4653.012	0.1%	10.758	6+0	775.502
4 android/view/ViewRoot.draw (Z)V	29.9%	3790.733	0.0%	2.449	5+0	758.147
5 com/android/internal/policy/impl/PhoneWindow$DecorView.dra	29.7%	3768.862	0.0%	0.394	5+0	753.772
6 android/widget/FrameLayout.draw (Landroid/graphics/Canvas;)V	29.7%	3768.468	0.0%	1.356	5+7	314.039
7 android/view/View.draw (Landroid/graphics/Canvas;)V	29.7%	3768.078	0.2%	28.358	5+39	85.638
8 android/view/ViewGroup.dispatchDraw (Landroid/graphics/Canv;	29.5%	3745.518	0.1%	12.476	5+27	117.047
9 android/view/ViewGroup.drawChild (Landroid/graphics/Canvas;L	29.5%	3744.036	0.2%	31.226	5+42	79.660
10 com/google/android/maps/MapView.onDraw (Landroid/graphic	26.4%	3350.741	0.0%	3.000	5+0	670.148
11 java/lang/Thread.run ()V	22.6%	2866.000	0.0%	0.220	3+0	955.333
12 com/google/common/DataRequestDispatcher$DispatcherServer	22.5%	2857.907	0.0%	1.535	1+0	2857.907
13 com/google/common/DataRequestDispatcher.serviceRequests (	22.5%	2855.970	0.0%	2.377	1+0	2855.970
14 com/google/common/io/android/AndroidHttpConnectionFact	18.2%	2311.515	0.0%	0.064	1+0	2311.515

Figure 5-14. Traceview list of methods

move the mouse from left to right, the timeline cursor shows the sequence of method calls, and the method names are called out in the upper right.

The bottom part of the Traceview display lists each method, in declining order by the amount of time spent in it. The first part of that list is shown in Figure 5-14.

The columns in this display have the following meanings:

Name

You can't see colors here, but on the screen, the color in the color-coded box to the left of each name tracks to the timeline shown in Figure 5-12. The 15 colors get reused in order by inclusive time, as you go down the list.

Incl% and Inclusive

The time (and percentage of total time) spent in this method, including all the methods that it called. The times are in milliseconds, but they should be interpreted with care. Because tracing slows down execution considerably, these times do not represent the true runtimes under normal execution. They do provide accurate relative timing information when comparing the runtimes of two methods.

Excl% and Exclusive

The time (and percentage of total time) spent actually executing in this method. In other words, any time spent in nested functions is removed from these two fields. The same timing caveats apply to Exclusive times as to Inclusive.

Calls+Recursive calls

Two values: the number of times this method was called externally and the number of times it called itself.

Time/Call

Simply the quotient of the second column divided by the sum of the numbers in the sixth column.

When you select a method by clicking on its name in the Profile Panel, Traceview adjusts the pane to bring that method to the top of the view, and opens a list of Parent and Child methods, as shown in Figure 5-15. "Parents" are methods that call this method. "Children" are methods called by this method.

Name	Incl %	Inclusive	Exc...	Exclu...	Calls+...	Tim...
8 android/view/ViewGroup.dispatchDraw (Landroid/graphics/Canv	29.5%	3745.518	0.1%	12.476	5+27	117.047
Parents						
7 android/view/View.draw (Landroid/graphics/Canvas;)V	100.0%	3745.518			5/32	
Children						
self	0.0%	1.161				
9 android/view/ViewGroup.drawChild (Landroid/graphics/C	100.0%	3744.036			5/47	
1398 android/view/View.getDrawingTime ()J	0.0%	0.321			5/37	
Parents while recursive						
Children while recursive						
9 android/view/ViewGroup.drawChild (Landroid/graphics/Canvas;L	29.5%	3744.036	0.2%	31.226	5+42	79.660
10 com/google/android/maps/MapView.onDraw (Landroid/graphic	26.4%	3350.741	0.0%	3.000	5+0	670.148
11 java/lang/Thread.run ()V	22.6%	2866.000	0.0%	0.220	3+0	955.333

Figure 5-15. Traceview zoom into Profile Panel

Clearly, there is a lot of information available in the Traceview records, and a full exploration is beyond the scope of this book. We'll leave other features of Traceview for you to explore, such as the use of Native Tracing to trace the QEMU emulator itself, the use of the other Debug methods to get timing information, and the use of the **dmtracedump** utility to generate call graphs.

Summary

Debugging and profiling are large topics within themselves, and we have only scratched the surface of the tools and methods available to you to develop Android applications. Some references follow to other sources of information that might prove useful:

- Debugging with the Eclipse Platform, *http://www.ibm.com/developerworks/library/os-ecbug/*
- For information about using the platform, *http://www.eclipse.org*
- Debugging Tasks (part of the Android SDK documentation), *http://d.android.com/guide/developing/debug-tasks.html*
- Developing on a Device (part of the Android SDK documentation), *http://d.android.com/guide/developing/device.html*
- Using Dalvik Debug Monitoring Service (DDMS) (part of the Android SDK documentation), *http://d.android.com/guide/developing/tools/ddms.html*
- Traceview: A Graphical Log Viewer (part of the Android SDK documentation), *http://d.android.com/guide/developing/tools/traceview.html*

CHAPTER 6

The ApiDemos Application

The ApiDemos application comes with the Android SDK, and can be found in the *samples/ApiDemos* subdirectory. It's a treasure trove of code that shows an application developer how to use a lot of the Android API. Unfortunately, it's left up to the student to figure out how it works. That's where this chapter comes in. Here, we'll show you the ropes of the ApiDemos application, and how to find the code that implements a feature that you see. Once you get the hang of it, it's a very useful place to find out how to use Android.

For the remainder of this chapter, we'll make a couple of assumptions when talking about files and directories:

- Non-Java source files and subdirectories can be found in the *samples/ApiDemos* subdirectory of the directory where you install the Android SDK.

- Java files are in the *src/com/example/android/apis* directory under the *samples/ApiDemos* directory.

Application Setup in the Manifest File

Like every other Android application, the best place to get a sense of how the application is strung together is the application's *AndroidManifest.xml* file. Let's take a look at part of the *AndroidManifest.xml* file for ApiDemos, near the beginning of the file:

```
<manifest xmlns:android="http://schemas.android.com/apk/res/android"❶
    package="com.example.android.apis">❷

    <uses-permission android:name="android.permission.READ_CONTACTS" />❸
    <uses-permission android:name="android.permission.WRITE_CONTACTS" />
    <uses-permission android:name="android.permission.CAMERA" />
    <uses-permission android:name="android.permission.VIBRATE" />
    <uses-permission android:name="android.permission.ACCESS_COARSE_LOCATION" />
    <uses-permission android:name="android.permission.INTERNET" />

    <application android:name="ApiDemosApplication"❹
            android:label="@string/activity_sample_code"
            android:icon="@drawable/app_sample_code" >
```

```
<uses-library android:name="com.google.android.maps" />

<activity android:name="ApiDemos">❺
    <intent-filter>
        <action android:name="android.intent.action.MAIN" />
        <category android:name="android.intent.category.DEFAULT" />
        <category android:name="android.intent.category.LAUNCHER" />
    </intent-filter>
</activity>
```

Here are some of the highlights of the code:

❶ Indicates that this XML file is an Android manifest.

❷ Defines the default package for the application. This allows the developer to refer to classes without expressing the fully qualified class each time. In terms of directories, it tells Android that classes for this application will be in *samples/ApiDemos/src/com/example/android/apis* or some subdirectory thereof.

❸ Sets up the various permissions required by this application. On a real phone, when the user attempts to install the applications, she is asked whether she wants the application to have the permissions listed. This way she knows that the application has the potential to read and write contacts, use the camera, make the phone vibrate, find the general area where the phone is at any given time, and use the Internet. If the user does not trust the developer, she may decide not to install the application after viewing the requested permissions.

❹ Defines the application-wide parameters. The most interesting of these is ApiDemosApplication, discussed in the following text.

❺ Defines the startup Activity for the application, ApiDemos. This activity can be found in the *ApiDemos.java* file. Its job is to discover all of the other demos in the application and display them on a menu for the user to select. The ApiDemos class uses information from *res/strings.xml* and *AndroidManifest.xml* to aid in this discovery (look at the call to queryIntentActivities).

The ApiDemosApplication class, found in the top-level directory of the source code, extends the Application class and has two methods: onCreate and onTerminate. The onCreate method executes before any activities start. Application-level global variables should be defined and initialized by the onCreate method. It's also a good place to set up any application-level default values.

There are several subdirectories under *samples/ApiDemos/src/com/example/android/apis*, each corresponding to a high-level functional area of the Android API:

App
  Examples of application-level constructs such as Activities, Alarms, Dialogs, and Services.

Content

Describes how to read assets from a file, from resources, and from an XML file.

Graphics

Many types of graphics examples, such as arcs bitmap manipulation, clipping, layers, and OpenGL.

Media

Examples of the MediaPlayer and the VideoView.

OS

Examples of how to invoke operating system services. As of this writing, it shows how to use the `VIBRATOR_SERVICE` and `SENSOR_SERVICE`.

Text

Cool text tricks. The "Linkify" demo shows how to use the `autoLink` attribute of the `TextView` to automatically set up links in text: the user clicks on a URL and the browser comes up, or clicks on a phone number and the dialer appears. The "Log-TextBox" demo shows how to create a simple screen log with a `LogTextBox` View.

Views

All of the various Android views: buttons, text boxes, autocompletion, date widgets, etc. You can find the dozens of different Android GUI elements here, along with their many options.

Finding the Source to an Interesting Example

The ApiDemos application has a lot of interesting examples that will help you learn how to program an Android application. However, it's not entirely obvious how to find the source to any particular screen. The following procedure will help you find the source to any ApiDemo you're interested in. To understand the process, we'll trace a couple of demos: the "App/Activity/Custom Title" and the "Text/Linkify" examples.

Custom Title Demo

This technique works when the ApiDemos application stores information about the demo in the *res/strings.xml* resource file:

1. After starting the ApiDemos application, find the particular demo by clicking on the menu, and remember the path you took through the menu system. In this case, you click on *App*, then *Activity*, and finally *Custom Title*.

2. Open the *res/values/strings.xml* file in a text editor such as Eclipse (actually, any text editor that can do regular expression searches should work fine). Carry out a regular expression search (Ctrl-F Ctrl-X in Eclipse) for each of the menu words from step 1. Use the regular expression ".*" to separate the words. Thus, the search term in our example is `App.*Activity.*Custom.*Title`. The search should return zero or one result.

If you don't find any results, use the procedure in the following section of this chapter. Otherwise, the single result should be the contents of a string element. The value of the `name` attribute of that string element is our search term for the next step. For our example, this is `activity_custom_title`.

3. Open the *AndroidManifest.xml* file and search it for the string you found in the previous step: `activity_custom_title`. The search should return only one result, which should be part of the the value of the `android:label` attribute within an `activity` element. That activity element should also contain an `android:name` attribute. The value of this attribute contains the path to the `Activity` class that implements the demo. In our example it's `.app.CustomTitle`. This translates to the *CustomTitle.java* files in the *app* subdirectory of the source tree.

In the end, therefore, the source for the App → Activity → Custom Title menu item can be found in *samples/ApiDemos/src/com/example/android/apis/app/CustomTitle.java*.

Linkify Demo

This technique should work for demos that you can't find with the previous method. If the ApiDemos application doesn't store information about the demo in *res/strings.xml*, it gets its information directly from *AndroidManifest.xml*—and so will we.

1. After starting the ApiDemos application, find the particular demo through clicking on the menu, and remember the path you took through the menu system. In this case, you click on Text and then Linkify.

2. Open the *AndroidManifest.xml* file and search for the menu elements as in the previous example. But this time the menu elements must be separated by slashes instead of ".*" regular expressions. So in this case, search for the text `Text/Linkify` (it doesn't have to be a regular expression search).

   The search should return only one result, which should be part of the the value of the `android:label` attribute within an `activity` element. That element should also contain an `android:name` attribute. The value of this attribute contains the path to the `Activity` class that implements the demo. In our example, the path is `.text.Link`. This translates to the *Link.java* file within the *text* subdirectory of the source tree.

So in this example, the source for the Text → Linkify menu item can be found in *samples/ApiDemos/src/com/example/android/apis/text/Linkify.java*.

Adding Your Own Examples to ApiDemos

The ApiDemos application is a handy sandbox for your own testing, and adding a new menu entry and Activity to it is quite easy. But remember that whenever you upgrade your API, all of your changes will be lost. Don't add code to the ApiDemo that you might want to save after an upgrade. It really is just a sandbox for quick tests.

With that caveat in mind, this section shows you how to add a new menu and screen to the ApiDemos application. We'll do that by adding a new ToastTest Activity with a matching toast_test layout. We'll then hook them into the ApiDemos application by adding them to the *AndroidManifest.xml* file.

First, create a file named *toast_test.xml* in the *res/layouts* directory and add the following content to lay out the widgets:

```xml
<?xml version="1.0" encoding="utf-8"?>
<RelativeLayout android:id="@+id/RelativeLayout01"
    android:layout_width="wrap_content "
    android:layout_height="wrap_content"
    xmlns:android="http://schemas.android.com/apk/res/android">
    <TextView android:id="@+id/TextView01"
        android:layout_width="wrap_content"
        android:layout_height="wrap_content"
        android:text="Guess my favorite color:" />
    <RadioGroup android:id="@+id/RadioGroup01"
        android:layout_below="@id/TextView01"
        android:layout_width="wrap_content"
        android:layout_height="wrap_content">
        <RadioButton android:id="@+id/redButton"
            android:layout_width="wrap_content"
            android:layout_height="wrap_content" android:text="Red" />
        <RadioButton android:id="@+id/greenButton"
            android:layout_width="wrap_content"
            android:layout_height="wrap_content" android:text="Green" />
        <RadioButton android:id="@+id/blueButton"
            android:layout_width="wrap_content"
            android:layout_height="wrap_content" android:text="Blue" />
    </RadioGroup>
</RelativeLayout>
```

This layout creates a RelativeLayout layout manager named `RelativeLayout01`, specifying up a `TextView` and a `RadioGroup`. The `TextView` presents the user with the text "Guess My Favorite Color" while the `RadioGroup`, named `RadioGroup01`, contains three `RadioButton` widgets: `redButton`, `greenButton`, and `blueButton`. They have the text "Red", "Green", and "Blue", respectively.

Next, create the *view/ToastTest.java* file. It simply responds to clicks from the layout:

```java
package com.example.android.apis.view;

//Need the following import to get access to the app resources, since this
//class is in a sub-package.
import com.example.android.apis.R;

import android.app.Activity;
import android.os.Bundle;
import android.view.View;
import android.widget.RadioButton;
import android.widget.Toast;

public class ToastTest  extends Activity{
```

```
/** Called when the activity is first created. */
@Override
public void onCreate(Bundle savedInstanceState) {
    super.onCreate(savedInstanceState);❶
    setContentView(R.layout.toast_test);❷

    final RadioButton redButton = (RadioButton) findViewById(R.id.redButton);❸
    redButton.setOnClickListener(new View.OnClickListener(){❹
        public void onClick(View v){
            Toast.makeText(ToastTest.this, "Ooooh, red", Toast.LENGTH_SHORT).show();
        }
    });
}
}
```

Here are some of the highlights of the code:

❶ Calls the method from the superclass, which is the `Activity` class itself.

❷ Sets the `ContentView` to use the `toast_test` layout, defined in the layout file you created earlier.

❸ Creates one of the `RadioButton` widgets, also going to the layout file.

❹ Sets up the `OnClickListener` of the `redButton` to show a piece of "Toast" that says "Ooooh, red" for a short period of time. Chapter 12 covers graphics programming on Android.

Like toast in a toaster, this text pops up when activated. This technique can be quite handy for debug code.

Finally, add a new activity element to the *AndroidManifest.xml* file:

```xml
<activity android:name=".view.ToastTest" android:label="Views/ToastTest" >
    <intent-filter>
        <action android:name="android.intent.action.MAIN" />
        <category android:name="android.intent.category.SAMPLE_CODE" />
    </intent-filter>
</activity>
```

This activity element should be added right after the TextSwitcher1 demo.

CHAPTER 7

Signing and Publishing Your Application

Writing and running Android applications for your own amusement is all well and good, but the point of creating new applications is to share them with others, whether you charge money for them or give them away for free. Google has created Android Market just for that purpose. Anyone with a connected Android phone can open the Android Market application and immediately download any of hundreds (soon to be thousands) of applications expressly designed for Android. These applications range from the very practical (Navigation, Timesheets, File Managers, etc.) to the downright silly (applications that make rude noises for the fun of it). There are a number of steps any application developer will go through in preparing and submitting an application to Android Market:

1. Thoroughly test the application—at least with the Android emulator, but also with as many actual Android devices as you can lay your hands on. There is no substitute for testing applications on real phones under real mobile network conditions to prove that they work as you intend. The last thing you want is thousands of people upset with you because your application doesn't work the way they expect it to.

2. Decide whether you'd like to add an End User License Agreement (EULA) to your application. This is normal practice in the industry (it's the "click to accept" license that you see when you download an application, even on desktops), and is strongly advised. You can create your own license using one you've seen that you like, or you can have a lawyer create a new one for you. Again, you don't have to have a EULA to submit your application, but it is strongly advised.

3. Create the icon and label you want displayed for your application in the Application Launcher, and attach them to your application.

4. Clean up the application for release: turn off debugging, get rid of any extraneous print or logging statements that you had in for debug, and take a final look at the code to clean it up.

5. Make sure you've included a version number and a version name in your manifest file, and of course, bump the version number if this is a new version of a previously released application.

6. Create a signing certificate, and, if needed, a Map API Key, as described in this chapter.

7. Recompile your application for release using Android Tools.

8. Sign your application using **jarsigner** and your signing certificate.

9. Retest your signed application to be sure no errors were entered during the process.

Test Your Application

You've probably been developing your application using the Android Emulator that is part of the Android Developers Kit. If you haven't already done so, take the time to load your application on a real Android device (such as the T-Mobile G1 phone), and test the application again. The emulator is very good, but there are a number of things that can be different between the desktop emulation and a real device:

Screen resolution
> The Android SDK emulates a device like the T-Mobile G1, with a half VGA screen (320×480), roughly 3.2 inches in diagonal measure. Real Android devices will have a variety of screen shapes, sizes, and resolutions, so you need to know how your application will function on those different devices.

Screen orientation
> The SDK emulates only portrait mode, with the screen taller than it is wide. Many Android devices (including the T-Mobile G1) support switching screen orientation, and you need to be sure your application behaves appropriately in all orientations.

Touchscreen operation
> The emulator uses mouse clicks and movements to mimic the touchscreen on a real device, but there's nothing like a real touchscreen. On a real device you can get a much better sense of what it will be like for users to interact with your application.

CPU and network performance
> On the emulator, you are using your PC or Mac to emulate an ARM processor. The application's speed is tied to the speed of your underlying host processor, which typically consists of multiple multigigahertz multiprocessors. If your application is at all performance sensitive, you'll want to see how it functions on real devices. Similarly, the emulator is using your host's network connection, which may be broadband, to access the Internet. On a real device your network connection will either be WiFi or a mobile network (GPRS, EDGE, HSPA, or 3G, depending on your location), and the connection's speed and latency will be changing

as the phone moves around. You want to know how these factors affect the operation of your application, and how it appears to the user.

The emulator is quite flexible, and some of these things can be tested to some degree by manipulating the emulator setup in DDMS (see "DDMS: Dalvik Debug Monitor Service" on page 74 for more about DDMS). But again, it is important to stress that nothing can replace testing on real Android devices.

Attach an End User License Agreement If Desired

Virtually every application that you download onto a desktop or notebook computer will contain an End User License Agreement. You should seriously consider whether you want to attach such a license to your application and have users agree to it before they install the application on their phone. Typically it limits what users are allowed to do with the application, defines whether it can be used for commercial purposes, specifically does not allow reverse engineering, and tries to protect you, the author, should something go wrong and someone has reason to bring a lawsuit against you. There are many such EULAs available on the Internet. You can either adopt one of those as your own or hire a lawyer to create a unique one for you, but the use of a EULA is strongly advised.

Create and Attach an Icon and Label

When your application is installed (on either the emulator or a real device), an icon and a label are placed on the Application Launcher that is part of your Android Desktop. This is how most users will launch your application, so you need a small graphic (in the form of a PNG file) for the icon, and a short label for your program. Icons are small square (64×64 pixel) pictures. Figure 7-1 shows the one we used for MJAndroid.

Figure 7-1. MJAndroid icon

The icon and the label are both assigned in the *AndroidManifest.xml* file. Here is the section of the file for MJAndroid that defines the icon (in the file *icon2.png*, located under the *res/drawable* directory) and the label (from the *strings.xml* file under *res/ values*):

```
<application android:icon="@drawable/icon2" android:debuggable="true">
  <uses-library android:name="com.google.android.maps" />
    <activity android:name=".MicroJobs" android:label="@string/app_name">
       <intent-filter>
...
```

Clean Up for Release

If you're like most developers, your path to completing your application was not linear. You tried some things, kept some, stopped using others, put in diagnostics when things didn't work quite right, named some things that you later wished you'd named differently, and so forth. Now is the time to clean all that up. Once your application is out in the real world, you'll have to support this version, and it would be good for you if the code were as clean as possible:

- Turn off debug and logging code. You don't really want your deployed application eating up precious mobile phone storage by generating logfiles, and the user won't be able to understand your debug messages anyway. If you haven't already, create a boolean to switch them off and leave them off for now. And remove `android:debuggable=true` from the *AndroidManifest.xml* file (see the earlier example) to make sure debug is turned off.

- Clean up your code wherever possible. Make the naming consistent, reorder methods in some reasonable way, and try to improve readability. Even if you're the next person to look at it, you won't remember what you did six months from now.

- Remove any test data that you included—particularly anything that's private or proprietary (like your name and address in a Contacts database).

- Delete any extraneous files from the project: old logfiles, source files that you no longer include in the application, etc.

Version Your Application

All applications submitted to Android Market must be versioned and named. You do that with simple statements in *AndroidManifest.xml*, as shown in the following segment of MJAndroid's manifest:

```
<?xml version="1.0" encoding="utf-8"?>
<manifest xmlns:android="http://schemas.android.com/apk/res/android"
    package="com.microjobsinc.mjandroid" android:versionCode="1"
        android:versionName="1.0">
```

Obviously you want the version numbering and naming to make sense. Android Market really only cares about the `versionCode`, which needs to be monotonically increasing for each release of your application, so a downloading device will know when to upgrade to new versions.

Obtaining a Signing Certificate and API Key

Before you can publish your application to Android Market and have every Android user in the world download it, you first must sign your application. In fact, you've been signing your application all along, because the Android Software Development Kit generates a debug signature that is used every time you run your application from Eclipse. The catch is that you cannot use the debug signature to publish your application to the world at large; you must generate a new signature.

If you're familiar with other mobile development environments (J2ME, Symbian, BREW, etc.), you're probably an old hand at signing applications. But if you're new to developing mobile applications, you may be asking yourself what all this signing stuff is for, anyway. Android uses application signing for only one purpose: to ensure that applications that claim to be from the same developer actually are. Applications from the same developer have special capabilities, discussed in the next section.

Google has stated that one of its intentions with Android was to minimize the hassle of getting applications signed. You don't have to go to a central signing authority to get a signing certificate; you can create the certificate yourself. Once you generate the certificate, you can sign your application using the **jarsigner** tool that comes with the Java JDK. Once again, you don't need to apply for or get anyone's approval. As you'll see, it's about as straightforward as signing can be.

Getting a Signing Certificate for an Application You Are Going to Ship

To sign your application, you are going to create an encrypted signing certificate and use it to sign your application. You can sign every Android application you develop with the same signing certificate. You can create as many signing certificates as you want, but you really need only one for all your applications. And using one certificate for all your applications lets you do some things that you couldn't do otherwise:

Simplify upgrades
> Signing certificates are tied to the application package name, so if you change the signing certificate you use with subsequent versions of your application, you'll have to change the package name, too. Changing certificates is manageable, but messy.

Multiple applications per process
> When all your applications share the same signing certificate, they can run in the same Linux process. You can use this to separate your application into smaller modules (each one an Android application) that together make up the larger application. If you were to do that, you could update the modules separately and they could still communicate freely.

Code/data sharing
> Android lets you enable or restrict access to parts of your application based on the requester's signing certificate. If all your applications share the same certificate, it's easy for you to reuse parts of one application in another.

One of the things you'll be asked when you generate a key pair and certificate is the validity period you desire for the certificate. Google recommends that you set it for at least 25 years, and in fact, if you're going to use Android Market to distribute your application, it requires a validity date at least until October 22, 2033 (25 years to the day from when they opened Android Market) for your certificate.

Generating a key pair (public and private keys) and a signing certificate

To generate a pair of public/private keys, use a tool called **keytool**, which came with the Sun JDK when you installed it onto your development computer. **keytool** asks you for some information and uses that to generate the pair of keys:

- A private key that will be kept in a keystore on your computer, secured with passwords. You will use the private key to sign your application, and if you need a Map API Key for your application, you will use the MD5 fingerprint of the signing certificate to generate the Map API Key.[*]

- A public key that Android can use to decrypt your signing certificate. You will send the public key along with your published application so that it can be made available in the runtime environment. Signing certificates are actually checked only at install time, so once installed, your application is good to run, even if the certificate or keys expire.

keytool is pretty straightforward. From your operating system's command line, enter something like:

```
$ keytool -genkey -v -keystore microjobs.keystore -alias mjkey -keyalg RSA
   -validity 10000
```

This asks **keytool** to generate a key pair and self-signed certificate (-genkey) in verbose mode (-v), so you get all the information, and put it in a keystore called *microjobs.keystore* (-keystore). It also says that in the future you want to refer to that key by the name mjkey (-alias), and that **keytool** should use the RSA algorithm for generating public/private key pairs (-keyalg). Finally, we say that we'd like the key to be valid for 10,000 days (-validity), or about 27 years.

keytool will prompt you for some things it uses to build the key pair and certificate:

- A password to be used in the future when you want to access the keystore
- Your first and last names
- Your organizational unit (the name for your division of your company, or something like "self" if you aren't developing for a company)
- Your organization name (the name of your company, or anything else you want to use)
- The name of your city or locality

---

[*] If you're not familiar with MD5, you can find many references on the Internet. For our purposes, you can think of it as a hash algorithm that creates a 128-bit fingerprint of an arbitrarily long string. It is often used to validate downloaded files on the Internet, and here it is a way of conveniently validating and condensing a signing certificate so it can be easily verified and compared by Google Maps.

- The name of your state or province
- The two-letter country code where you are located

keytool will then echo all this information back to you to make sure it's accurate, and if you confirm the information, will generate the key pair and certificate. It will then ask you for another password to use for the key itself (and give you the option of using the same password you used for the keystore). Using that password, **keytool** will store the key pair and certificate in the keystore.

You can get more information about security, key pairs, and the **keytool** utility on Sun's website at *http://java.sun.com/j2se/1.5.0/docs/tooldocs/#security*.

Getting a Signing Certificate While Debugging

When you're creating and debugging your application that uses a MapView, or when you're running a demo application like MJAndroid, you still need a valid Map API Key to get map tiles from Google Maps, and you need the fingerprint of your debug signing certificate to obtain a Map API Key. You can't just use the apiKey that we have coded into the MJAndroid source files, because it is tied to the signing certificate that was generated by our debug environment. Your debug environment will generate its own, different signing certificate for you to use, so you need to obtain a Map API Key to match.

There are two steps to getting the key:

1. Get a copy of the MD5 fingerprint for your Debug signing certificate.
2. Use that fingerprint to obtain a valid Map API Key from Google and enter it into *AndroidManifest.xml*.

Getting the MD5 fingerprint of your Debug signing certificate

When the Android SDK automatically generates a Debug signing certificate for you, it places it in a keystore called *debug.keystore*. The trick is to find this keystore. At least for the current version of the SDK, as this is being written, the location is operating system dependent:

- Under Linux and Mac OS X, it is in the *.android* subdirectory under your home directory: *~/.android/debug.keystore*.
- Under Windows Vista, it's a little harder to find; it's under your personal Application Data directory: *C:\Users\your_username\AppData\Local\Android \debug.keystore*.
- Windows XP is similar to Vista: *C:\Documents and Settings\your_username\Local Settings\Application Data\Android\debug.keystore* (unlike Vista, you will need to use a quoted string for the XP shell).

Once you've found *debug.keystore*, **keytool** can give you the MD5 fingerprint of your Debug signing certificate. Under Linux or OS X you'd type:

```
$ keytool -list -alias androiddebugkey -keystore ~/.android/debug.keystore -storepass
    android -keypass android
```

For Vista or XP, just substitute the correct location in the -keystore option. **keytool** prints the date the Debug signing certificate was created and the MD5 fingerprint. As an interesting note, Debug signing certificates are good for 365 days after creation.

What Happens When My Debug Signing Certificate Expires?

After your certificate expires, you'll get a build error whenever you try to build your application. The error will be displayed on the Android console (one of the tabs in the bottom pane of the Java and DDMS Perspectives), and it will say something like:

```
debug:
[echo] Packaging bin/samples-debug.apk, and signing it with a debug key...
[exec] Debug Certificate expired on 8/4/08 3:43 PM
```

To fix it, just delete your *debug.keystore* file (see the earlier list for its location in different host operating systems). The next time you build, the Android SDK will generate a new *debug.keystore* with a new Debug signing certificate, and your application can build and run.

Now that you have the MD5 fingerprint of your Debug Signing Certificate, you can use it to get a valid Map API Key for your system.

Getting a Map API Key from Google

Now that you have a signing certificate to use for your application, you can apply to Google for a Map API Key. Map API Keys are tied to a signing certificate, so obviously the Map API Key you get will work only with applications signed with the same certificate (another good reason for sticking with the same certificate for all your applications). Getting the key is pretty easy, and it's free.

When an application that contains a MapView runs, it requests map "tiles" from Google Maps via the Internet. As part of that request, it sends the Map API Key that was obtained when the developer signed up with Google, as well as the MD5 fingerprint of the application's signing certificate. Google Maps checks to see that the key is registered to a developer, and then checks to see that the Map API Key matches the one on file for applications with that signing certificate fingerprint. If they match, it sends the requested tiles. If they don't match, no tiles are sent.

So we're going to need the MD5 fingerprint of the signing certificate that we just created. Fortunately, **keytool** can get that for us:

```
$ keytool -list -alias mjkey -keystore microjobs.keystore
```

---

keytool asks for the passwords to the keystore (and key, if they're different), and prints out the MD5 fingerprint in hexadecimal. Use your mouse to copy the fingerprint so you can paste it into the Google page later.

Now you can go to the Google Map API Key website at *http://code.google.com/android/ maps-api-signup.html* to actually get the Map API Key. The Terms of Service are shown in a text box. Read them, and if appropriate, click on the checkbox that indicates you accept. Paste the MD5 fingerprint into the form, click the "Generate API key" button, and the website will ask you to log into your Google account. If you don't have a Google account, you can quickly create one on the spot.

Once you log in, the website returns the Map API Key, which can be used with any application that uses the signing certificate whose fingerprint you entered. It's a long alphanumeric string, so you will want to copy it into your clipboard and paste it into the XML layout file for your Map Activity.

As an example, the XML layout file for MJAndroid's Map Activity (called MicroJobs) has the following section defining the MapView and the API Key that matches our debug environment:

```
<com.google.android.maps.MapView
    android:id="@+id/mapmain"
    android:layout_width="fill_parent"
    android:layout_height="fill_parent"
    android:clickable="true"
    android:apiKey="0P18KOTAEOdO2GifdtbuScgEGLWe3p4CYUQngMg"
/>
```

Of course, you will have to substitute your own **apiKey** for ours.

Signing Your Application

We're almost ready to sign your application, but first you need to create an *unsigned* version that you can sign with your signature certificate. To do that, in the Package Explorer window of Eclipse, right-click on your project name. You'll get a long pop-up menu; toward the bottom, click on **Android Tools**. You should see another menu that includes the item you want: "Export Unsigned Application Package...". This item takes you to a File Save dialog box, where you can pick the place to save the unsigned version of your *apk* file. It doesn't matter where you put it—just pick a place you can remember.

Now that you have an unsigned version of your *apk* file, we can go ahead and sign it using **jarsigner**. Open a terminal or command window in the directory where you stored the unsigned *apk* file. Here's the line we used to sign MJAndroid, using the key we generated earlier in the keystore **microjobs.keystore**:

```
$ jarsigner -verbose -keystore microjobs.keystore MJAndroid.apk mjkey
```

Congratulations! You now have a signed version of your application that can be loaded and run on any Android device. But before you send it in to Android Market, there's one more intervening step....

Retesting Your Application

If everything went smoothly, your application is now signed and will function just as well as it did before you went through this process. But to be sure things went smoothly, it is wise to retest your application, again testing on real Android devices where possible. You really don't want thousands of people downloading a broken application attributed to you, so just to be safe, retest on as many Android devices as you can get your hands on.

Publishing on Android Market

After you're satisfied that your application runs as expected on real Android devices, you're ready to upload to Android Market, Google's service for publishing and downloading Android applications. The procedure is pretty straightforward:

1. Sign up as an Android Developer (if you're not already signed up).
2. Upload your signed application.

Signing Up As an Android Developer

Go to Google's website at *http://market.android.com/publish*, and fill out the forms provided. As this is written, Android Market is still in beta, and you will be asked to:

- Use your Google account to log in (if you don't have a Google account, you can get one for free by following the Create Account link on the login page).
- Agree to the Android Market Terms of Service.
- Pay a one-time fee of $25 (payable by credit card via Google Checkout; again, if you don't have an account set up, you can do so quickly).

The forms ask for a minimal amount of information—your name, phone number, etc.—and you are signed up.

Uploading Your Application

Now you can go to *http://market.android.com/publish/Home* to upload your application. To identify and categorize your application, you will be asked for the following:

Application apk file Name and Location
  The *apk* file of your application, signed with your private signature certificate.

Title and Description

These are very important, because they are the core of your marketing message to potential users. Try to make the title descriptive and catchy at the same time, and describe the application in a way that will make your target market want to download it.

Application Type

There are currently two choices: Applications or Games.

Category

The allowable list of categories varies depending on Application Type. The currently available categories for Applications are: Communications, Demo, Entertainment, Finance, Lifestyle, Multimedia, News & Weather, Productivity, Reference, Shopping, Social, Software Libraries, Tools, and Travel. For Games, the currently available categories include: Arcade & Action, Brain & Puzzle, Cards & Casino, and Casual.

Price

This must be "Free" under the beta version of Android Market. Google has said they will enable charging for applications in the near future (maybe by the time you read this).

Geography

You can limit where your application is available, or choose to make it available everywhere.

Finally, you are asked to confirm that your application meets the Android Content Guidelines and that it does not knowingly violate any export laws. After that, you can upload your *apk* file, and within a few days your application will appear on the Android Market online catalog, accessible from any connected Android device. There is currently no way to access Android Market directly from your PC or Mac, so you'll have to use your Android phone to find out when your application is available for download.

PART II

Programming Topics

After getting ready to write your own programs by reading Part I, you can learn how to make the most of Android's libraries in this part of the book. We cover databases, graphics, inter-process communication, and telephony.

CHAPTER 8

Persistent Data Storage: SQLite Databases and Content Providers

To accomplish many of the activities offered by modern mobile phones, such as tracking contacts, events, and tasks, the operating system and applications must be adept at storing and keeping track of large quantities of data. Most of this data is structured like a spreadsheet, in the form of rows and columns. Each Android application is like an island unto itself, in that each application is only allowed to read and write data that it has created, but sharing data across application boundaries is necessary. Android supports the content provider feature mentioned in Chapter 1 so that applications can share data.

In this chapter we examine two distinct data access APIs that the Android framework offers:

SQLiteDatabase
> Android's Java interface to its relational database, SQLite. It supports an SQL implementation rich enough for anything you're likely to need in a mobile application, including a cursor facility.

ContentProvider
> An interface used between applications. The server application that hosts the data manages it through basic create, read, update, and delete (CRUD) operations. The client application uses a similar API, but the Android framework transmits the client's requests to the server. We'll show both the server API and the client API in this chapter.

Databases

Data is best stored in a relational database format if it can include many instances of the same type of thing. Take a contact list, for instance. There are many contacts, all of whom potentially have the same types of information (address, phone number, etc.). Each "row" of data stores information about a different person, while each "column" stores a specific attribute of each person: names in one column, addresses in another column, and home phone numbers in a third.

Android uses the SQLite database engine, a self-contained, transactional database engine that requires no separate server process. It is used by many applications and environments beyond Android, and is being actively developed by a large community.

The process that initiates a database operation, such as a SELECT or UPDATE, does the actual work of reading or writing the disk file that contains the database in order to fulfill the request. With SQLite, the database is a simple disk file. All of the data structures making up a relational database—tables, views, indexes, etc.—are within this file.

SQLite is not a Google project, although Google has contributed to it. SQLite has an international team of software developers who are dedicated to enhancing the software's capabilities and reliability. Some of those developers work full time on the project.

Reliability is a key feature of SQLite. More than half of the code in the project is devoted to testing the library. The library is designed to handle many kinds of system failures, such as low memory, disk errors, and power failures. In no case should the database be left in an unrecoverable state: this would be a showstopper on a mobile phone, where critical data is often stored in a database. If that database were susceptible to easy corruption, the mobile phone could become an expensive paperweight if the battery were to fail at an inopportune time.

This is not a book on SQL, so we will not go into much detail about the database commands themselves. Ample documentation about SQL in general and SQLite in particular can be found on the Web. But the SQL we use in our examples should be a good starting point for your own applications.

We'll use the *MicroJobsDatabase.java* file from our MicroJobs example application to discuss how to create and use a SQLite database using Android. This is the subject of the next section.

Basic Structure of the MicroJobsDatabase Class

In our example, the *MicroJobsDatabase.java* file completely encapsulates all of the SQL logic necessary to work with the database. All of the other Java classes in the MicroJobs application work with standard Java classes or Cursors and are unaware of how the data is actually stored. This is good programming practice and should be emulated in all of your Android applications that use databases.

Before we delve too deeply into the guts of creating a database and selecting data from it, it's important to understand the general layout of the MicroJobsDatabase class.

MicroJobsDatabase inherits from the abstract SQLiteOpenHelper class, and therefore must override the onCreate and onUpgrade methods. The onCreate method is automatically called when the application starts for the first time; its job is to create the database.

As newer versions of the application are shipped, the database on the phone tends to be updated, a task that falls to the onUpgrade method. When you ship a new version of a database, you must also increment the version number, as we'll explain.

The general elements in MicroJobsDatabase code are:

Constants

The MicroJobsDatabase class defines two important constants:

DATABASE_NAME

This holds the filename of the database, "MicroJobs" in this case.

> Here is the full path to the MicroJobs file: */data/data/ com.microjobsinc.mjandroid/databases/MicroJobs*. You can use the **adb pull** command line on your desktop (see the discussion of **adb** in "The Tools" on page 57) to pull the database from the emulator or developer device and then debug it using the *SQLite3* executable on the desktop.

DATABASE_VERSION

This defines the database version understood by the software that defines the constant. If the version of the database on the machine is less than DATABASE_VERSION, the application should run onUpgrade to upgrade the database to the current level.

Constructor

The constructor for the database in this program, MicroJobsDatabase, uses the **super** function to call its parent's constructor. The parent does most of the work of creating the database object. One thing our MicroJobsDatabase constructor has to do is store the Context object. This step is not required in applications whose database code is encapsulated within an enclosing content provider class, because the ContentProvider class has a getContext call that will provide the Context object when necessary. Since MicroJobs is a standalone database class, it has to keep the Context object around in its own private variable. In the case of MicroJobs, the Context object is really the Activity object that opens the database. An Activity is a Context. The Context object is the interface to application-global resources and classes as well as application-level operations, such as broadcasting Intents and launching activities.

onCreate

When an Android application attempts to read or write data to a database that does not exist, the framework executes the onCreate method. The onCreate method in the MicroJobsDatabase class shows one way to create the database. Because so much SQL code is required to create the database and populate it with sample data, we've chosen to segregate all of the SQL code invoked by onCreate into the *strings.xml* resource file; this makes the Java code much more readable but forces the developer to look in two separate files to see what's really going on. When we look at the custom Cursor classes later in this chapter, we'll see that SQL can be embedded into the application source code as well. It's really a matter of style.

To actually create the database, the first line of the onCreate method loads the SQL string referenced by the `MicroJobsDatabase_onCreate` resource identifier into a `String` array named `sql`. Note the following code snippets from *MicroJobsDatabase.java*:

```
String[] sql =
    mContext.getString(R.string.MicroJobsDatabase_onCreate).split("\n");
```

and from *strings.xml*:

```
<string name="MicroJobsDatabase_onCreate">"
CREATE TABLE jobs (_id INTEGER PRIMARY KEY AUTOINCREMENT, employer_id INTEGER,
    title TEXT, description TEXT, start_time INTEGER, end_time INTEGER,
        status INTEGER);
CREATE TABLE employers( _id INTEGER, employer_name TEXT, ...
CREATE TABLE workers( _id INTEGER PRIMARY KEY AUTOINCREMENT, ...
CREATE TABLE status( _id INTEGER PRIMARY KEY AUTOINCREMENT, ...
INSERT INTO status (_id , status) VALUES (NULL, 'Filled');
INSERT INTO status (_id , status) VALUES (NULL, 'Applied For');
INSERT INTO status (_id , status) VALUES (NULL, 'Open');
...
"</string>
```

The single `getString` line of Java code loads the SQL required to create the database, along with a reasonable amount of test data.

 One crucial piece of information mentioned only briefly in the Android documentation is that you must either escape all single quotes and double quotes with a backslash (\" or \') within a resources string or enclose the entire string in either single or double quotes. If single and double quotes are mixed in a resource string, they must be escaped. In the case of the `MicroJobs Database_onCreate` string just shown, notice that the entire thing is surrounded with double quotes.

The rest of the onCreate method runs each line of SQL. The entire process runs under a transaction so that it will either execute completely or be rolled back and have no effect at all on the database.

onUpdate

In the MicroJobs application, the onUpdate method is very similar in structure to the onCreate method. However, the contents of the *strings.xml* resource file are quite different:

```
<string name="MicroJobsDatabase_onUpgrade">"
DROP TABLE IF EXISTS jobs
DROP TABLE IF EXISTS employers
```

```
DROP TABLE IF EXISTS workers
DROP TABLE IF EXISTS status
"</string>
```

The opening `<string>` tag is followed by a double quotation mark to start a string, and a closing quotation mark ends the strings before the `</string>` tag. Within the string are four rather drastic SQL commands. To support the demonstration code in this book, we cheat a little. The "upgrade" code removes the old database and re-creates it with whatever is in the current version of the code. Although this is nice for a book, it won't work very well in real life. Your customers won't be very happy if they have to re-key their information each time they upgrade software versions! A real application would have several upgrade scripts, one for each version that might be out in the wild. We would execute each upgrade script, one at a time, until the phone's database is completely up-to-date.

The structural parts of `MicroJobsDatabase.java` follow. The custom Cursors and the public functions that return them are discussed next.

```java
MicroJobsDatabase.java (structure):
package com.microjobsinc.mjandroid;

import ...

/**
 * Provides access to the MicroJobs database. Since this is not a Content Provider,
 * no other applications will have access to the database.
 */
public class MicroJobsDatabase extends SQLiteOpenHelper {
    /** The name of the database file on the file system */
    private static final String DATABASE_NAME = "MicroJobs";
    /** The version of the database that this class understands. */
    private static final int DATABASE_VERSION = 1;
    /** Keep track of context so that we can load SQL from string resources */
    private final Context mContext;

    /** Constructor */
    public MicroJobsDatabase(Context context) {❶
        super(context, DATABASE_NAME, null, DATABASE_VERSION);
        this.mContext = context;
    }

    /** Called when it is time to create the database */
    @Override
    public void onCreate(SQLiteDatabase db) {
        String[] sql =
          mContext.getString(R.string.MicroJobsDatabase_onCreate).split("\n");❷
        db.beginTransaction();❸
        try {
            // Create tables and test data
            execMultipleSQL(db, sql);
            db.setTransactionSuccessful();❹
        } catch (SQLException e) {
            Log.e("Error creating tables and debug data", e.toString());
```

```
            throw e;
        } finally {
            db.endTransaction();
        }
    }

    /** Called when the database must be upgraded */
    @Override
    public void onUpgrade(SQLiteDatabase db, int oldVersion, int newVersion) {❺
        Log.w(MicroJobs.LOG_TAG, "Upgrading database from version " + oldVersion +
            " to " +
            newVersion + ", which will destroy all old data");

        String[] sql =
            mContext.getString(R.string.MicroJobsDatabase_onUpgrade).split("\n");
        db.beginTransaction();
        try {
            execMultipleSQL(db, sql);
            db.setTransactionSuccessful();
        } catch (SQLException e) {
            Log.e("Error upgrading tables and debug data", e.toString());
            throw e;
        } finally {
            db.endTransaction();
        }

        // This is cheating.  In the real world, you'll need to add columns, not
            rebuild from scratch.
        onCreate(db);
    }

    /**
     * Execute all of the SQL statements in the String[] array
     * @param db The database on which to execute the statements
     * @param sql An array of SQL statements to execute
     */
    private void execMultipleSQL(SQLiteDatabase db, String[] sql){❻
        for( String s : sql )
            if (s.trim().length()>0)
                db.execSQL(s);
    }
}
```

Here are some of the highlights of the code:

❶ Constructs the MicroJobsDatabase object. We pass the parent class the database name and version, and it keeps track of when to simply open the database and when to upgrade the version. The database itself is not opened here—that happens in response to a getReadableDatabase or getWritableDatabase call. We also keep a private reference to the Context object in the constructor.

❷ Retrieves strings containing SQL code, which we have chosen to store in a resource file for easier readability and maintenance.

❸ Begins the transaction within which all the SQL statements will execute to create the database.

❹ Ends the transaction, creating the database.

❺ Function to call in order to upgrade the database.

❻ Function that executes each SQL statement retrieved by item 2.

Reading Data from the Database

There are many ways to read data from an SQL database, but they all come down to a basic sequence of operations:

1. Create an SQL statement that describes the data that you need to retrieve.
2. Execute that statement against the database.
3. Map the resulting SQL data into data structures that the language you're working in can understand.

This process can be very complex in the case of object-relational mapping software, or relatively simple when writing the queries directly into your application. The difference is fragility. Complex ORM tools shield your code from the complexities of database programming and object mapping by moving that complexity elsewhere. The result is that your code is more robust in the face of database changes, but at the cost of complex ORM setup and maintenance.

The simple approach of writing queries directly into your application works well only for very small projects that will not change much over time. Applications with database code in them are very fragile because as the database changes, any code that references those changes must be examined and potentially changed.

A common middle-ground approach is to sequester all of the database logic into a set of objects whose sole purpose is to translate application requests into database requests and deliver the results back to the application. This is the approach we have taken with the MicroJobs application; all of the database code is contained in a single class in the file *MicroJobsDatabase.java*.

Android gives us the ability to customize Cursors, and we use that ability to further reduce code dependencies by hiding all of the information about each specific database operation inside a custom cursor. Each custom cursor is a class within the `MicroJobsDatabase` class; the one that we'll look at in this chapter is the `JobsCursor`.

The interface to the caller in the `getJobs` method of `MicroJobsDatabase` appears first in the code that follows. The method's job is to return a `JobsCursor` filled with jobs from the database. The user can choose (through the single parameter passed to `getJobs`) to sort jobs by either the `title` column or the `employer_name` column:

```
public class MicroJobsDatabase extends SQLiteOpenHelper {
...
```

```
/** Return a sorted JobsCursor
 * @param sortBy the sort criteria
 */
public JobsCursor getJobs(JobsCursor.SortBy sortBy) {❶
    String sql = JobsCursor.QUERY + sortBy.toString();❷
    SQLiteDatabase d = getReadableDatabase();❸
    JobsCursor c = (JobsCursor) d.rawQueryWithFactory(❹
        new JobsCursor.Factory(),
        sql,
        null,
        null);
    c.moveToFirst();❺
    return c;❻
}
...
public static class JobsCursor extends SQLiteCursor{❼
    public static enum SortBy{❽
        title,
        employer_name
    }
    private static final String QUERY =
        "SELECT jobs._id, title, employer_name, latitude, longitude, status "+
        "FROM jobs, employers "+
        "WHERE jobs.employer_id = employers._id "+
        "ORDER BY ";
    private JobsCursor(SQLiteDatabase db, SQLiteCursorDriver driver,
            String editTable, SQLiteQuery query) {❾
        super(db, driver, editTable, query);
    }
    private static class Factory implements SQLiteDatabase.CursorFactory{❿
        @Override
        public Cursor newCursor(SQLiteDatabase db,⓫
                SQLiteCursorDriver driver, String editTable,
                SQLiteQuery query) {
            return new JobsCursor(db, driver, editTable, query);⓬
        }
    }
    public long getColJobsId()
     {return getLong(getColumnIndexOrThrow("jobs._id"));}⓭
    public String getColTitle()
     {return getString(getColumnIndexOrThrow("title"));}
    public String
      getColEmployerName()
       {return getString(getColumnIndexOrThrow("employer_name"));}
    public long getColLatitude()
        {return getLong(getColumnIndexOrThrow("latitude"));}
    public long getColLongitude()
        {return getLong(getColumnIndexOrThrow("longitude"));}
    public long getColStatus(){return getLong(getColumnIndexOrThrow("status"));}
}
```

Here are some of the highlights of the code:

❶ Function that fashions a query based on the user's requested sort column (the sortBy parameter) and returns results as a cursor.

❷ Creates the query string. Most of the string is static (the QUERY variable), but this line tacks on the sort column. Even though QUERY is private, it is still available to the enclosing class. This is because the getJobs method and the the JobsCursor class are both within the MicroJobsDatabase class, which makes JobsCursor's private data members available to the getJobs method.

To get the text for the sort column, we just run toString on the enumerated value passed by the user. The enumeration is defined at item 8. We could have defined an associative array, which would give us more flexibility in naming variables, but this solution is simpler. Additionally, the names of the columns pop up quite nicely in Eclipse's autocompletion.

❸ Retrieves a handle to the database.

❹ Creates the JobsCursor cursor using the SQLiteDatabase object's rawQueryWith Factory method. This method lets us pass a factory method that Android will use to create the exact type of cursor we need. If we had used the simpler rawQuery method, we would get back a generic Cursor that lacked the special features of JobsCursor.

❺ As a convenience to the caller, moves to the first row in the result. This way, the cursor is returned ready to use. A common mistake is forgetting the moveToFirst call and then pulling your hair out trying to figure out why the Cursor object is throwing exceptions.

❻ The cursor is the return value.

❼ Class that creates the cursor returned by getJobs.

❽ Simple way to provide alternate sort criteria: store the names of columns in an enum. This variable is used in item 2.

❾ Constructor for the customized cursor. The final argument is the query passed by the caller.

❿ Factory class to create the cursor, embedded in the JobsCursor class.

⓫ Creates the cursor from the query passed by the caller.

⓬ Returns the cursor to the enclosing JobsCursor class.

⓭ Convenience functions that extract particular columns from the row under the cursor. For instance, getColTitle returns the value of the title column in the row currently referenced by the cursor. This separates the database implementation from the calling code and makes that code easier to read.

A sample use of the database follows. The code gets a cursor, sorted by title, through a call to getJobs. It then iterates through the jobs.

```
MicroJobsDatabase db = new MicroJobsDatabase(this);❶
JobsCursor cursor = db.getJobs(JobsCursor.SortBy.title);❷
```

```
for( int rowNum=0; rowNum<cursor.getCount(); rowNum++){ ❸
    cursor.moveToPosition(rowNum);
    doSomethingWith(cursor.getColTitle()); ❹
}
```

Here are some of the highlights of the code:

❶ Creates a `MicroJobsDatabase` object. The argument, `this`, represents the context, as discussed previously.

❷ Creates the `JobsCursor` cursor, referring to the `SortBy` enumeration discussed earlier.

❸ Uses generic Cursor methods to iterate through the cursor.

❹ Still within the loop, invokes one of the custom accessor methods provided by `JobsCursor` to "do something" chosen by the user with the value of each row's title column.

Modifying the Database

Android Cursors are great when you want to read data from the database, but the Cursors API does not provide methods for creating, updating, or deleting data. The `SQLiteDatabase` class provides two basic interfaces that you can use for both reading and writing:

- A set of four methods called simply `insert`, `query`, `update`, and `delete`
- A more general `execSQL` method that takes any SQL statement and runs it against the database

We recommend using the first method when your operations fit its capabilities. We'll show you both ways using the MJAndroid operations.

Inserting data into the database

The SQL `INSERT` statement is used whenever you want to insert data into an SQL database. The `INSERT` statement maps to the "create" operation of the CRUD methodology.

In the MJAndroid application, the user can add jobs to the list by clicking on the Add Job menu item when looking at the Jobs list. The user can then fill out a form to input the employer, job title, and description. After the user clicks on the Add Job button on the form, the following line of code is executed:

```
db.addJob(employer.id, txtTitle.getText().toString(),
    txtDescription.getText().toString());
```

This code calls the `addJob` function, passing in the employer ID, the job title, and the job description. The `addJob` function does the actual work of writing the job out to the database.

Example 8-1 shows you how to use the `insert` method.

Example 8-1. Using the insert method

```
/**
 * Add a new job to the database.  The job will have a status of open.
 * @param employer_id    The employer offering the job
 * @param title          The job title
 * @param description     The job description
 */
public void addJob(long employer_id, String title, String description){
    ContentValues map = new ContentValues();❶
    map.put("employer_id", employer_id);
    map.put("title", title);
    map.put("description", description);
    try{
        getWritableDatabase().insert("jobs", null, map);❷
    } catch (SQLException e) {
        Log.e("Error writing new job", e.toString());
    }
}
```

Here are some of the highlights of the code in Example 8-1:

❶ The ContentValues object is a map of column names to column values. Internally, it's implemented as a HashMap<String,Object>. However, unlike a simple HashMap, ContentValues is strongly typed. You can specify the data type of each value stored in a ContentValues container. When trying to pull values back out, ContentValues will automatically convert values to the requested type if possible.

❷ The second parameter to the insert method is nullColumnHack. It's used only when the third parameter, the map, is null and therefore the row would otherwise be completely empty.

Example 8-2 shows you how to use the execSQL method.

Example 8-2. Using the execSQL method

```
/**
 * Add a new job to the database.  The job will have a status of open.
 * @param employer_id    The employer offering the job
 * @param title          The job title
 * @param description     The job description
 */
public void addJob(long employer_id, String title, String description){
    String sql = ❶
        "INSERT INTO jobs (_id, employer_id, title, description, start_time, end_time,
            status) " +
        "VALUES (        NULL, ?,          ?,    ?,           0,          0,          3)";
    Object[] bindArgs = new Object[]{employer_id, title, description};
    try{
        getWritableDatabase().execSQL(sql, bindArgs);❷
    } catch (SQLException e) {
        Log.e("Error writing new job", e.toString());
    }
}
```

Here are some of the highlights of the code in Example 8-2:

❶ First, we build a SQL string template named `sql` that contains bindable parameters that will be filled in with user data. The bindable parameters are marked by a question mark in the string. Next, we build an object array named **bindArgs** that contains one object per element in our SQL template. There are three question marks in the template, and therefore there must be three elements in the object array.

❷ Executes the SQL command by passing the SQL template string and the bind arguments to `execSQL`. Using a SQL template and bind arguments is much preferred over building up the SQL statement, complete with parameters, into a `String` or `StringBuilder`. By using a template with parameters, you protect your application from SQL injection attacks. These attacks occur when a malicious user enters information into a form that is deliberately meant to modify the database in a way that was not intended by the developer. This is normally done by ending the current SQL command prematurely, using SQL syntax characters, and then adding new SQL commands directly in the form field. The template-plus-parameters approach also protects you from more run-of-the-mill errors, such as invalid characters in the parameters.

Updating data already in the database

The MicroJobs application enables the user to edit a job by clicking on the job in the Jobs list and choosing the Edit Job menu item. The user can then modify the strings for employer, job title, and description in the `editJob` form. After the user clicks on the Update button on the form, the following line of code is executed:

```
db.editJob((long)job_id, employer.id, txtTitle.getText().toString(),
    txtDescription.getText().toString());
```

This code calls the `editJob` method, passing the job ID and the three items the user can change: employer ID, job title, and job description. The `editJob` method does the actual work of modifying the job in the database.

Example 8-3 shows you how to use the `update` method.

Example 8-3. Using the update method

```
/**
 * Update a job in the database.
 * @param job_id        The job id of the existing job
 * @param employer_id   The employer offering the job
 * @param title         The job title
 * @param description   The job description
 */
public void editJob(long job_id, long employer_id, String title, String description) {
    ContentValues map = new ContentValues();
    map.put("employer_id", employer_id);
    map.put("title", title);
    map.put("description", description);
    String[] whereArgs = new String[]{Long.toString(job_id)};
```

```
    try{
        getWritableDatabase().update("jobs", map, "_id=?", whereArgs);❶
    } catch (SQLException e) {
        Log.e("Error writing new job", e.toString());
    }
}
```

Here are some of the highlights of the code in Example 8-3:

❶ The first parameter to update is the name of the table to manipulate. The second is the map of column names to new values. The third is a small snippet of SQL; in this case, it's a SQL template with one parameter. The parameter is marked with a question mark, and is filled out with the contents of the fourth argument.

Example 8-4 shows you how to use the execSQL method.

Example 8-4. Using the execSQL method

```
/**
 * Update a job in the database.
 * @param job_id         The job id of the existing job
 * @param employer_id    The employer offering the job
 * @param title          The job title
 * @param description    The job description
 */
public void editJob(long job_id, long employer_id, String title, String description) {
    String sql =
        "UPDATE jobs " +
        "SET employer_id = ?, "+
        " title = ?,  "+
        " description = ? "+
        "WHERE _id = ? ";
    Object[] bindArgs = new Object[]{employer_id, title, description, job_id};
    try{
        getWritableDatabase().execSQL(sql, bindArgs);
    } catch (SQLException e) {
        Log.e("Error writing new job", e.toString());
    }
}
```

For the application in Example 8-4, we show the simplest possible function. This makes it easy to understand in a book, but is not enough for a real application. In a real application, you would want to check input strings for invalid characters, verify that the job exists before trying to update it, verify that the employer_id value is valid before using it, do a better job of catching errors, etc. You would also probably authenticate the user for any application that is shared by multiple people.

Deleting data in the database

The MicroJobs application enables the user to delete a job as well as create and change it. From the main application interface, the user clicks on the List Jobs button to get a list of jobs, and then clicks on a particular job to see the job detail. At this level, the user can click on the "Delete this job" menu item to delete the job. The application asks the user if he really wants to delete the job. When the user hits the "Delete" button in response, the following line of code in the *MicroJobsDetail.java* file is executed:

```
db.deleteJob(job_id);
```

This code calls the `deleteJob` method of the `MicroJobsDatabase` class, passing it the job ID to delete. The code is similar to the functions we've already seen and lacks the same real-world features.

Example 8-5 shows you how to use the `delete` method.

Example 8-5. Using the delete method

```
/**
 * Delete a job from the database.
 * @param job_id        The job id of the job to delete
 */
public void deleteJob(long job_id) {
    String[] whereArgs = new String[]{Long.toString(job_id)};
    try{
        getWritableDatabase().delete("jobs", "_id=?", whereArgs);
    } catch (SQLException e) {
        Log.e("Error deleteing job", e.toString());
    }
}
```

Example 8-6 shows you how to use the `execSQL` method.

Example 8-6. Using the execSQL method

```
/**
 * Delete a job from the database.
 * @param job_id        The job id of the job to delete
 */
public void deleteJob(long job_id) {
    String sql = String.format(
            "DELETE FROM jobs " +
            "WHERE _id = '%d' ",
            job_id);
    try{
        getWritableDatabase().execSQL(sql);
    } catch (SQLException e) {
        Log.e("Error deleteing job", e.toString());
    }
}
```

Content Providers

Much of the time, an application's data is tightly bound to that application. For instance, a book reader application will typically have one datafile per book. Other applications on the mobile phone will have no interest in the files that the book reader uses to store books, so those files are tightly bound to the application, and there is no need to make any effort to share the book data. In fact, the Android OS enforces this tight binding so that applications can't read or write data across packages at all.

However, some applications want to share their data; that is, they want other applications to be able to read and write data within their database. Perhaps the most obvious example is contact data. If each application that required contacts forced the user to maintain a separate database for that specific application, the phone would be all but useless.

Android enables applications to share data using the content provider API. This API enables each client application to query the OS for data it's interested in, using a uniform resource identifier (URI) mechanism, similar to the way a browser requests information from the Internet.

The client does not know which application will provide the data; it simply presents the OS with a URI and leaves it to the OS to start the appropriate application to provide the result.

The content provider API enables full CRUD access to the content. This means the application can:

- Create new records
- Retrieve one, all, or a limited set of records
- Update records
- Delete records if permitted

This section shows how to use the content provider API by examining the inner workings of the NotePad application provided with the Android SDK. Assuming the SDK was installed in the /sdk directory, all file references within the NotePad project are relative to /sdk/samples/NotePad; thus, when the AndroidManifest.xml file is referenced in this section, the /sdk/samples/NotePad/AndroidManifest.xml file is assumed. By studying NotePad's implementation, you'll be able to create and manage content providers of your own.

 Throughout this chapter we make the assumption that the backend of a content provider is a SQLite database. This will almost always be the case, and the API uses standard database operations, such as create, read, update, and delete. However, it is possible to use the API to store and retrieve data using any backend that will support the required operations. For instance, a flat file that just does inserts and queries that return some subset of the file is possible. However, in most cases an SQLite database will be on the backend of a content provider, so we use those terms and concepts in this chapter.

Introducing NotePad

The Android NotePad application is a very simple notebook. It allows the user to type textual notes on lined note paper and store them under a textual title of any length. A user can create notes, view a list of notes, and update and delete notes. As an application, NotePad is usable, but just barely; its main purpose is to show programmers how to build and use content providers.

Activities

The NotePad application has three distinct Activities: NoteList, NoteEditor, and TitleEditor. Instead of communicating directly to the NotePad database, each of these Activities use the content provider API, so the NotePad application is both a content provider client and a server. This makes it perfect for exploring content providers.

The purpose of each activity is reasonably obvious from its name. The NoteList activity presents the user with a list of notes, and allows her to add a new note or edit the title or body of an existing note.

The NoteEditor allows a user to create a new note or modify the body of an existing note. Finally, the TitleEditor is a dialog box that allows a user to modify the title of an existing note.

Database

The NotePad database is created with the following SQL statement:

```
CREATE TABLE notes (
    _id INTEGER PRIMARY KEY,
    title TEXT,
    note TEXT,
    created INTEGER,
    modified INTEGER
);
```

The _id column is not required, but recommended by the Android SDK documentation. The documentation suggests that the column should be defined with the SQL attributes INTEGER PRIMARY KEY AUTOINCREMENT. Unless you have an application-specific identifier that you can guarantee to be unique, you might as well make use of the AUTOINCREMENT feature to assign arbitrary integers robustly.

The title and note columns store the note title and note body data, respectively. The main *raison d'être* for the NotePad application is to manipulate the contents of these columns.

Finally, the created and modified columns keep track of when the note was created and when it was last modified. In the NotePad application itself, these columns are never seen by the user. However, other applications can read them using the content provider API.

Structure of the source code

This section briefly examines each relevant file within the NotePad application:

AndroidManifest.xml

> Chapter 3 described the purpose of the *AndroidManifest.xml* file that is part of every Android application. It describes important attributes of the application, such as the Activities and Intents that the application implements. The *AndroidManifest.xml* file for the NotePad application reveals the three activities—NotesList, NoteEditor, and TitleEditor—along with the various Intents that these activities consume. Finally, the `<provider>` element shows that the application is a content provider. We'll discuss the `<provider>` element in detail later in this section.

res/drawable/app_notes.png

> This file is the icon for the application. The `<application>` element within the *AndroidManifest.xml* file sets the icon using the `android:icon` attribute.

res/layout/.xml*

> These three layout files use XML to describe how each activity screen is laid out. Chapter 2 covers these concepts.

res/values/strings.xml

> All of the user-visible strings in the NotePad application appear in this file. Over time, as the application gains acceptance in the user community, users from non-English-speaking countries will want the application adapted to their languages. This job is much easier if all user-facing strings start out in *strings.xml*.

src/com/example/android/notepad/NoteEditor.java

> The `NoteEditor` class extends the `Activity` class and allows the user to edit a note in the `notes` database. This class never manipulates the `notes` database directly, but instead uses the `NotePadProvider` content provider.

src/com/example/android/notepad/NotePad.java

> The `NotePad` class contains the `AUTHORITY` attribute (discussed later) and the `Notes` class, which defines the names of the content provider columns. Because the database columns are named the same as the content provider columns, the `Note` class also is also used to define the names of the database columns. Neither the `NotePad` class nor the `Notes` class contain any executable code. The relevant portion of the *NotePad.java* file follows:

```
public final class NotePad {
    public static final String AUTHORITY = "com.google.provider.NotePad";
    private NotePad() {}// This class cannot be instantiated
    /** Notes table */
    public static final class Notes implements BaseColumns {
        // This class cannot be instantiated
        private Notes() {} // This class cannot be instantiated
        public static final Uri CONTENT_URI =
                Uri.parse("content://" + AUTHORITY + "/notes");
        public static final String CONTENT_TYPE =
                "vnd.android.cursor.dir/vnd.google.note";
```

```
                    public static final String CONTENT_ITEM_TYPE=
                            "vnd.android.cursor.item/vnd.google.note";
                    public static final String TITLE = "title";
                    public static final String NOTE = "note";
                    public static final String CREATED_DATE = "created";
                    public static final String MODIFIED_DATE = "modified";
                }
            }
```

src/com/example/android/notepad/NotePadProvider.java

> The `NotePadProvider` class is the content provider for the notes database. It inter-
> cepts URIs for each of the CRUD actions and returns data appropriate to the action
> requested. This file is examined in detail later in this chapter.

src/com/example/android/notepad/NotesList.java

> The `NotesList` class is an Activity that allows the user to view a list of notes. The
> user can add a new note or edit the title or body of an existing note

src/com/example/android/notepad/TitleEditor.java

> The `TitleEditor` class is an Activity that implements a dialog box that allows a user
> to modify the title of an existing note. Since this is a very simple class, it is quite
> helpful to examine it closely, to understand how to query and modify data in a
> content provider.

Content Providers

Now that we've examined the general structure of the NotePad application, it's time
to look at how the application both implements and consumes the `NotePadProvider`
content provider.

Implementing a content provider

The Android SDK contains a document that describes nine steps to creating a content
provider. In summary, they are:

1. Extend the `ContentProvider` class.
2. Define the `CONTENT_URI` for your content provider.
3. Create the data storage for your content.
4. Create the column names for communication with clients.
5. Define the process by which binary data is returned to the client.
6. Declare public static Strings that clients use to specify columns.
7. Implement the CRUD methods of a Cursor to return to the client.
8. Update the *AndroidManifest.xml* file to declare your `<provider>`.
9. Define MIME types for any new data types.

In the following sections, we'll examine each step in detail using the NotePad application as our guide.

Extend ContentProvider. Within *NotePadProvider.java*, the `NotePadProvider` class extends `ContentProvider`, as shown here:

```
public class NotePadProvider extends ContentProvider
```

Classes that extend `ContentProvider` must provide implementations for the following methods:

onCreate
> This method is called during the content provider's startup. Any code you want to run just once, such as making a database connection, should reside in this method.

getType
> This method, when given a URI, returns the MIME type of the data that this content provider provides at that URI. The URI comes from the client application interested in accessing the data.

insert
> This method is called when the client code wishes to insert data into the database your content provider is serving. Normally, the implementation for this method will either directly or indirectly result in a database insert operation.

query
> This method is called whenever a client wishes to read data from the content provider's database. It is normally called through `ContentProvider`'s `managedQuery` method. Normally, here you retrieve data using a SQL SELECT statement and return a cursor containing the requested data.

update
> This method is called when a client wishes to update one or more rows in the `ContentProvider`'s database. It translates to a SQL UPDATE statement.

delete
> This method is called when a client wishes to delete one or more rows in the `ContentProvider`'s database. It translates to a SQL DELETE statement.

NotePadProvider class and instance variables. As usual, it's best to understand the major class and instance variables used by a method before examining how the method works. The variables we need to understand for the NotePad's `ContentProvider` class are:

```
private static final String DATABASE_NAME = "note_pad.db";
private static final int DATABASE_VERSION = 2;
private static final String NOTES_TABLE_NAME = "notes";
private DatabaseHelper mOpenHelper;
```

DATABASE_NAME
> The name of the database file on the device. For the NotePad project, the full path to the file is */data/data/com.example.android.notepad/databases/note_pad.db*.

DATABASE_VERSION

The version of the database this code works with. If this number is higher than the version of the database itself, the application calls the `DatabaseHelper.onUpdate` method. See "Create the data storage" on page 122 for more information.

NOTES_TABLE_NAME

The name of the `notes` table within the `notes` database.

mOpenHelper

This instance variable is initialized during `onCreate`. It provides access to the database for the `insert`, `query`, `update`, and `delete` methods.

In addition to these class and instance variables, the `NotePadContentProvider` class also has a static initialization block that performs complex initializations of static variables that can't be performed as simple one-liners:

```
private static HashMap<String, String> sNotesProjectionMap;
private static final UriMatcher sUriMatcher;
private static final int NOTES = 1;
private static final int NOTE_ID = 2;
...
static {
    sUriMatcher = new UriMatcher(UriMatcher.NO_MATCH);
    sUriMatcher.addURI(NotePad.AUTHORITY, "notes", NOTES);
    sUriMatcher.addURI(NotePad.AUTHORITY, "notes/#", NOTE_ID);

    sNotesProjectionMap = new HashMap<String, String>();
    sNotesProjectionMap.put(Notes._ID, Notes._ID);
    sNotesProjectionMap.put(Notes.TITLE, Notes.TITLE);
    sNotesProjectionMap.put(Notes.NOTE, Notes.NOTE);
    sNotesProjectionMap.put(Notes.CREATED_DATE, Notes.CREATED_DATE);
    sNotesProjectionMap.put(Notes.MODIFIED_DATE, Notes.MODIFIED_DATE);
}
```

The meanings of these variables follow:

sNotesProjectionMap

The projection map used by the query method. This `HashMap` maps the content provider's column names to database column names. A projection map is not required, but when used it must list all column names that might be returned by the query. In `NotePadContentProvider`, the content provider column names and the database column names are identical, so the `sNotesProjectionMap` is not required.

sUriMatcher

This data structure is loaded with several URI templates that match URIs clients can send the content provider. Each URI template is paired with an integer that the `sUriMatcher` returns when it's passed a matching URI. The integers are used as cases of a switch in other parts of the class. `NotePadContentProvider` has two types of URIs, represented by the `NOTES` and `NOTES_ID` integers.

NOTES

`sUriMatcher` returns this value for note URIs that do not include a note ID.

`NOTES_ID`
> `sUriMatcher` returns this value when the notes URI includes a note ID.

Define `CONTENT_URI`. When a client application uses a content resolver to request data, a URI that identifies the desired data is passed to the content resolver. Android tries to match the URI with the `CONTENT_URI` of each content provider it knows about to find the right provider for the client. Thus, the `CONTENT_URI` defines the type of URIs your content provider can process.

A `CONTENT_URI` consists of these parts:

`content://`
> This initial string tells the Android framework that it must find a content provider to resolve the URI.

The authority
> This string uniquely identifies the content provider and consists of up to two sections: the organizational section and the provider identifier section. The organizational section uniquely identifies the organization that created the content provider. The provider identifier section identifies a particular content provider that the organization created. For content providers that are built into Android, the organizational section is omitted. For instance, the built-in "media" authority that returns one or more images does not have the organizational section of the authority. However any content providers that are created by developers outside of Google's Android team must define both sections of the content provider. Thus, the Notepad example application's authority is `com.google.provider.NotePad`. The organizational section is `com.google.provider`, and the provider identifier section is `NotePad`. The Google documentation suggests that the best solution for picking the authority section of your `CONTENT_URI` is to use the fully qualified class name of the class implementing the content provider.

> The authority section uniquely identifies the particular content provider that Android will call to respond to queries that it handles.

The path
> The content provider can interpret the rest of the URI however it wants, but it must adhere to some requirements:

> - If the content provider can return multiple data types, the URI must be constructed so that some part of the path specifies the type of data to return.

>   For instance, the built-in "Contacts" content provider provides many different types of data: People, Phones, ContactMethods, etc. The Contacts content provider uses strings in the URI to differentiate which type of data the user is requesting. Thus, to request a specific person, the URI will be something like this:

>   `content://contacts/people/1`

>   To request a specific phone number, the URI could be something like this:

>   `content://contacts/people/1/phone/3`

In the first case, the MIME data type returned will be `vnd.android.cursor.item/person`, whereas in the second case, it will be `vnd.android.cursor.item/phone`.

- The content provider must be capable of returning either one item or a set of item identifiers. The content provider will return a single item when an item identifier appears in the final portion of the URI. Looking back at our previous example, the URI *content://contacts/people/1/phone/3* returned a single phone number of type `vnd.android.cursor.item/phone`. If the URI had instead been *content://contacts/people/1/phone*, the application would have returned a list of all of the phone numbers for the person having the person identifier number 1, and the MIME type of the data returned would be `vnd.android.cursor.dir/phone`.

As mentioned earlier, the content provider can interpret the path portion of the URI however it wants. This means that it can use items in the path to filter data to return to the caller. For instance, the built-in "media" content provider can return either internal or external data, depending on whether the URI contains the word "internal" or "external" in the path.

The full `CONTENT_URI` for NotePad is *content://com.google.provider.NotePad/notes*.

The `CONTENT_URI` must be of type `public static final Uri`. It is defined in the `NotePad` class of the NotePad application. First, a string named `AUTHORITY` is defined:

```
public final class NotePad {
    public static final String AUTHORITY = "com.google.provider.NotePad";
```

Then, the `CONTENT_URI` itself is defined:

```
public static final class Notes implements BaseColumns {
    public static final Uri CONTENT_URI = Uri.parse("content://" + AUTHORITY +
        "/notes");
```

Create the data storage. A content provider can store data in any way it chooses. Because content providers use database semantics, the `SQLite` database is most commonly used. The `onCreate` method of the `ContentProvider` class (`NotePadProvider` in the NotePad application) creates this data store. The method is called during the content provider's initialization. In the NotePad application, the `onCreate` method creates a connection to the database, creating the database first if it does not exist.

```
@Override
public boolean onCreate() {
    mOpenHelper = new DatabaseHelper(getContext());❶
    return true;
}

private static class DatabaseHelper extends SQLiteOpenHelper {

    DatabaseHelper(Context context) {
        super(context, DATABASE_NAME, null, DATABASE_VERSION);
    }

    @Override
```

```
        public void onCreate(SQLiteDatabase db) {
            db.execSQL("CREATE TABLE " + NOTES_TABLE_NAME + " ("
                    + Notes._ID + " INTEGER PRIMARY KEY,"
                    + Notes.TITLE + " TEXT,"
                    + Notes.NOTE + " TEXT,"
                    + Notes.CREATED_DATE + " INTEGER,"
                    + Notes.MODIFIED_DATE + " INTEGER"
                    + ");");
        }

        @Override
        public void onUpgrade(SQLiteDatabase db, int oldver, int newver) {
            // destroy the old version -- not nice to do in a real app!
            db.execSQL("DROP TABLE IF EXISTS notes");
            onCreate(db);
        }
    }
}
```

Here are some of the highlights of the code:

❶ Creates a new object of the DatabaseHelper class, which is derived from SQLiteOpen
Helper. The constructor for DatabaseHelper knows to call onCreate or onUpgrade if it
has to create or upgrade the database.

This is standard database code for Android, very similar to the database creation code
from the MJAndroid project. A handle for the new DatabaseHelper class is assigned to
the mOpenHelper class variable, which is used by the rest of the content provider to
manipulate the database.

This method embeds raw SQL into a call to execSQL. As we'll see, further calls don't
need to use SQL; instead, their simple CRUD operations use calls provided by the
framework.

Data Store for Binary Data

The Android SDK documentation suggests that when your content provider stores
binary data, such as a bitmap or music clip, the data should be stored outside of the
database in a file, and the content provider should store a content:// URI in the database that points to the file. Client applications will query your content provider to
retrieve that content:// URI and then retrieve the actual byte stream from the file it
specifies.

The reason for this circuitous route is easy to understand after some examination. Because filesystem I/O is much faster and more versatile than dealing with SQLite blobs,
it's better to use the Unix filesystem instead of SQL blobs. But since an Android application cannot read or write files that another application has created, a content provider must be used to access the blobs. Therefore, when the first content provider
returns a pointer to a file containing a blob, that pointer must be in the form of a
content:// URI instead of a Unix filename. The use of a content:// URI causes the file
to be opened and read under the permissions of the content provider that owns the file,
not the client application (which does not have access rights to the file).

To implement the file approach, instead of creating a hypothetical user table like this:

```
CREATE TABLE user (
    _id INTEGER PRIMARY KEY AUTOINCREMENT,
    name TEXT,
    password TEXT,
    picture BLOB
);
```

the documentation suggests two tables that look like this:

```
CREATE TABLE user (
    _id INTEGER PRIMARY KEY AUTOINCREMENT,
    name TEXT,
    password TEXT,
    picture TEXT
);

CREATE TABLE userPicture (
    _id INTEGER PRIMARY KEY AUTOINCREMENT,
    _data TEXT
);
```

The picture column of the user table will store a content:// URI that points to a row in the userPicture table. The _data column of the userPicture table will point to a real file on the Android filesystem.

If the path to the file were stored directly in the user table, clients would get a path but be unable to open the file, because it's owned by the application serving up the content provider and the clients don't have permission to read it. In the solution shown here, however, access is controlled by a ContentResolver class, which we'll examine later.

The ContentResolver class looks for a column named _data when processing requests. If the file specified in that column is found, the class's openOutputStream method opens the file and returns a java.io.OutputStream to the client. This is the same object that would be returned if the client were able to open the file directly. The ContentResolver class is part of the same application as the content provider, and therefore is able to open the file when the client cannot.

Create the column names. Content providers exchange data with their clients in much the same way an SQL database exchanges data with database applications: using Cursors full of rows and columns of data. A content provider must define the column names it supports, just as a database application must define the columns it supports. When the content provider uses an SQLite database as its data store, the obvious solution is to give the content provider columns the same name as the database columns, and that's just what NotePadProvider does. Because of this, there is no mapping necessary between the NotePadProvider columns and the underlying database columns.

Not all applications make all of their data available to content provider clients, and some more complex applications may want to make derivative views available to content provider clients. The projection map described in "NotePadProvider class and instance variables" on page 119 is available to handle these complexities.

Supporting binary data. We already explained the recommended data structure for serving binary data in the sidebar "Data Store for Binary Data" on page 123. The other piece of the solution lies in the `ContentResolver` class, discussed later.

Declare column specification strings. The `NotePadProvider` columns are defined in the `NotePad.Notes` class, as mentioned in "NotePadProvider class and instance variables" on page 119. Every content provider must define an `_id` column to hold the record number of each row. The value of each `_id` must be unique within the content provider; it is the number that a client will append to the content provider's *vnd.android.cursor.item* URI when attempting to query for a single record.

When the content provider is backed by an SQLite database, as is the case for `NotePadProvider`, the `_id` should have the type `INTEGER PRIMARY KEY AUTOINCREMENT`. This way, the rows will have a unique `_id` number and `_id` numbers will not be reused, even when rows are deleted. This helps support referential integrity by ensuring that each new row has an `_id` that has never been used before. If row `_id`s are reused, there is a chance that cached URIs could point to the wrong data.

Implement the Cursor. A content provider implementation must override the CRUD methods of the `ContentProvider` base class: `insert`, `query`, `update`, and `delete`. For the NotePad application, these methods are defined in the `NotePadProvider` class.

Create data (insert). Classes that extend `ContentProvider` must override its `insert` method. This method receives values from a client, validates them, and then adds a new row to the database containing those values. The values are passed to the `ContentProvider` class in a `ContentValues` object:

```
@Override
public Uri insert(Uri uri, ContentValues initialValues) {
    // Validate the requested uri
    if (sUriMatcher.match(uri) != NOTES) {
        throw new IllegalArgumentException("Unknown URI " + uri);
    }
    ContentValues values;
    if (initialValues != null)
        values = new ContentValues(initialValues);
    else
        values = new ContentValues();

    Long now = Long.valueOf(System.currentTimeMillis());

    // Make sure that the fields are all set
    if (values.containsKey(NotePad.Notes.CREATED_DATE) == false)
        values.put(NotePad.Notes.CREATED_DATE, now);

    if (values.containsKey(NotePad.Notes.MODIFIED_DATE) == false)
        values.put(NotePad.Notes.MODIFIED_DATE, now);

    if (values.containsKey(NotePad.Notes.TITLE) == false) {
        Resources r = Resources.getSystem();
        values.put(NotePad.Notes.TITLE,r.getString(android.R.string.untitled));
    }
```

```
    if (values.containsKey(NotePad.Notes.NOTE) == false) {
        values.put(NotePad.Notes.NOTE, "");
    }

    SQLiteDatabase db = mOpenHelper.getWritableDatabase();
    long rowId = db.insert(NOTES_TABLE_NAME, Notes.NOTE, values);
    if (rowId > 0) {
      Uri noteUri=ContentUris.withAppendedId(NotePad.Notes.CONTENT_URI,rowId);
      getContext().getContentResolver().notifyChange(noteUri, null);
      return noteUri;
    }
    throw new SQLException("Failed to insert row into " + uri);
}
```

Read/select data (query). NotePadProvider must override the query method and return a Cursor containing the data requested. It starts by creating an instance of the SQLite QueryBuilder class, using both static information from the class and dynamic information from the URI. It then creates the Cursor directly from the database using the SQLiteQueryBuilder query. Finally, it returns the Cursor that the database created.

When the URI contains a note identification number, the NOTE_ID case is used. In this case, text is added to the WHERE clause so that only the note identified by the URI is included in the Cursor returned to the NotePadProvider client:

```
@Override
public Cursor query(Uri uri, String[] projection, String selection,
    String[] selectionArgs, String sortOrder)
{
    SQLiteQueryBuilder qb = new SQLiteQueryBuilder();

    switch (sUriMatcher.match(uri)) {
    case NOTES:
        qb.setTables(NOTES_TABLE_NAME);
        qb.setProjectionMap(sNotesProjectionMap);
        break;

    case NOTE_ID:
        qb.setTables(NOTES_TABLE_NAME);
        qb.setProjectionMap(sNotesProjectionMap);
        qb.appendWhere(Notes._ID + "=" + uri.getPathSegments().get(1));
        break;

    default:
        throw new IllegalArgumentException("Unknown URI " + uri);
    }

    // If no sort order is specified use the default
    String orderBy;
    if (TextUtils.isEmpty(sortOrder)) {
        orderBy = NotePad.Notes.DEFAULT_SORT_ORDER;
    } else {
        orderBy = sortOrder;
    }
```

```
// Get the database and run the query
SQLiteDatabase db = mOpenHelper.getReadableDatabase();
Cursor c=qb.query(db,projection,selection,selectionArgs,null,null,orderBy);

// Tell cursor what uri to watch, so it knows when its source data changes
c.setNotificationUri(getContext().getContentResolver(), uri);
return c;
}
```

Update data. NotePadProvider's update method receives values from a client, validates them, and modifies relevant rows in the database given those values. It all boils down to the *SQLiteDatabase's* update method. The first value passed to update is the table name. This constant is defined elsewhere in the class. The second parameter, `values`, is a ContentValues object formed by the client of the ContentProvider. The final two arguments, `where` and `whereArgs`, are used to form the WHERE clause of the SQL UPDATE command.

The ContentValues object is created by the ContentProvider's client. It contains a map of database column names to new column values that is passed through to the SQLiteDatabase's update method.

The `where` string and the `whereArgs` string array work together to build the WHERE clause of the SQLite UPDATE command. This WHERE clause limits the scope of the UPDATE command to the rows that match its criteria. The `where` string can be built either to contain all of the information necessary to build the WHERE clause, or to contain a template that is filled out at runtime by inserting strings from the `whereArgs` string. The easiest way to understand this is with a couple of examples.

Let's suppose that you want to update only those rows where the `dogName` column is equal to `'Jackson'`. As the content provider's client, you could create a single `where` string consisting of `"dogName='Jackson'"` and pass it along to the update method. This works well and is what many applications do. But unless you check your input very well, this method is subject to an SQL injection attack, as described earlier in the chapter.

The better approach is to pass a template as the `where` clause, something like `"dogName=?"`. The question mark marks the location for the value of `dogName`, and the actual value is found in the `whereArgs` string array. The first question mark is replaced by the first value in the `whereArgs` string array. If there were a second question mark, it would be replaced with the second value, and so forth:

```
@Override
public int update(Uri uri,ContentValues values,String where,String[] whereArgs) {
    SQLiteDatabase db = mOpenHelper.getWritableDatabase();
    int count;
    switch (sUriMatcher.match(uri)) {
    case NOTES:
        count = db.update(NOTES_TABLE_NAME, values, where, whereArgs);
        break;
```

```
        case NOTE_ID:
            String noteId = uri.getPathSegments().get(1);
            count = db.update(NOTES_TABLE_NAME, values, Notes._ID + "=" + noteId
                    + (!TextUtils.isEmpty(where)?" AND ("+where+')':""), whereArgs);
            break;

        default:
            throw new IllegalArgumentException("Unknown URI " + uri);
        }

        getContext().getContentResolver().notifyChange(uri, null);
        return count;
    }
```

Delete data. NotePadProvider's `delete` method is very similar to the `update` method, but instead of updating the rows with new data, it simply deletes them:

```
@Override
public int delete(Uri uri, String where, String[] whereArgs) {
    SQLiteDatabase db = mOpenHelper.getWritableDatabase();
    int count;
    switch (sUriMatcher.match(uri)) {
    case NOTES:
        count = db.delete(NOTES_TABLE_NAME, where, whereArgs);
        break;

    case NOTE_ID:
        String noteId = uri.getPathSegments().get(1);
        count = db.delete(NOTES_TABLE_NAME, Notes._ID + "=" + noteId
            + (!TextUtils.isEmpty(where)?" AND ("+where+')':""), whereArgs);
        break;

    default:
        throw new IllegalArgumentException("Unknown URI " + uri);
    }

    getContext().getContentResolver().notifyChange(uri, null);
    return count;
}
```

Updating AndroidManifest.xml. The *AndroidManifest.xml* file defines all external access to the application, including any content providers. Within the file, the `<provider>` tag declares the content provider.

The *AndroidManifest.xml* file within the NotePad project has the following `<provider>` tag:

```
<provider android:name="NotePadProvider"
    android:authorities="com.google.provider.NotePad"
/>
```

An `android:authorities` attribute must be defined within the `<provider>` tag. Android uses this attribute to identify the URIs that this content provider will fulfill.

The `android:name` tag is also required, and identifies the name of the content provider class. Note that this string matches the `AUTHORITY` string in the `NotePad` class, discussed earlier.

In sum, this section of the *AndroidManifest.xml* file can be translated to the following English statement: "This content provider accepts URIs that start with *content://com.google.provider.notepad/* and passes them to the `NotePadProvider` class."

Define MIME types. Your content provider must override the `getType` method. This method accepts a URI and returns the MIME type that corresponds to that URI. For the `NotePadProvider`, two types of URIs are accepted, so two types of URIs are returned:

- The *content://com.google.provider.NotePad/notes* URI will return a directory of zero or more notes, using the `vnd.android.cursor.dir/vnd.google.note` MIME type.

- A URI with an appended ID, of the form *content://com.google.provider.NotePad/notes/N*, will return a single note, using the `vnd.android.cursor.item/vnd.google.note` MIME type.

The client passes a URI to the Android framework to indicate the database it wants to access, and the Android framework calls your `getType` method internally to get the MIME type of the data. That helps Android decide what to do with the data returned by the content provider.

Your `getType` method must return the MIME type of the data at the given URI. In NotePad, the MIME types are stored as simple string variables, shown earlier in "Structure of the source code" on page 117. The return value starts with `vnd.android.cursor.item` for a single record and `vnd.android.cursor.dir` for multiple items:

```
@Override
public String getType(Uri uri) {
  switch (sUriMatcher.match(uri)) {
  case NOTES:
    return Notes.CONTENT_TYPE;      // vnd.android.cursor.dir/vnd.google.note

  case NOTE_ID:
    return Notes.CONTENT_ITEM_TYPE; // vnd.android.cursor.item/vnd.google.note

  default:
    throw new IllegalArgumentException("Unknown URI " + uri);
  }
}
```

Consuming a Content Provider

The NotePad application both implements and consumes the `NotePadProvider` content provider. The previous sections described how the `NotePadProvider` allows any application on the Android device to access the notes database. This section explains how the various Activities use the `NotePadProvider` to manipulate the database. Since these activities are part of the same application as the `NotePadProvider`, they could simply manipulate the database directly, but instead they use the `ContentProvider`. This does not impose any performance penalty, so not only does it work well as an example for our purposes, but it is also good programming practice for all applications implementing a content provider.

The following sections follow the CRUD functions in order. First, data is created using the SQL INSERT statement. That data is then typically read using an SQL SELECT query. Sometimes the data must be updated using the SQL UPDATE statement or deleted using the SQL DELETE statement.

Create data (insert)

The following code is from the `NoteEditor` class in the NotePad application. Code that was not relevant to the discussion was removed in the listing:

```java
@Override
protected void onCreate(Bundle savedInstanceState) {
    super.onCreate(savedInstanceState);

    final Intent intent = getIntent();

    // Do some setup based on the action being performed.
    final String action = intent.getAction();
    if (Intent.ACTION_EDIT.equals(action)) {
        ...
    } else if (Intent.ACTION_INSERT.equals(action)) {
        // Requested to insert: set that state, and create a new entry
        // in the container.
        mUri = getContentResolver().insert(intent.getData(), null);

        if (mUri == null) {
            // Creating the new note failed
            finish();
            return;
        }
        // Do something with the new note here.
        ...

    }
    ...
}
```

The NotePad application starts out in the `NotesList` Activity. `NotesList` has an "Add Note" menu entry, shown in Figure 8-1.

When the user presses the Add Note button, the NoteEditor Activity is started with the `ACTION_INSERT` Intent. NoteEditor's onCreate method examines the Intent to determine why it was started. When the Intent is `ACTION_INSERT`, a new note is created by calling the `insert` method of the content resolver:

```java
mUri = getContentResolver().insert(intent.getData(), null);
```

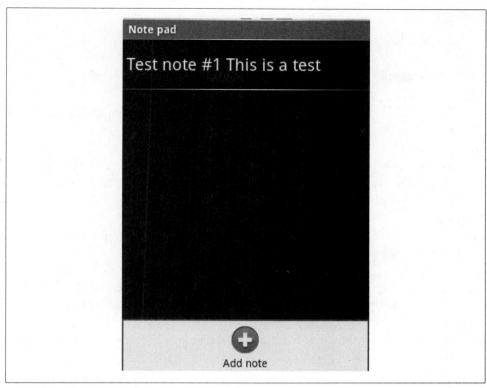

Figure 8-1. NotesList Activity

In brief, this line's job is to create a new blank note and return its URI to the `mUri` variable. The value of the `mUri` variable is the URI of the note being edited.

So how does this sequence of calls work? First, note that `NotesList`'s parent class is `ListActivity`. All `Activity` classes are descended from `ContextWrapper`. So, the first thing the line does is call `ContextWrapper.getContentResolver` to return a `ContentResolver` instance. The `insert` method of that `ContentResolver` is then immediately called with two parameters:

URI of the content provider in which to insert the row
> Our argument, `intent.getData`, resolves to the URI of the Intent that got us here in the first place, *content://com.google.provider.NotePad/notes*.

Data to insert
> Here, by passing `null`, we're inserting a record with no data. The data is added later with a call to the `update` method when the user types something in.

`ContentResolver`'s job is to manipulate objects that URIs point to. Almost all of its methods are verbs that take a URI as their first argument. `ContentResolver`'s methods include all of the CRUD methods, stream methods for file I/O, and others.

Read/query data

To read data, use the `managedQuery` method. This is an `Activity` method that calls `query` internally. It manages the query for the developer, closing the Cursor and re-querying it when necessary. The parameters passed to `managedQuery` are:

uri
> The URI to query. This will map to a specific content provider, and in NotePad's case, to the NotePad content provider.

projection
> A `String` array with one element for each column you want returned in the query. Columns are numbered and correspond to the order of the columns in the underlying database.

selection
> Indicates which rows to retrieve through an SQL WHERE clause; it is passed as a single `String` variable. Can be `NULL` if you want all rows.

selectionArgs
> A `String` array containing one argument for each parameter or placeholder (a question mark in the SQL SELECT statement). Pass `NULL` if there are no arguments.

sortOrder
> A `String` variable containing a full `ORDER BY` argument, if sorting is desired. Can be `NULL`.

The NotePad application queries the `NotePadProvider` to fill in the list of notes to display to the user:

```
public class NotesList extends ListActivity {

    ...

    private static final String[] PROJECTION = new String[] {❶
            Notes._ID, // 0
            Notes.TITLE, // 1
    };

    ...

    @Override
    protected void onCreate(Bundle savedInstanceState) {
        super.onCreate(savedInstanceState);

        setDefaultKeyMode(DEFAULT_KEYS_SHORTCUT);❷

        // If no data was given in the Intent (because we were started
        // as a MAIN activity), then use our default content provider.
        Intent intent = getIntent();❸
        if (intent.getData() == null) {
            intent.setData(Notes.CONTENT_URI);
        }
```

```
        // Inform the list we provide context menus for items
        getListView().setOnCreateContextMenuListener(this);

        // Perform a managed query. The Activity will handle closing
        // and requerying the cursor when needed.
        Cursor cursor = managedQuery(getIntent().getData(),❹
                PROJECTION, null, null, Notes.DEFAULT_SORT_ORDER);

        // Used to map notes entries from the database to views
        SimpleCursorAdapter adapter = new SimpleCursorAdapter(❺
            this,
            R.layout.noteslist_item,
            cursor,
            new String[] { Notes.TITLE },
            new int[] { android.R.id.text1 });
        setListAdapter(adapter);❻
    }
```

Here are some of the highlights of the code:

❶ Creates the projection, the first parameter to `managedQuery`. In this case, the array contains the note ID and title.

❷ Sets the Activity's default key handling mode to `DEFAULT_KEYS_SHORTCUTS`. This lets the user execute shortcut commands from the options menu without having to press the menu key first.

❸ Gets the client's request, passed in the Intent. This should contain the content provider URI, but if it doesn't, the next line sets it to the NotePad URI.

❹ The `managedQuery` call, which returns a cursor.

❺ To use the data in the Cursor as the input for a ListActivity, an Adapter is required. In this case, a SimpleCursorAdapter has all the functionality that is necessary.

❻ After you have created the Adapter, issue the ListActivity's `setListAdapter` method to display the data from the Cursor on the screen.

Update data

To understand how to update data, we'll take a look at the `TitleEditor` class. Because it's small, looking at it in its entirety is instructive. Relatively few lines are needed to manipulate the content provider, and most of the function connects the user's clicks to changes in the content provider. The user interaction uses basic manipulations of graphic elements, which were briefly introduced in Chapter 4 and will be fully discussed in Chapter 10 and subsequent chapters. The rest of this section prints the `TitleEditor` class in blocks, following each block with explanations.

```
    public class TitleEditor extends Activity implements View.OnClickListener {

        /** An array of the columns we are interested in. */
        private static final String[] PROJECTION = new String[] {
            NotePad.Notes._ID, // 0
```

```
        NotePad.Notes.TITLE, // 1
};

/** Index of the title column */
private static final int COLUMN_INDEX_TITLE = 1;

/** Cursor providing access to the note whose title we are editing. */
private Cursor mCursor;

/** The EditText field from our UI. Used to extract the text when done. */
private EditText mText;

/** The content URI to the note that's being edited. */
private Uri mUri;
```

This first section of the TitleEditor Activity class sets up all of its private data. The following private variables are declared:

PROJECTION
> Used by the managedQuery function to describe the columns to return in the query, as shown in the previous section.

COLUMN_INDEX_TITLE
> Defines the number of the column, in the order returned by the query, from which the title must be pulled. The numbers start at 0, so the value of 1 shown is the index of the TITLE within the PROJECTION string.

mUri
> Holds the URI of the note whose title we're going to edit. An example URI might be *content://com.google.provider.NotePad/notes/2*.

mCursor
> The cursor that holds the results of the query.

mText
> The EditText field on the form.

Next, the Activity's onCreate method sets up the Activity:

```
@Override
public void onCreate(Bundle savedInstanceState) {
    super.onCreate(savedInstanceState);

    setContentView(R.layout.title_editor);❶

    // Get the uri of the note whose title we want to edit
    mUri = getIntent().getData();

    // Get a cursor to access the note
    mCursor = managedQuery(mUri, PROJECTION, null, null, null);❷

    // Set up click handlers for the text field and button
    mText = (EditText) this.findViewById(R.id.title);❸
    mText.setOnClickListener(this);
```

```
        Button b = (Button) findViewById(R.id.ok);
        b.setOnClickListener(this);
    }
```

Here are some of the highlights of the code:

❶ Finds the `ContentView` in the *res/layout/title_editor.xml* layout file, using the `setContentView` method.

❷ Runs the `managedQuery` method to load results into a Cursor.

❸ Sets click handlers for both the button and the text box. This will direct any clicks on the button or the text box to the `onClick` method, which we'll see shortly.

When `onCreate` finishes, the `onResume` method is called. This method pulls the current value of the note title from the cursor and assigns it to the value of the text box:

```
@Override
protected void onResume() {
    super.onResume();

    // Initialize the text with the title column from the cursor
    if (mCursor != null) {
        mCursor.moveToFirst();
        mText.setText(mCursor.getString(COLUMN_INDEX_TITLE));
    }
}
```

The `onPause` method is where the application writes the data back to the database. In other words, NotePad follows the typical Android practice of saving up writes until the application is suspended. We'll see soon where this method is called:

```
@Override
protected void onPause() {
    super.onPause();

    if (mCursor != null) {
        // Write the title back to the note
        ContentValues values = new ContentValues();❶
        values.put(Notes.TITLE, mText.getText().toString());❷
        getContentResolver().update(mUri, values, null, null);❸
    }
}
```

Here are some of the highlights of the code:

❶ Creates a new `ContentValues` object to hold the set of values to pass to the `ContentResolver`.

❷ Puts the column name and the new value of the column in the `values` object.

❸ Stores the updated value by creating a `ContentResolver` and passing the URI and new vales to its update method.

The last method in `TitleEditor` is the common callback for handling user clicks, named `onClick`:

```
public void onClick(View v) {
    // When the user clicks, just finish this activity.
    // onPause will be called, and we save our data there.
    finish();
}
```

The comment describes what is going on pretty well. Once the user clicks either the OK button or the text box within the dialog box, the Activity calls the `finish` method. That method calls `onPause`, which writes the contents of the dialog box back to the database, as we showed earlier.

Delete data

A user who pulls up a list of notes from the `NotesList` class can choose the Delete option on the context menu to run the following method:

```
@Override
public boolean onContextItemSelected(MenuItem item) {
    AdapterView.AdapterContextMenuInfo info;
    info = (AdapterView.AdapterContextMenuInfo) item.getMenuInfo()❶;

    switch (item.getItemId()) {
      case MENU_ITEM_DELETE: {
        // Delete the note that the context menu is for
        Uri noteUri = ContentUris.withAppendedId(getIntent().getData(), info.id);❷
        getContentResolver().delete(noteUri, null, null);❸
        return true;
      }
    }
    return false;
}
```

Here are some of the highlights of the code:

❶ When the menu for the job was created, the job ID was stuffed into the extra information variable for the menu. That extra information section is retrieved from the `MenuItem` on this line and used in the next part of the highlighted code.

❷ Builds a URI by extracting the URI from the user's Intent, as usual, and appending the number of the item to delete, taken from the menu.

❸ Creates a `ContentResolver` and pass the URI to its `delete` method.

CHAPTER 9

Location and Mapping

Ever since mobile phones started incorporating devices that made them aware of their geographic locations, developers have foreseen a new era of location-based applications. Location awareness improves many applications and makes possible totally new applications. If your application is looking up restaurants, it's clearly better if you can restrict your search to the area around you. It's even better if you can see a map of the restaurants' locations, and perhaps be able to look up driving or walking directions. If you're looking for a temporary job, as in the MJAndroid application highlighted in this book, it's clearly an advantage to be able to see where the opportunities are.

And navigation is really just the first generation of Location-Based Services (LBS). Developers foresee the day you'll be able to opt-in to receive advertisements from nearby retailers as you walk down a street, and your music player will suggest songs based on your current location. The world of LBS is just beginning to take off, and as we'll see, Google's Android offers powerful features that make the development of these applications very easy.

In economic terms, location-based applications are a major factor in mobile telephony, constituting half the revenue from mobile applications, and growing fast. Because they are based on the ability of the mobile network to locate devices and the relationship of mobility and location, location-based applications are as fundamental to mobile telephony as communication.

Location is usually combined with search: Where are my contacts? Where are services or products I'm looking for? Where are people with common interests?

Location-Based Services

Mobile phones use several related methods, alone and in combination, to determine where they are:

Cell ID
> Regardless of whether you're actually talking on the phone, as long as it's powered up, your mobile phone carries on a constant conversation with nearby cell towers.

It has to do this in order to be able to respond when someone calls you, so every few seconds it "pings" the cell tower it was using last to tell it that it's still in range and to note network parameters such as the current time, the current signal strength (uplink and downlink), etc.

If you happen to be moving, your phone may do a handover to another cell tower, all in the background without a need for you to intervene. Each cell tower worldwide has a unique identifier, called (appropriately enough) its Cell ID, and each tower knows its latitude and longitude, so it's easy enough for a mobile phone to know "approximately" where you are located by taking note of the current Cell ID's geographic location. Cell sizes vary depending on the expected traffic in an area, but in the U.S., their radius ranges from a half mile (cities) to five miles or more (wide-open spaces).

Triangulation

Most of the time your mobile phone is in range of more than one cell tower. In 2G and later mobile technologies, the cell tower has the ability to tell what direction your signal is coming from. If there are two or three towers that can see your phone, together they can triangulate on your phone's location. With some operators, your phone then has the ability to query the network to find out where it's been located. This sounds a little backward, but it can be very accurate, and doesn't depend on any extra hardware on the mobile phone.

GPS

The satellite-based Global Positioning System (GPS) is ubiquitous these days, found in car navigation units, handheld navigators, and mobile phones. The good news is that, using GPS, your mobile phone can determine its location very accurately, including its altitude if that's important for some particular application. There are several downsides to GPS, but it is gaining popularity nonetheless. The downsides:

Increased cost

GPS radios and processors are fairly inexpensive, but still, an increase of even $10 in the bill-of-materials cost of a mobile phone is considerable.

Reduced battery life

There have been great strides in reducing the power required by GPS radios and processors, but they still suck battery power. Most phones that include GPS also have a feature that lets the user turn it on and off. If your application depends on GPS accuracy, it's good to remember that your application might have to check whether the GPS device is turned on and notify the user if it isn't.

Unreliable availability

Nothing "always works," but GPS in particular depends on your mobile device being able to see the satellites currently overhead. If you're in the basement of a high-rise building, surrounded by steel-reinforced concrete, you probably aren't going to be able to use GPS.

It's reasonable to expect that all Android phones will include one or all of these location-finding methods. The T-Mobile G1 in particular can use them all. So now we'll proceed to techniques for using the location capabilities.

Mapping

Google is most famous for their search engine, but not far behind that comes the fame of Google Maps. When creating Android, the folks at Google could easily see the potential in LBS and how well that fit with their mapping expertise. Most LBS applications end up displaying a map. Meanwhile, Google already had the technology to display and update interactive maps, and the business processes in place to allow others to use those maps and add features for their own websites. It still required a leap to make that mapping technology available to application developers for mobile phones, but thankfully Google accomplished just that.

The Google Maps Activity

One of the applications that comes with Android is Google Maps itself. If it's appropriate, you can start Google Maps from your application the same way you start any other Activity:

1. Create an Intent (`new Intent(String action, Uri uri)`) that says you need to display a Map. The parameters are:
   - An `action`, for which you must specify `ACTION_VIEW`.
   - A `Uri`, for which you should specify one of the following URI Schemes, substituting your data:
     — geo:*latitude,longitude*
     — geo:*latitude,longitude*?z=*zoom*
     — geo:0,0?q*my_street_address*
     — geo:0,0?q*business_near_city*
2. Call `startActivity(Intent intent)`, using the Intent you just created.

An example that creates a map is:

```
Intent intent = new Intent(ACTION_VIEW, "geo:37.422006,-122.084095");
startActivity(intent);
```

This is certainly easy, and gets you all the power of Google Maps, but you can't really integrate the map into your application this way. Google Maps is an application unto itself, and there's no way for you to change anything about the user interface or add overlay graphics to the map to point out whatever is of interest to your users. Android provides more flexible packages to add that power.

The MapView and MapActivity

This book's MJAndroid application needs to be able to add overlays that show the locations for jobs in the area. So instead of using the Google Maps application, we will use a MapView, which we can overlay with as many graphics as we want. You can have only one MapView per Activity, however, and your activity has to extend MapActivity. As you'll see, that's a small price to pay for all the functionality that comes for free.

There are a couple of unique prerequisites for using MapViews in your application, and we touched on both of them when we looked at the initialization of MJAndroid in Chapter 4.

Include the MapViews library
> The MapView is not included in the default Android libraries, so you need to specify in *AndroidManifest.xml* that we are using this additional library:

```
<application android:icon="@drawable/icon2">
        <uses-library android:name="com.google.android.maps" />
```

> You can't put the `uses-library` line just anywhere in *AndroidManifest.xml*; it needs to be within the `<application>` tag and outside of the `<activity>` tag definitions.

Sign your application and obtain a Map apiKey from Google
> When you use a MapView in your application, you are using actual Google Maps data to draw the map. For legal reasons, Google needs to track who is using their map data. They don't care what your application does with it, but they need to have you register with them for an API key and agree to appropriate Terms of Service. This tells them your application is using mapping data, and whether you are also using the routing data that is available from Google Maps. Chapter 7 covered the processes of signing your application and getting an `apiKey`.

 Remember that programs using a MapView must be signed. To make it easy for you to try out the MJAndroid example from this book, we've included an *.apk* file as described in the sidebar "Running the MJAndroid Code" on page 35 in Chapter 3. If you change the code or do any coding of your own, you need to get your own key, as described in Chapter 7.

Working with MapViews

The MapView encapsulates a lot of very complex mapping software and is available for you in your Android applications—for free. Here are some of the things you can do with a MapView, with only a little programming on your part:

- Show a street map of any area in the world, with up-to-date mapping information courtesy of Google

- Change the MapView to show:

  Street view
  > Photographs taken at street level for many areas in North America

  Satellite view
  > An aerial, photographic view of the area

  Traffic view
  > Real-time traffic information superimposed on the map or satellite views

- Move the map under program control
- Plot your own graphics in overlays on top of the map
- Respond to user touch events on the map

MapView and MyLocationOverlay Initialization

The map in MicroJobs has two modes:

- At startup, and when we select "Current Location" from the Spinner, we want to display a map of our current location, and we want that map to track us as we move around. For this map we will use the `MyLocationOverlay` class.

- When we select a specific location from the Spinner, we want to display a map of that location, turn off location updates, and not track movement.

Let's look again at the code in *MicroJobs.java* that initializes the MapView and the MyLocationOverlay that tracks our current location:

```
@Override
public void onCreate(Bundle savedInstanceState) {

...

    mvMap = (MapView) findViewById(R.id.mapmain);❶

    // get the map controller
    final MapController mc = mvMap.getController();❷

    mMyLocationOverlay = new MyLocationOverlay(this, mvMap);❸
    mMyLocationOverlay.runOnFirstFix(❹
        new Runnable() {
            public void run() {
                mc.animateTo(mMyLocationOverlay.getMyLocation());❺
                mc.setZoom(16);
            }
    });

Drawable marker = getResources().getDrawable(R.drawable.android_tiny_image);❻
marker.setBounds(0, 0, marker.getIntrinsicWidth(), marker.getIntrinsicHeight());
    mvMap.getOverlays().add(new MJJobsOverlay(marker));

    mvMap.setClickable(true);❼
    mvMap.setEnabled(true);
```

```
        mvMap.setSatellite(false);
        mvMap.setTraffic(false);
        mvMap.setStreetView(false);

        // start out with a general zoom
        mc.setZoom(16); ❽
...
    /**
     * Required method to indicate whether we display routes
     */
    @Override
    protected boolean isRouteDisplayed() { return false; } ❾
```

Here are some of the highlights of the code:

❶ We first find the MapView in the *main.xml* layout file, the same way we find any other view, and assign it to the variable mvMap of type MapView, so we can refer to it when we need to.

❷ We also get a handle on the MapController associated with MapView. We'll use that to pan (animate) the map, zoom in, zoom out, change views, etc.

❸ To use MyLocationOverlay, we create a new instantiation, giving it the highly creative name mMyLocationOverlay.

❹ The first thing we do with mMyLocationOverlay is define a method that Android will call when we receive our first location fix from the location provider.

❺ This runOnFirstFix method moves the map to the current location (given by mMyLocationOverlay.getMyLocation()) and zooms to a reasonable level for us to see nearby job prospects.

❻ Next, we identify a marker that we've decided to use on mMyLocationOverlay to mark available jobs. We use an image that's stored in our *res/drawable* directory, called *android_tiny_image*. It's a picture of a little Android robot. We define the bounds of the Drawable marker, as described in Chapter 12, and add the marker overlay to the list of overlays for the MapView mvMap.

❼ Now we'd like to set some initial attributes for mvMap, described later in this section. We'll allow the user to change most of these through menu buttons.

❽ Then, following a belt-and-suspenders philosophy, just in case there isn't a location provider to trigger runOnFirstFix, we'll set the zoom level again here.

❾ Finally, MapView requires us to override the isRouteDisplayed() method to indicate whether we are displaying route information on our map. We are not, so we return false.

MyLocationOverlay encapsulates a wealth of location and mapping code. In our single call to the constructor we:

• Ask Android to figure out what location providers are available in our environment (GPS, Cell ID, triangulation).

- Connect to the "best" of those location providers.
- Ask the location provider to send us periodic location updates as our handset moves.
- Link to routines that will automatically move our map as needed to track any changes in location.

MyLocationOverlay also allows us to place a compass rose on the MapView and have that updated as well, but we won't be using that in MJAndroid.

The map attributes set by the code are:

setClickable

We want users to be able to click (tap) on a job to cause MJAndroid to display more detail about that job, so we set this to true.

setEnabled

This method is actually inherited from android.view.View. Google doesn't tell us exactly what this means in the case of a MapView, but presumably it enables the standard map functions (zooming, panning, etc.).

setSatellite

Setting this flag adds a satellite view from the composite map, whereas clearing the flag removes the view. To start with, we don't want the satellite information on the map.

setTraffic

Similarly, setting or clearing this flag adds or removes current traffic information from the map, respectively. Again, we don't want to start with traffic information on the map.

setStreetView

We don't want street views right now either, although we'll let the user enable them later.

Zooming in Android Maps

Android maps come already equipped with support for zooming in and out. The "i" key zooms in on the map, and the "o" key zooms out. Maps can also zoom in and out under program control, through the MapController.

There are several methods defined for zooming, all via the MapController. Android defines 21 zoom levels for maps. At zoom level 1, the equator of the earth is 256 pixels long. Every step up in zoom level multiplies that by 2. Google warns that the higher-resolution maps are not available worldwide. All of the zoom methods clamp the zoom level to the range 1 through 21 if you ask MapController to go beyond those limits.

The methods that control zoom, along with their parameters, are:

zoomIn

Zooms in one level.

---

zoomOut
:   Zooms out one level.

setZoom(int zoomlevel)
:   Zooms to the given level, restricting it to the range 1 to 21.

zoomInFixing(int xpixel, int ypixel), zoomOutFixing(int xpixel, int ypixel)
:   Zoom in one level, but keep the given point fixed on the screen. Normally when you zoom in and out, the center of the screen is the only point that stays fixed. These routines let you pick any point on the map to be the fixed point.

zoomToSpan(int latSpanE6, int longSpanE6)
:   Attempts to zoom so the given span is displayed on the map. What it actually does is select the zoom level that is the closest match for the span requested. The latitude and longitude span parameters are expressed as integers with a value 10^6 times the actual value in degrees. For instance, a latitude/longitude span of 2.5 degrees by 1.0 degrees would be expressed as zoomToSpan(2500000, 1000000).

Pausing and Resuming a MapActivity

Mobile applications have unique requirements, due mostly to the constrained resources available to execute applications. For now let's focus on MapActivities and talk about a way we can help save battery power. The good news is that Android makes it pretty easy.

In a mobile environment, battery life is everything, and if we're not the application that is currently being displayed, we want to do everything we can to minimize the power we consume. You recall from the discussion of the Android lifecycle (Chapter 1) that when an Activity (such as MicroJobs) starts another Activity (such as MicroJobsList) the new Activity takes over the screen, and the calling Activity gets pushed onto a stack of Activities that are waiting to run. At that time, Android calls the onPause() routine in the calling Activity so it can prepare itself to go into hibernation. At this point in *MicroJobs.java* (or just about any MapActivity that uses location updates), we want to turn off location updates. Doing so will at least save the cycles devoted to doing the update, and may allow the handset to save even more power by putting the location provider in a quiescent state.

When the called Activity (in our case, MicroJobsList) exits and the calling Activity is popped off the stack and takes control of the screen, the framework calls the onResume method in the calling Activity. In a MapActivity, we want to turn on location updates again when this method is invoked.

In MicroJobs, the onPause and onResume methods are straightforward:

```
/**
 * @see com.google.android.maps.MapActivity#onPause()
 */
@Override
public void onPause() {
```

```
        super.onPause();
        mMyLocationOverlay.disableMyLocation();
    }

    /**
     * @see com.google.android.maps.MapActivity#onResume()
     */
    @Override
    public void onResume() {
        super.onResume();
        mMyLocationOverlay.enableMyLocation();
    }
```

Note that if we'd had a compass rose as part of our MyLocationOverlay, we would have to disable and enable it as well. Otherwise, the system would be updating the direction of the compass rose even when it wasn't being displayed, thereby wasting cycles and battery power.

Controlling the Map with Menu Buttons

We want to give the user the ability to turn on satellite, traffic, and street views of the map. In addition, we'll throw in a few menu buttons to enable zooming and another way of getting to the Jobs List.

Android has a sophisticated set of menu capabilities that includes three types of menus (options, context, and submenus), each with its own capabilities, icon menu buttons, and other advanced features. We just use text-based menu buttons, and so we need to do two things:

1. Create the menu of buttons that will be displayed.
2. Catch the menu events and invoke appropriate actions.

The following code creates the menu in *MicroJobs.java*:

```
    /**
     * Set up menus for this page
     *
     * @see android.app.Activity#onCreateOptionsMenu(android.view.Menu)
     */
    @Override
    public boolean onCreateOptionsMenu(Menu menu) {
        boolean supRetVal = super.onCreateOptionsMenu(menu);
        menu.add(Menu.NONE, 0, Menu.NONE, getString(R.string.map_menu_zoom_in));
        menu.add(Menu.NONE, 1, Menu.NONE, getString(R.string.map_menu_zoom_out));
        menu.add(Menu.NONE, 2, Menu.NONE, getString(R.string.map_menu_set_satellite));
        menu.add(Menu.NONE, 3, Menu.NONE, getString(R.string.map_menu_set_map));
        menu.add(Menu.NONE, 4, Menu.NONE, getString(R.string.map_menu_set_traffic));
        menu.add(Menu.NONE, 5, Menu.NONE, getString(R.string.map_menu_show_list));
        return supRetVal;
    }
```

We create menu buttons by overriding the `onCreateOptionsMenu` method, where we are passed a menu parameter for the Activity's menu. After dutifully allowing the superclass a chance to do what it needs to do, we simply add items (buttons) to the menu using `menu.add`. The version of `menu.add` that we've chosen takes four parameters:

int groupid
> Android allows you to group menu items so you can quickly change the whole menu at once. We don't have a need for that in MicroJobs, so `Menu.NONE` says we don't need it.

int itemid
> We need a unique identifier for this menu item so we can tell later whether it was picked.

int order
> The `itemid` we defined in the second parameter does not imply order. If we cared about the order in which the items were presented, we'd do that with this parameter. Since we don't care, we use `Menu.NONE` again.

int titleRes
> The ID of the string resource we want to use for the button title. Note that this is an integer, not a string, so the menu strings need to be predefined in *string.xml*, under the *res* directory. You recall that Android takes care of compiling the strings in *res/strings.xml* into a *.java* file (*R.java*) that assigns an integer to each string. The `getString` method retrieves that integer for you (despite the name, the method returns an integer, not a string).

To catch the menu events, we override the `onOptionsItemSelected` method:

```
/**
 * @see android.app.Activity#onOptionsItemSelected(android.view.MenuItem)
 */
@Override
public boolean onOptionsItemSelected(MenuItem item) {
        switch (item.getItemId()) {
            case 0:
                // Zoom in
                zoomIn();
                return true;
            case 1:
                // Zoom out
                zoomOut();
                return true;
            case 2:
                // Toggle satellite views
                mvMap.setSatellite(!mvMap.isSatellite());
                return true;
            case 3:
                // Toggle street views
                mvMap.setStreetView(!mvMap.isStreetView());
                return true;
            case 4:
```

```
                // Toggle traffic views
                mvMap.setTraffic(!mvMap.isTraffic());
                return true;
            case 5:
                // Show the job list activity
                startActivity(new Intent(MicroJobs.this, MicroJobsList.class));
                return true;
        }
        return false;
    }
```

We are passed the selected `MenuItem`, and the switch has a case for each button that we defined for the menu. The code for each case is similar to code that we've seen before.

Controlling the Map with the KeyPad

Some users might prefer to control the map through the keypad (generally one "click," versus two "clicks" to cause a Menu event). Enabling this behavior also demonstrates how to respond to KeyPad events in general, so we've added some code to zoom in, zoom out, and back out of the current Activity:

```
/**
 * @see android.app.Activity#onKeyDown(int, android.view.KeyEvent)
 */
@Override
public boolean onKeyDown(int keyCode, KeyEvent event) {
    switch (keyCode) {
        case KeyEvent.KEYCODE_DPAD_UP: // zoom in
            zoomIn();
            return true;
        case KeyEvent.KEYCODE_DPAD_DOWN: // zoom out
            zoomOut();
            return true;
        case KeyEvent.KEYCODE_BACK: // go back (meaning exit the app)
            finish();
            return true;
        default:
            return false;
    }
}
```

To catch key down events, we simply override `onKeyDown` and provide a switch for the different keys that are of interest. In addition to the keycodes you would expect (`KEYCODE_A`, ...`KEYCODE_Z` and things like `KEYCODE_SPACE`, `KEYCODE_SHIFT_LEFT`, and `KEYCODE_SHIFT_RIGHT`), Android includes keycodes that may or may not appear on any particular device (e.g., `KEYCODE_CAMERA` and `KEYCODE_VOLUME_UP`). A complete set of keycodes can be found at *http://code.google.com/android/reference/android/view/Key Event.html*.

Location Without Maps

What if your Activity needs to access location information, but it doesn't include a MapView? When you use a MapView, Android makes everything very easy with MyLocationOverlay, but even if you don't need a map, it isn't difficult to get location information. The code in this section is not part of MJAndroid, but it shows how you would go about getting location information without a map.

Let's look at a very simple, one-Activity application that displays the current location in a TextView.

The Manifest and Layout Files

An appropriate *AndroidManifest.xml* file follows. We created this file using the Android SDK and the Android Manifest Editor that comes as part of the SDK. The only change we needed to make with the editor was to add the `uses-permission` tag for `android.permission.ACCESS_FINE_LOCATION` (in the next-to-last line of the file). We always need this permission in order to get location information from a GPS location provider:

```xml
<?xml version="1.0" encoding="utf-8"?>
<manifest xmlns:android="http://schemas.android.com/apk/res/android"
        package="com.microjobsinc.dloc"
        android:versionCode="1"
        android:versionName="1.0.0">
    <application android:icon="@drawable/icon" android:label="@string/app_name">
        <activity android:name=".Main"
                android:label="@string/app_name">
            <intent-filter>
                <action android:name="android.intent.action.MAIN" />
                <category android:name="android.intent.category.LAUNCHER" />
            </intent-filter>
        </activity>
    </application>

<uses-permission android:name="android.permission.ACCESS_FINE_LOCATION">
    </uses-permission>
</manifest>
```

We'll use a very simple layout file with four TextViews: one label and one text box each for latitude and longitude:

```xml
<?xml version="1.0" encoding="utf-8"?>
<LinearLayout xmlns:android="http://schemas.android.com/apk/res/android"
    android:orientation="vertical"
    android:layout_width="fill_parent"
    android:layout_height="fill_parent"
    >
<TextView
    android:id="@+id/lblLatitude"
    android:layout_width="fill_parent"
    android:layout_height="wrap_content"
```

```
            android:text="Latitude:"
            />
        <TextView
            android:id="@+id/tvLatitude"
            android:layout_width="fill_parent"
            android:layout_height="wrap_content"
            />
        <TextView
            android:id="@+id/lblLongitude"
            android:layout_width="fill_parent"
            android:layout_height="wrap_content"
            android:text="Longitude:"
            />
        <TextView
            android:id="@+id/tvLongitude"
            android:layout_width="fill_parent"
            android:layout_height="wrap_content"
            />
    </LinearLayout>
```

Connecting to a Location Provider and Getting Location Updates

Let's start with an Activity that just connects with the GPS LocationProvider and gets and displays our current location (no updates). The procedure is pretty straightforward:

```
package com.microjobsinc.dloc;

import android.app.Activity;
import android.content.Context;
import android.location.Location;
import android.location.LocationManager;
import android.os.Bundle;
import android.widget.TextView;

public class Main extends Activity {
    /** Called when the activity is first created. */
    @Override
    public void onCreate(Bundle savedInstanceState) {
        super.onCreate(savedInstanceState);
        setContentView(R.layout.main);

        // find the TextViews
        TextView tvLatitude = (TextView)findViewById(R.id.tvLatitude);
        TextView tvLongitude = (TextView)findViewById(R.id.tvLongitude);

        // get handle for LocationManager
        LocationManager lm = (LocationManager)
          getSystemService(Context.LOCATION_SERVICE);❶

        // connect to the GPS location service
        Location loc = lm.getLastKnownLocation("gps");❷

        // fill in the TextViews
        tvLatitude.setText(Double.toString(loc.getLatitude()));❸
        tvLongitude.setText(Double.toString(loc.getLongitude()));
```

```
        }
    }
```

Here are some of the highlights of the code:

❶ Connect to the `LocationManager` using `getSystemService(Context.LOCATION_SERV
ICE)`.

❷ Ask the `LocationManager` where we are using `getLastKnownLocation("`*provider*`")`.

❸ Get the latitude and longitude from the location returned and use it as needed.

But we also want to get periodic location updates from the `LocationManager` so we can
track our location as we move about. For that we need to add a listener routine and
ask the `LocationManager` to call it when it has an update.

Location updates from the `LocationManager` are accessible to an application through a
`DispLocListener` class, so we will create an instance of this class in the `onCreate` method
of our main Activity. We are required to override a number of methods in
`DispLocListener` to meet the `LocationListener` interface definition, but we don't need
them for this application, so we'll leave the definitions empty.

The full implementation follows:

```
package com.microjobsinc.dloc;

import android.app.Activity;
import android.content.Context;
import android.location.Location;
import android.location.LocationListener;
import android.location.LocationManager;
import android.os.Bundle;
import android.widget.TextView;

public class Main extends Activity {
    private LocationManager lm;
    private LocationListener locListenD;
    public TextView tvLatitude;
    public TextView tvLongitude;

    /** Called when the activity is first created. */
    @Override
    public void onCreate(Bundle savedInstanceState) {
        super.onCreate(savedInstanceState);
        setContentView(R.layout.main);

        // find the TextViews
        tvLatitude = (TextView)findViewById(R.id.tvLatitude);
        tvLongitude = (TextView)findViewById(R.id.tvLongitude);

        // get handle for LocationManager
        LocationManager lm = (LocationManager)
          getSystemService(Context.LOCATION_SERVICE);

        // connect to the GPS location service
```

```
        Location loc = lm.getLastKnownLocation("gps");

        // fill in the TextViews
        tvLatitude.setText(Double.toString(loc.getLatitude()));
        tvLongitude.setText(Double.toString(loc.getLongitude()));

        // ask the Location Manager to send us location updates
        locListenD = new DispLocListener();
        lm.requestLocationUpdates("gps", 30000L, 10.0f, locListenD);
    }

    private class DispLocListener implements LocationListener {

        @Override
        public void onLocationChanged(Location location) {
            // update TextViews
            tvLatitude.setText(Double.toString(location.getLatitude()));
            tvLongitude.setText(Double.toString(location.getLongitude()));
        }

        @Override
        public void onProviderDisabled(String provider) {
        }

        @Override
        public void onProviderEnabled(String provider) {
        }

        @Override
        public void onStatusChanged(String provider, int status, Bundle extras) {
        }
    }
}
```

Our onCreate method creates an instance of DispLocListener and requests that the
LocationManager update it as needed using requestLocationUpdates. This method takes
four parameters:

String provider
   Which location provider to use. We assume GPS is available in this case.

long minTime
   Minimum update time, in milliseconds. The LocationManager will wait at least this
   long between updates. Here's an opportunity to tune your application for battery
   life: more frequent updates means more battery usage.

float minDistance
   Minimum distance, in meters, required to trigger an update. The Location
   Manager will update us only if we've moved at least this far since the last update.

LocationListener listener
   The name of the listener method to call when there is an update. This is the
   DispLocListener instance we just created.

Finally, we want to add the onPause and onResume code to turn off location updates when we're not actually displaying on the user's screen, and then turn them back on when we are:

```
/**
 * Turn off location updates if we're paused
 */
@Override
public void onPause() {
    super.onPause();
    lm.removeUpdates(locListenD);
}

/**
 * Resume location updates when we're resumed
 */
@Override
public void onResume() {
    super.onResume();
    lm.requestLocationUpdates("gps", 30000L, 10.0f, locListenD);
}
```

Updating the Emulated Location

While you are developing and debugging an application like the one just shown, you're normally running on the emulator. It would be nice (maybe even essential) to be able to update the current location that the emulator uses as it's running your code. Such a Mock Location Provider can get very fancy, but Android provides some built-in ways of updating the emulated location:

- The geo program built into the Android shell
- One-time updates via DDMS
- Tracks that are sequentially updated via DDMS

We'll look at each of these.

Using geo to update location

The **geo** utility is built into the Android image that runs on the emulator. It has a number of capabilities, the most important of which is geo fix:

geo fix

> You can use the **geo fix** command to send a location to Android by telnetting to the console of the emulated Android. The LocationProvider will then use this as the current location:
>
> ```
> telnet localhost 5554
> Android Console: type 'help' for a list of commands
> OK
> geo fix -122.842232 38.411908 0
> OK
> ```

geo fix takes three parameters:

longitude
> Specified in decimal

latitude
> Also specified in decimal

altitude
> Specified in meters

Using DDMS to update location

We talked a lot about DDMS (the Dalvik Debug Monitor Service) in Chapter 5, but two features are related to location updates. The Emulator Control pane of the DDMS screen provides several ways of controlling the running emulator. After switching to the DDMS perspective (click on DDMS in the upper right of the Eclipse window), you should see the Emulator Control pane in the middle left of the DDMS window (Figure 9-1). You will probably have to scroll down in that pane to see the controls related to Location Controls.

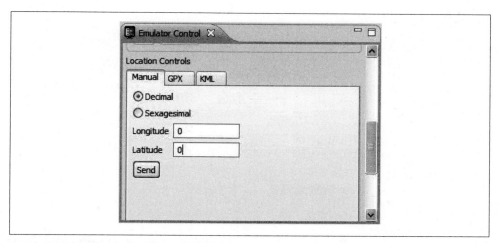

Figure 9-1. DDMS Emulator Control pane

To send a one-time update of a location to the emulator, just enter the longitude and latitude in the appropriate boxes and click Send.

If you click on the GPX or KML tabs, you will be able to load a GPX or KML file that describes a path, as shown in Figure 9-2. Here we've already loaded the file *OR.kml*, which is included on the website for this book. It traces a path near O'Reilly headquarters in Sebastopol, California.

You can create GPX tracks with many GPS navigation software tools, and KML tracks with Google Earth or many other navigation programs. The *OR.kml* file was generated

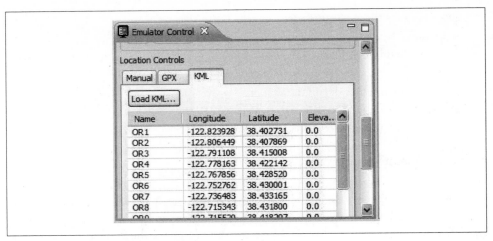

Figure 9-2. DDMS Emulator with KML location updates

by plotting a series of Google Earth Placemarks and concatenating them together into a single file. Here's an excerpt from *OR.kml*:

```xml
<?xml version="1.0" encoding="UTF-8"?>
<kml xmlns="http://earth.google.com/kml/2.2">
<Document>
    <name>OR1.kml</name>
    <StyleMap id="msn_ylw-pushpin">
        <Pair>
            <key>normal</key>
            <styleUrl>#sn_ylw-pushpin</styleUrl>
        </Pair>
        <Pair>
            <key>highlight</key>
            <styleUrl>#sh_ylw-pushpin</styleUrl>
        </Pair>
    </StyleMap>
    <Style id="sh_ylw-pushpin">
        <IconStyle>
            <scale>1.3</scale>
            <Icon>
              <href>http://maps.google.com/mapfiles/kml/pushpin/ylw-pushpin.png</href>
            </Icon>
            <hotSpot x="20" y="2" xunits="pixels" yunits="pixels"/>
        </IconStyle>
        <ListStyle>
        </ListStyle>
    </Style>
    <Style id="sn_ylw-pushpin">
        <IconStyle>
            <scale>1.1</scale>
            <Icon>
              <href>http://maps.google.com/mapfiles/kml/pushpin/ylw-pushpin.png</href>
            </Icon>
            <hotSpot x="20" y="2" xunits="pixels" yunits="pixels"/>
        </IconStyle>
```

```
        <ListStyle>
        </ListStyle>
    </Style>
    <Placemark>
        <name>OR1</name>
        <LookAt>
            <longitude>-122.7583711698369</longitude>
            <latitude>38.38922415809942</latitude>
            <altitude>0</altitude>
            <range>14591.7166300043</range>
            <tilt>0</tilt>
            <heading>0.04087372005871314</heading>
            <altitudeMode>relativeToGround</altitudeMode>
        </LookAt>
        <styleUrl>#msn_ylw-pushpin</styleUrl>
        <Point>
            <coordinates>-122.8239277647483,38.40273084940345,0</coordinates>
        </Point>
    </Placemark>
    <Placemark>
        <name>OR2</name>
        <LookAt>
            <longitude>-122.7677364592949</longitude>
            <latitude>38.3819544049429</latitude>
            <altitude>0</altitude>
            <range>11881.3330990845</range>
            <tilt>0</tilt>
            <heading>-8.006283077460853e-010</heading>
            <altitudeMode>relativeToGround</altitudeMode>
        </LookAt>
        <styleUrl>#msn_ylw-pushpin</styleUrl>
        <Point>
            <coordinates>-122.8064486052584,38.40786910573772,0</coordinates>
        </Point>
    </Placemark>
    <Placemark>
        <name>OR3</name>
        <LookAt>
            <longitude>-122.7677364592949</longitude>
            <latitude>38.3819544049429</latitude>
            <altitude>0</altitude>
            <range>11881.3330990845</range>
            <tilt>0</tilt>
            <heading>-8.006283077460853e-010</heading>
            <altitudeMode>relativeToGround</altitudeMode>
        </LookAt>
        <styleUrl>#msn_ylw-pushpin</styleUrl>
        <Point>
            <coordinates>-122.7911077944045,38.41500788727795,0</coordinates>
        </Point>
    </Placemark>
    ...
```

CHAPTER 10

Building a View

Android comes with many requirements that herald complexity in the user interface: it's a multiprocessing system that supports multiple concurrent applications, accepts multiple forms of input, is highly interactive, and must be flexible enough to support a wide range of devices now and in the future. The user interface is impressively rich and easy to use, given all that it has to do. But you need to understand how it works in order to use it without crashing your application, making it look awful on some devices, or imposing a performance penalty on the system.

This chapter gives you basic techniques for writing a graphical interface on Android. It explains the architecture of the Android UI toolkit, while showing you in practical terms how to enable and lay out basic interface elements such as buttons and text boxes. It also covers event handling and other critical topics, such as using multiple threads to offload long tasks so that the UI doesn't freeze.

Android GUI Architecture

The Android environment adds yet another Graphical User Interface (GUI) toolkit to the Java ecosphere, joining AWT, Swing, SWT, and J2ME (leaving aside the web UI toolkits). If you've worked with any of these, the Android framework will look familiar. Like them, it is single-threaded, event-driven, and built on a library of nestable components.

The Android UI framework is, like the other UI frameworks, organized around the common Model-View-Controller pattern illustrated in Figure 10-1. It provides structure and tools for building a Controller that handles user input (like key presses and screen taps) and a View that renders graphical information to the screen.

The Model

The Model is the guts of your application: what it actually does. It might be, for instance, the database of tunes on your device and the code for playing them. It might be your list of contacts and the code that places phone calls or sends IMs to them.

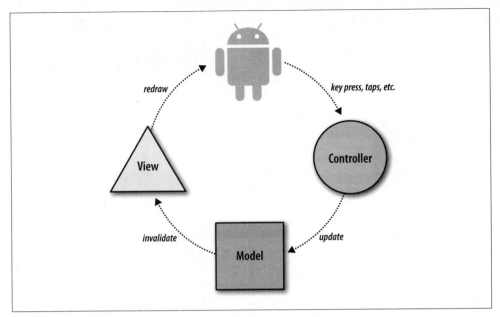

Figure 10-1. Model-View-Controller concept

While a particular application's View and Controller will necessarily reflect the Model they manipulate, a single Model might be used by several different applications. Think, for instance, of an MP3 player and an application that converts MP3 files into WAV files. For both applications, the Model includes the MP3 file format and codecs for it. The former application, however, has the familiar Stop, Start, and Pause controls, and plays the track. The latter may not produce any sound at all; instead, it will have controls for setting bitrate, etc. The Model is all about the data. It is the subject of most of the rest of this book.

The View

The View is the application's feedback to the user. It is the portion of the application responsible for rendering the display, sending audio to speakers, generating tactile feedback, and so on. The graphical portion of the Android UI framework's View, described in detail in Chapter 12, is implemented as a tree of subclasses of the View class. Graphically, each of these objects represents a rectangular area on the screen that is completely within the rectangular area represented by its parent in the tree. The root of this tree is the application window.

As an example, the display in a hypothetical MP3 player might contain a component that shows the album cover for the currently playing tune. Another component might display the name of the currently playing song, while a third contains subcomponents such as the Play, Pause, and Stop buttons.

The UI framework paints the screen by walking the View tree, asking each component to draw itself in a *preorder traversal*. In other words, each component draws itself and then asks each of its children to do the same. When the whole tree has been rendered, the smaller, nested components that are the leaves of the tree—and that were, therefore, painted later—appear to be painted on top of the components that are nearer to the root and that were painted first.

The Android UI framework is actually quite a bit more efficient than this oversimplified description suggests. It does not paint an area of a parent view if it can be certain that some child will later paint the same area, because it would be a waste of time to paint background underneath an opaque object! It would also be a waste of time to repaint portions of a view that have not changed.

The Controller

The Controller is the portion of an application that responds to external actions: a keystroke, a screen tap, an incoming call, etc. It is implemented as an event queue. Each external action is represented as a unique event in the queue. The framework removes each event from the queue in order and dispatches it.

For example, when a user presses a key on his phone, the Android system generates a KeyEvent and adds it to an *event queue*. Eventually, after previously enqueued events have been processed, the KeyEvent is removed from the queue and passed as the parameter of a call to the dispatchKeyEvent method of the View that is currently selected.

Once an event is dispatched to the in-focus component, that component may take appropriate action to change the internal state of the program. In an MP3 player application, for instance, when the user taps a Play/Pause button on the screen and the event is dispatched to that button's object, the handler method might update the Model to resume playing some previously selected tune.

This chapter describes the construction of a Controller for an Android application.

Putting It Together

We now have all the concepts necessary to describe the complete UI system. When an external action occurs (for example, when the user scrolls, drags, or presses a button; a call comes in; or an MP3 player arrives at the end of its playlist), the Android system enqueues an event representing the action on the event queue. Eventually the event is dequeued—first in, first out—and dispatched to an appropriate event handler. The handler, probably code you write as part of your application, responds to the event by notifying the Model that there has been a change in state. The Model takes the appropriate action.

Nearly any change in Model state will require a corresponding change in the View. In response to a key press, for instance, an EditText component must show the newly typed character at the insertion point. Similarly, in a phone book application, clicking on a contact will cause that contact to be highlighted and the previously highlighted contact to have its highlighting removed.

In order to update the display, the Model must notify the UI Framework that some portion of the display is now stale and has to be redrawn. The redraw request is, actually, nothing more than another event enqueued in the same framework event queue that held the Controller event a moment ago. The redraw event is processed, in order, like any other UI event.

Eventually, the redraw event is removed from the queue and dispatched. The event handler for a redraw event is the View. The View tree is redrawn, and each View object is responsible for rendering its current state at the time it is drawn.

To make this concrete, we can trace the cycle through a hypothetical MP3 player application:

1. When the user taps the screen image of the Play/Pause button, the framework creates a new MotionEvent containing, among other things, the screen coordinates of the tap. The framework enqueues the new event at the end of the event queue.

2. As described in "The Controller" on page 159, when the event percolates through the queue, the framework removes it and passes it down the View tree to the leaf widget within whose bounding rectangle the tap occurred.

3. Because the button widget represents the Play/Pause button, the application button handling code tells the core (the Model) that it should resume playing a tune.

4. The application Model code starts playing the selected tune. In addition, it sends a redraw request to the UI framework.

5. The redraw request is added to the event queue and eventually processed as described in "The View" on page 158.

6. The screen gets redrawn with the Play button in its playing state, and everything is again in sync.

UI component objects such as buttons and text boxes actually implement both View and Controller methods. This only makes sense. When you add a Button to your application's UI, you want it to appear on the screen as well as do something when the user pushes it. Even though the two logical elements of the UI—the View and the Controller—are implemented in the same object, you should take care that they do not directly interact. Controller methods, for instance, should never directly change the display. Leave it to the code that actually changes state to request a redraw, and trust that later calls to rendering methods will allow the component to reflect its new state. Coding in this way minimizes synchronization problems and helps to keep your program robust and bug-free.

There is one more aspect of the Android UI framework that it is important to understand: it is single-threaded. There is a single thread removing events from the event queue to make Controller callbacks and to render the View. This is significant for several reasons.

The simplest consequence of a single-threaded UI is that it is not necessary to use `synchronized` blocks to coordinate state between the View and the Controller. This is a valuable optimization.

Another advantage of a single-threaded UI is the guarantee that each event on the event queue is processed completely and in the order in which it was enqueued. That may seem fairly obvious, but its implications make coding the UI much easier. When a UI component is called to handle an event, it is guaranteed that no additional UI processing will take place until it returns. That means, for instance, that when a component requests multiple changes in the program state—each of which causes a corresponding request that the screen be repainted—it is guaranteed that the repaint will *not* start until it has completed processing, performed all of its updates, and returned. In short, UI callbacks are atomic.

There is a third reason to remember that there is only a single thread dequeuing and dispatching events from the UI event queue: if your code stalls that thread, for any reason, your UI will freeze! If a component's response to an event is simple (changing the state of variables, creating new objects, etc.), it is perfectly correct to do that processing on the main event thread. If, on the other hand, the handler must retrieve a response from some distant network service or run a complex database query, the entire UI will become unresponsive until the request completes. That definitely does not make for a great user experience! Long-running tasks must be delegated to another thread, as described in "Advanced Wiring: Focus and Threading" on page 179.

Assembling a Graphical Interface

The Android UI framework provides both a complete set of drawing tools with which to build a UI and a rich collection of prebuilt components based on these tools. As we will see in Chapter 12, the framework graphics tools provide plenty of support for applications that need to create their own controls or render special views. On the other hand, many applications may work very well using only canned widgets from the toolkit. In fact, as we saw in Chapter 9, the `MapActivity` and `MyLocationOverlay` classes make it possible to create extremely sophisticated applications without doing any custom drawing at all.

We've already used the term "widget" once or twice, without explicitly defining it. Recall that the screen is a rendered by a tree of components. In the Android UI framework, these components are all subclasses of `android.view.View`. The components that are leaves or nearly leaves do most of the actual drawing and are, in the context of an application UI, commonly called widgets.

The internal nodes, sometimes called *Container Views*, are special components that can have other components as children. In the Android UI framework, Container Views are subclasses of `android.view.ViewGroup`, which, of course, is in turn a subclass of `View`. Typically, they do very little drawing. Instead, they are responsible for arranging their child components on the screen and keeping them arranged as the display changes shape, orientation, and so on. Doing this can be quite complex.

You have already seen a very simple `View` coded up in "Writing Hello-World" on page 22. That application created a trivial `TextView` and displayed it. There is no way to add anything to that application, because the root `View` is a `TextView`, which cannot be a container for other components. To create more complex displays, it is necessary to assemble a tree of containers. Example 10-1 shows an application with a view tree that is three layers deep. A vertical linear layout contains two horizontal linear layouts. Each of the horizontal layouts, in turn, contains two widgets.

Example 10-1. A complex view tree

```
package com.oreilly.android.intro;

import android.app.Activity;
import android.graphics.Color;
import android.os.Bundle;
import android.view.Gravity;
import android.view.ViewGroup;
import android.widget.Button;
import android.widget.EditText;
import android.widget.LinearLayout;


public class AndroidDemo extends Activity {
    private LinearLayout root;

    @Override
    public void onCreate(Bundle state) {
        super.onCreate(state);

        LinearLayout.LayoutParams containerParams
            = new LinearLayout.LayoutParams(
                ViewGroup.LayoutParams.FILL_PARENT,
                ViewGroup.LayoutParams.WRAP_CONTENT,
                0.0F);

        LinearLayout.LayoutParams widgetParams
            = new LinearLayout.LayoutParams(
                ViewGroup.LayoutParams.FILL_PARENT,
                ViewGroup.LayoutParams.FILL_PARENT,
                1.0F);

        root = new LinearLayout(this);
        root.setOrientation(LinearLayout.VERTICAL);
        root.setBackgroundColor(Color.LTGRAY);
        root.setLayoutParams(containerParams);
```

```
LinearLayout ll = new LinearLayout(this);
ll.setOrientation(LinearLayout.HORIZONTAL);
ll.setBackgroundColor(Color.GRAY);
ll.setLayoutParams(containerParams);
root.addView(ll);

EditText tb = new EditText(this);
tb.setText(R.string.defaultLeftText);
tb.setFocusable(false);
tb.setLayoutParams(widgetParams);
ll.addView(tb);

tb = new EditText(this);
tb.setText(R.string.defaultRightText);
tb.setFocusable(false);
tb.setLayoutParams(widgetParams);
ll.addView(tb);

ll = new LinearLayout(this);
ll.setOrientation(LinearLayout.HORIZONTAL);
ll.setBackgroundColor(Color.DKGRAY);
ll.setLayoutParams(containerParams);
root.addView(ll);

Button b = new Button(this);
b.setText(R.string.labelRed);
b.setTextColor(Color.RED);
b.setLayoutParams(widgetParams);
ll.addView(b);

b = new Button(this);
b.setText(R.string.labelGreen);
b.setTextColor(Color.GREEN);
b.setLayoutParams(widgetParams);
ll.addView(b);

setContentView(root);
    }
}
```

Note that the code preserves a reference to the root of the View tree for later use.

This example uses three LinearLayout widgets. A LinearLayout, just as its name implies, is a View that displays its children in a row or column, as determined by its orientation property. The child views are displayed in the order in which they are *added* to the LinearLayout (regardless of the order in which they were *created*), in the directions familiar to Western readers: left to right and top to bottom. The button labeled "Green", for instance, is in the lower righthand corner of this layout, because it is the second thing added to the horizontal LinearLayout View, which was, in turn, the second thing added to the vertical LinearLayout (the root).

Figure 10-2 shows what the results might look like to the user. The seven Views in the tree are structured as shown in Figure 10-3.

Figure 10-2. *The View as it appears on the screen*

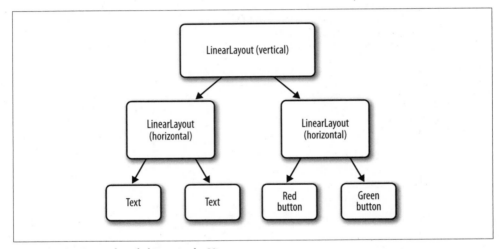

Figure 10-3. *Hierarchy of objects in the View*

Chapter 8 explained that the Android framework provides a convenient capability for separating data resources from code. This is particularly useful in building view component layouts. The previous example can be replaced with the dramatically simpler code in Example 10-2 and the XML definition of the layout in Example 10-3.

Example 10-2. Complex View using a layout resource

```
package com.oreilly.android.intro;

import android.app.Activity;
import android.os.Bundle;


/**
 * Android UI demo program
```

```
 */
public class AndroidDemo extends Activity {
    private LinearLayout root;

    @Override public void onCreate(Bundle state) {
        super.onCreate(state);
        setContentView(R.layout.main);
        root = (LinearLayout) findViewById(R.id.root);
    }
}
```

Example 10-3. Complex View layout resource

```
<LinearLayout xmlns:android="http://schemas.android.com/apk/res/android"
    android:id="@+id/root"
    android:orientation="vertical"
    android:background="@drawable/lt_gray"
    android:layout_width="fill_parent"
    android:layout_height="wrap_content">

  <LinearLayout
      android:orientation="horizontal"
      android:background="@drawable/gray"
      android:layout_width="fill_parent"
      android:layout_height="wrap_content">

    <EditText
        android:id="@+id/text1"
        android:text="@string/defaultLeftText"
        android:focusable="false"
        android:layout_width="fill_parent"
        android:layout_height="fill_parent"
        android:layout_weight="1"/>

    <EditText
        android:id="@+id/text2"
        android:text="@string/defaultRightText"
        android:focusable="false"
        android:layout_width="fill_parent"
        android:layout_height="fill_parent"
        android:layout_weight="1"/>
  </LinearLayout>

  <LinearLayout
      android:orientation="horizontal"
      android:background="@drawable/dk_gray"
      android:layout_width="fill_parent"
      android:layout_height="wrap_content">

    <Button
        android:id="@+id/button1"
        android:text="@string/labelRed"
        android:textColor="@drawable/red"
        android:layout_width="fill_parent"
        android:layout_height="fill_parent"
        android:layout_weight="1"/>
```

```
  <Button
      android:id="@+id/button2"
      android:text="@string/labelGreen"
      android:textColor="@drawable/green"
      android:layout_width="fill_parent"
      android:layout_height="fill_parent"
      android:layout_weight="1"/>
  </LinearLayout>
</LinearLayout>
```

This version of the code, like the first one, also preserves a reference to the root of the View tree. It does this by tagging a widget in the XML layout (the root `LinearLayout`, in this case) with an `android:id` tag, and then using the `findViewById` method from the `Activity` class to recover the reference.

It is a very good idea to get into the habit of using a resource to define your View tree layout. Doing so allows you to separate the visual layout from the code that brings it to life. This way, you can tinker with the layout of a screen without recompiling. Further, if the history of other UI frameworks is any indication, there will eventually be tools for Android that allow you to compose screens, creating their XML definitions, using a visual UI editor.

Wiring Up the Controller

"Assembling a Graphical Interface" on page 161 demonstrated a view with two buttons. Although the buttons look nice—they even highlight when clicked—they aren't very useful. Clicking them doesn't actually do anything.

The discussion of "The Controller" on page 159 described how the Android framework translates external actions (screen taps, key presses, etc.) into events that are enqueued and then passed into the application. Example 10-4 shows how to add an *event handler* to one of the buttons in the demo, so that it does something when it is clicked.

Example 10-4. Wiring up a button

```
@Override public void onCreate(Bundle state) {
    super.onCreate(state);
    setContentView(R.layout.main);

    final EditText tb1 = (EditText) findViewById(R.id.text1);
    final EditText tb2 = (EditText) findViewById(R.id.text2);

    ((Button) findViewById(R.id.button2)).setOnClickListener(
        new Button.OnClickListener() {
            @Override public void onClick(View arg0) {
                tb1.setText(String.valueOf(rand.nextInt(200)));
                tb2.setText(String.valueOf(rand.nextInt(200)));
            }
        }
    }
```

```
    );
}
```

When run, this version of the application still looks a lot like Figure 10-2. Unlike the earlier example, though, in this version every time a user clicks the button labeled "Green", the numbers in the `EditText` boxes change. This is illustrated in Figure 10-4.

Figure 10-4. Working button

Simply changing numbers isn't very interesting, but this small example demonstrates the standard mechanism that an application uses to respond to UI events. It is important to note that, appearances notwithstanding, this example does not violate the MVC separation of concerns. In response to the call to `setText`, in this implementation of an `OnClickListener`, the `EditText` object updates an internal representation of the text it should display, and then calls its own `invalidate` method. It does not immediately draw on the screen. There are very few rules in programming that are absolute, but the admonition to separate the Model, the View, and the Controller comes pretty close.

In the example, the instance of the `Button` class is wired to its behavior using its `setOnClickListener` method. `Button` is a subclass of `View`, which defines an interface named `OnClickListener` and a method named `setOnClickListener`, which registers the listener. The `OnClickListener` interface defines a single method, `onClick`. When a `Button` receives an event from the framework, in addition to any other processing it might do, it examines the event to see whether it qualifies as a "click." (The button in Example 10-1 would highlight when pressed, even before the listener was added.) If the event does qualify as a click and if a click listener has been installed, that listener's `onClick` method is invoked.

The click listener is free to implement any custom behavior that's needed. In the example, the custom behavior creates two random numbers between 0 and 200 and puts one into each of the two text boxes. Instead of subclassing `Button` and overriding its event processing methods, all that is necessary to extend its behavior is to register a click listener that implements the behavior. Certainly a lot easier!

The click handler is especially interesting because at the heart of the Android system—the framework event queue—there is no such thing as a click event. Instead, `View` event processing synthesizes the concept of a "click" from other events. If the device has a touch-sensitive screen, for instance, a single tap is considered a click. If the device has a center key in its D-pad or an "Enter" key, pressing and releasing either will also register as a click. `View` clients need not concern themselves with what a click is or how it is generated on a particular device. They need only handle the higher-level concept, leaving the details to the framework.

A `View` can have only one `OnClickListener`. Calling `setOnClickListener` a second time on a given `View` will remove the old listener and install the new one. On the other hand, a single listener can listen to more than one `View`. The code in Example 10-5, for instance, is part of another application that looks exactly like Example 10-2. In this version, though, pushing *either* of the buttons will update the text box.

This capability can be very convenient in an application in which several actions produce the same behavior. Do not be tempted, though, to create a single enormous listener to handle all your widgets. Your code will be easier to maintain and modify if it contains multiple smaller listeners, each of which implements a single, clear behavior.

Example 10-5. Listening to multiple buttons

```
@Override public void onCreate(Bundle state) {
    super.onCreate(state);
    setContentView(R.layout.main);

    final EditText tb1 = (EditText) findViewById(R.id.text1);
    final EditText tb2 = (EditText) findViewById(R.id.text2);

    Button.OnClickListener listener = new Button.OnClickListener() {
        @Override public void onClick(View arg0) {
            tb1.setText(String.valueOf(rand.nextInt(200)));
            tb2.setText(String.valueOf(rand.nextInt(200)));
        } };

    ((Button) findViewById(R.id.button1)).setOnClickListener(listener);
    ((Button) findViewById(R.id.button2)).setOnClickListener(listener);
}
```

Listening to the Model

The Android UI framework uses the handler installation pattern pervasively. Although our earlier examples were all `Button`s, many other Android widgets define listeners. The `View` class defines several events and listeners that are ubiquitous, and which we will explore in further detail later in this chapter. Other classes, however, define other specialized types of events and provide handlers for those events that are meaningful only for those classes. This is a standard idiom that allows clients to customize the behavior of a widget without having to subclass it.

This pattern (called the *Callback Pattern*) is also an excellent way for your program to handle its own external, asynchronous actions. Whether responding to a change in state on a remote server or an update from a location-based service, your application can define its own events and listeners to allow its clients to react.

The examples so far have been elementary and have cut several corners. Although they demonstrate connecting a View and a Controller, they have not had real Models. (Example 10-4 actually used a `String` owned by the implementation of `EditText` as a Model.) In order to proceed, we're going to have to take a brief detour to build a real, usable Model.

The two classes in Example 10-6 comprise a Model that will support extensions to the demo application for this chapter. They provide a facility for storing a list of objects, each of which has X and Y coordinates, a color, and a size. They also provide a way to register a listener, and an interface that the listener must implement.

Example 10-6. The Dots Model

```
package com.oreilly.android.intro.model;


/** A dot: the coordinates, color and size. */
public final class Dot {
    private final float x, y;
    private final int color;
    private final int diameter;

    /**
     * @param x horizontal coordinate.
     * @param y vertical coordinate.
     * @param color the color.
     * @param diameter dot diameter.
     */
    public Dot(float x, float y, int color, int diameter) {
        this.x = x;
        this.y = y;
        this.color = color;
        this.diameter = diameter;
    }

    /** @return the horizontal coordinate. */
    public float getX() { return x; }

    /** @return the vertical coordinate. */
    public float getY() { return y; }

    /** @return the color. */
    public int getColor() { return color; }

    /** @return the dot diameter. */
    public int getDiameter() { return diameter; }
}


package com.oreilly.android.intro.model;
```

```java
import java.util.Collections;
import java.util.LinkedList;
import java.util.List;


/** A list of dots. */
public class Dots {
    /** DotChangeListener. */
    public interface DotsChangeListener {
        /** @param dots the dots that changed. */
        void onDotsChange(Dots dots);
    }

    private final LinkedList<Dot> dots = new LinkedList<Dot>();
    private final List<Dot> safeDots = Collections.unmodifiableList(dots);

    private DotsChangeListener dotsChangeListener;

    /** @param l the new change listener. */
    public void setDotsChangeListener(DotsChangeListener l) {
        dotsChangeListener = l;
    }

    /** @return the most recently added dot, or null. */
    public Dot getLastDot() {
        return (dots.size() <= 0) ? null : dots.getLast();
    }

    /** @return the list of dots. */
    public List<Dot> getDots() { return safeDots; }

    /**
     * @param x dot horizontal coordinate.
     * @param y dot vertical coordinate.
     * @param color dot color.
     * @param diameter dot size.
     */
    public void addDot(float x, float y, int color, int diameter) {
        dots.add(new Dot(x, y, color, diameter));
        notifyListener();
    }

    /** Delete all the dots. */
    public void clearDots() {
        dots.clear();
        notifyListener();
    }

    private void notifyListener() {
        if (null != dotsChangeListener) {
            dotsChangeListener.onDotsChange(this);
        }
    }
}
```

In addition to using this model, the next example also introduces a widget used to view it, the DotView: it will be discussed later, in Example 12-3. For now we introduce it as a library widget. Its job is to draw the dots represented in the Model, in the correct color and at the correct coordinates. The complete source for the application is on the website for this book.

Example 10-7 shows the new demo application, after adding the new Model and View.

Example 10-7. Dots demo

```
package com.oreilly.android.intro;

import java.util.Random;

import android.app.Activity;
import android.graphics.Color;
import android.os.Bundle;
import android.view.View;
import android.widget.Button;
10 import android.widget.EditText;
import android.widget.LinearLayout;

import com.oreilly.android.intro.model.Dot;
import com.oreilly.android.intro.model.Dots;
import com.oreilly.android.intro.view.DotView;


/** Android UI demo program */
public class TouchMe extends Activity {
    public static final int DOT_DIAMETER = 6;

    private final Random rand = new Random();

    final Dots dotModel = new Dots();

    DotView dotView;

    /** Called when the activity is first created. */
    @Override public void onCreate(Bundle state) {
        super.onCreate(state);

        dotView = new DotView(this, dotModel);

        // install the view
        setContentView(R.layout.main);
        ((LinearLayout) findViewById(R.id.root)).addView(dotView, 0);

        // wire up the controller
        ((Button) findViewById(R.id.button1)).setOnClickListener(❶
            new Button.OnClickListener() {❷
                @Override public void onClick(View v) {
                    makeDot(dots, dotView, Color.RED);❸
                } });
        ((Button) findViewById(R.id.button2)).setOnClickListener(❶
```

```
                    new Button.OnClickListener() {❷
                        @Override public void onClick(View v) {❸
                            makeDot(dots, dotView, Color.GREEN);
                        } });

                final EditText tb1 = (EditText) findViewById(R.id.text1);
                final EditText tb2 = (EditText) findViewById(R.id.text2);
                dots.setDotsChangeListener(new Dots.DotsChangeListener() {❹
                    @Override public void onDotsChange(Dots d) {
                        Dot d = dots.getLastDot();
                        tb1.setText((null == d) ? "" : String.valueOf(d.getX()));
                        tb2.setText((null == d) ? "" : String.valueOf(d.getY()));
                        dotView.invalidate();
                    } });
            }


            /**
             * @param dots the dots we're drawing
             * @param view the view in which we're drawing dots
             * @param color the color of the dot
             */
            void makeDot(Dots dots, DotView view, int color) {❺
                int pad = (DOT_DIAMETER + 2) * 2;
                dots.addDot(
                    DOT_DIAMETER + (rand.nextFloat() * (view.getWidth() - pad)),
                    DOT_DIAMETER + (rand.nextFloat() * (view.getHeight() - pad)),
                    color,
                    DOT_DIAMETER);
            }
        }
```

Here are some of the highlights of the code:

❶ These two calls to setOnClickListener add new listeners to the layout obtained from the XML definition.

❷ Anonymous classes handle click event callbacks to the "Red" and "Green" buttons. These event handlers differ from those in the previous example only in that here their behavior has been factored out into the local method makeDot, described in item 5.

❸ Calls to makeDot within onClick (to take place when a button is clicked).

❹ The most substantial change to the example. This is where the Model is wired to the View, using the Callback pattern, by installing a dotsChangedListener. When the Model changes, this new listener is called. It installs the X and Y coordinates of the last dot into the left and right text boxes, respectively, and requests that the Dot View redraw itself (the invalidate call).

❺ Definition of makeDot. This new method creates a dot, checking to make sure it is within the DotView's borders, and adds it to the Model. It also allows the dot's color to be specified as a parameter.

Figure 10-5 shows what the application looks like when run.

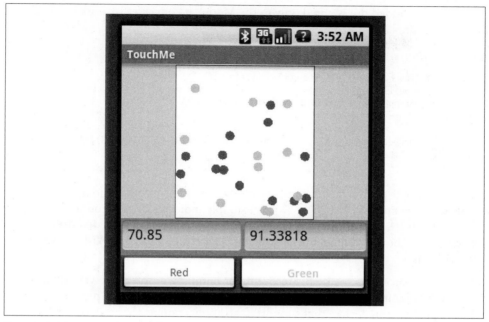

Figure 10-5. Running the Dots demo

Pushing the button labeled "Red" adds a new red dot to the `DotView`. Pushing the "Green" button adds a green one. The text fields contain the coordinates of the last dot added.

The basic structure of Example 10-2 is still recognizable, with some extensions. For example, here is the chain of events that results from clicking the "Green" button:

1. When the button is clicked, its `clickHandler` is called.
2. This causes a call to the anonymous class installed as an `OnClickHandler`. It, in turn, calls `makeDot` with the color argument `Color.GREEN`. The `makeDot` method generates random coordinates and adds a new green `Dot` to the Model at those coordinates.
3. When the Model is updated, it calls its `DotsChangedListener`.
4. The listener updates the values in the text views and requests that the `DotView` be redrawn.

Listening for Touch Events

Modifying the demo application to handle taps is just a matter of adding a tap handler. The code in Example 10-8 extends the demo application to place a cyan dot in the `DotView` at the point at which the screen is tapped. In the previous example, the code would be added at the beginning of the `onCreate` function right after the call to its parent method. Notice that, because the code that displays the X and Y coordinates of the most recently added dot is wired only to the Model, it continues to work correctly, no matter how dots are added.

Example 10-8. Touchable Dots

```
dotView.setOnTouchListener(new View.OnTouchListener() {
    @Override public boolean onTouch(View v, MotionEvent event) {
        if (MotionEvent.ACTION_DOWN != event.getAction()) {
            return false;
        }
        dots.addDot(event.getX(), event.getY(), Color.CYAN, DOT_DIAMETER);
        return true;
    } });
```

The `MotionEvent` passed to the handler has several other properties in addition to the location of the tap that caused it. As the example indicates, it also contains the event type, one of `DOWN`, `UP`, `MOVE`, or `CANCEL`. A simple tap actually generates one `DOWN` and one `UP` event. Touching and dragging generates a `DOWN` event, a series of `MOVE` events, and a final `UP` event.

The facilities provided by the `MotionEvent` for handling gestures are very interesting. The event contains the size of the touched area and the amount of pressure applied. That means that, on devices that support it, an application might be able to distinguish between a tap with one finger and a tap with two fingers, or between a very light brush and a firm push.

Efficiency is still important in the mobile world. A UI framework confronts the horns of a dilemma when tracking and reporting touchscreen events. Reporting too few events might make it impossible to follow motion with sufficient accuracy to do, for instance, handwriting recognition. On the other hand, reporting too many touch samples, each in its own event, could load the system unacceptably. The Android UI framework addresses this problem by bundling groups of samples together, reducing the load and still maintaining accuracy. To see all of the samples associated with an event, use the history facility implemented with the methods `getHistoricalX`, `getHistoricalY`, etc.

Example 10-9 shows how to use the history facility. It extends the demo program to track a user's gestures when she touches the screen. The framework delivers sampled X and Y coordinates to the `onTouch` method of an object installed as the `OnTouchListener` for the `DotView`. The method displays a cyan dot for each sample.

Example 10-9. Tracking motion

```
private static final class TrackingTouchListener
    implements View.OnTouchListener
{
    private final Dots mDots;

    TrackingTouchListener(Dots dots) { mDots = dots; }
```

```
@Override public boolean onTouch(View v, MotionEvent evt) {
    switch (evt.getAction()) {
        case MotionEvent.ACTION_DOWN:
            break;

        case MotionEvent.ACTION_MOVE:
            for (int i = 0, n = evt.getHistorySize(); i < n; i++) {❶
                addDot(
                    mDots,
                    evt.getHistoricalX(i),
                    evt.getHistoricalY(i),
                    evt.getHistoricalPressure(i),
                    evt.getHistoricalSize(i));
            }
            break;

        default:
            return false;
    }

    addDot(
        mDots,
        evt.getX(),
        evt.getY(),
        evt.getPressure(),
        evt.getSize());

    return true;
}

private void addDot(Dots dots, float x, float y, float p, float s) {
    dots.addDot(
        x,
        y,
        Color.CYAN,
        (int) ((p * s * Dot.DIAMETER) + 1));
}
}
```

Here are some highlights of the code:

❶ This loop handles batched historical events. When touch samples change more quickly than the framework can deliver them, it bundles them into a single event. The MotionEvent method getHistorySize returns the number of samples in the batch, and the various getHistory methods get the subevent specifics.

Figure 10-6 shows what the extended version of the application might look like after a few clicks and drags.

The implementation uses the size and pressure at a given location's sample to determine the diameter of the dot drawn there. Unfortunately, the Android emulator does not emulate touch pressure and size, so all of the dots have the same diameter. Size and pressure values are normalized across devices, as floating-point values between 0.0 and

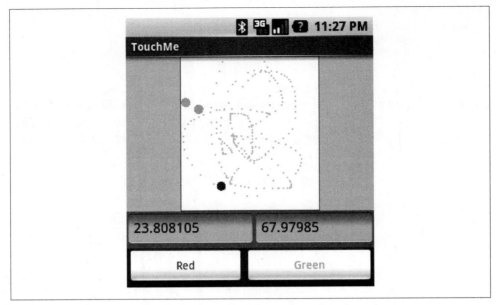

Figure 10-6. Running the Dots demo after adding the touch tracking feature

1.0, depending on the calibration of the screen. It is possible, however, that either value may actually be larger than 1.0. At the other end of the range, the emulator always reports the event size as zero.

Devices with trackballs also generate `MotionEvents` when the trackball is moved. These events are similar to those generated by taps on a touch-sensitive screen, but they are handled differently. Trackball `MotionEvents` are passed into the `View` through a call to `dispatchTrackballEvent`, not to `dispatchTouchEvent`, which delivered taps. Although `dispatchTrackballEvent` does pass the event to `onTrackballEvent`, it does not first pass the event to a listener! Not only are trackball-generated `MotionEvents` not visible through the normal tap-handling machinery, but, in order to respond to them, a widget must subclass `View` and override the `onTrackballEvent` method.

`MotionEvents` generated by the trackball are handled differently in yet another way. If they are not *consumed* (to be defined shortly) they are converted into D-pad key events (like those that would be generated by left, right, up and down arrow keys). This makes sense when you consider that most devices have either a D-pad or a trackball, but not both. Without this conversion, it wouldn't be possible to generate D-pad events on a device with only a trackball. Of course, it also implies that an application that handles trackball events must do so carefully, lest it break the translation.

Listening for Key Events

Handling keystroke input across multiple platforms can be very tricky. Some devices have many more keys than others, some require triple-tapping for character input, and so on. This is a great example of something that should be left to the framework (`EditText` or one of its subclasses) whenever possible.

To extend a widget's `KeyEvent` handling, use the `View` method `setOnKeyListener` to install an `OnKeyListener`. The listener will be called with multiple `KeyEvents` for each user keystroke, one for each action type: `DOWN`, `UP`, and `MULTIPLE`. The action types `DOWN` and `UP` indicate a key was pressed or released, just as they did for the `MotionEvent` class. A key action of `MULTIPLE` indicates that a key is being held down (autorepeating). The `KeyEvent` method `getRepeatCount` gives the number of keystrokes that a `MULTIPLE` event represents.

Example 10-10 shows a sample key handler. When added to the demo program, it causes dots to be added to the display at randomly chosen coordinates when keys are pressed and released: a magenta dot when the Space key is pressed and released, a yellow dot when the Enter key is pressed and released, and a blue dot when any other key is pressed and released.

Example 10-10. Handling keys

```
dotView.setFocusable(true);

dotView.setOnKeyListener(new OnKeyListener() {
    @Override public boolean onKey(View v, int keyCode, KeyEvent event) {
        if (KeyEvent.ACTION_UP != event.getAction()) {
            int color = Color.BLUE;
            switch (keyCode) {
                case KeyEvent.KEYCODE_SPACE:
                    color = Color.MAGENTA;
                    break;
                case KeyEvent.KEYCODE_ENTER:
                    color = Color.YELLOW;
                    break;
                default: ;
            }

            makeDot(dots, dotView, color);
        }

        return true;
    } });
```

Alternative Ways to Handle Events

You've probably noticed that the `on...` methods of all of the listeners introduced thus far—including `onKey`—return a `boolean` value. This is a pattern for listeners that allows them to control subsequent event processing by their caller.

When a Controller event is handed to a widget, the framework code in the widget dispatches it to an appropriate method, depending on its type: `onKeyDown`, `onTouchEvent`, etc. These methods, either in `View` or one its subclasses, implement the widget's behavior. As described earlier, though, the framework first offers the event to an appropriate listener (`OnTouchListener`, `OnKeyListener`, etc.) if one exists. The listener's return value determines whether the event is then dispatched to the `View` methods.

If the listener returns `false`, the event is dispatched to the `View` methods as if the handler did not exist. If, on the other hand, a listener returns `true`, the event is said to have been *consumed*. The `View` aborts any further processing for it. The `View` methods are never called and have no opportunity to process or respond to the event. As far as the `View` methods are concerned, it is as if the event did not exist.

There are three ways that an event might be processed:

No listener
> The event is dispatched to the `View` methods for normal handling. A widget implementation may, of course, override these methods.

A listener exists and returns true
> Listener event handling completely replaces normal widget event handling. The event is never dispatched to the `View`.

A listener exists and returns false
> The event is processed by the listener and then by the `View`. After listener event handling is completed, the event is dispatched to the `View` for normal handling.

Consider, for instance, what would happen if the key listener from Example 10-10 were added to an `EditText` widget. Since the `onKey` method always returns `true`, the framework will abort any further `KeyEvent` processing as soon as the method returns. That would prevent the `EditText` key-handling mechanism from ever seeing the key events, and no text would ever appear in the text box. That is probably not the intended behavior!

If the `onKey` method instead returns `false` for some key events, the framework will dispatch those events to the `EditText` widget for continued processing. The `EditText` mechanism will see the events, and the associated characters will be appended to the `EditText` box, as expected. Example 10-11 shows an extension of Example 10-10 that, besides adding new dots to the Model, also filters the characters passed to the hypothetical `EditText` box. It allows numeric characters to be processed normally but hides everything else.

Example 10-11. Handling keys

```
new OnKeyListener() {
    @Override public boolean onKey(View v, int keyCode, KeyEvent event) {
        if (KeyEvent.ACTION_UP != event.getAction()) {
            int color = Color.BLUE;
            switch (keyCode) {
                case KeyEvent.KEYCODE_SPACE:
                    color = Color.MAGENTA;
                    break;
                case KeyEvent.KEYCODE_ENTER:
                    color = Color.YELLOW;
```

```
                break;
            default: ;
        }

        makeDot(dotModel, dotView, color);
    }

    return (keyCode < KeyEvent.KEYCODE_0)
        ||(keyCode > KeyEvent.KEYCODE_9);
    }
}
```

If your application needs to implement entirely new ways of handling events (in other words, if it is something that cannot be implemented reasonably by augmenting behavior and filtering, using an OnKeyHandler), you will have to understand and override View key event handling. To summarize the process, events are dispatched to the View through the DispatchKeyEvent method. DispatchKeyEvent implements the behavior described previously, offering the event to the onKeyHandler first. If the handler returns false, it offers the event to the View methods implementing the KeyEvent.Callback interface: onKeyDown, onKeyUp, and onKeyMultiple.

Advanced Wiring: Focus and Threading

As demonstrated in Example 10-9 and "Listening for Touch Events" on page 173, MotionEvents are delivered to the widget whose bounding rectangle contains the coordinates of the touch that generated them. It isn't quite so obvious how to determine which widget should receive a KeyEvent. In order to do this, the Android UI framework, like most other UI frameworks, supports the concept of selection, or *focus*.

In order to accept focus, a widget's *focusable* attribute must be set to true. This can be done using either an XML layout attribute (the EditText Views in Example 10-3 have their focusable attribute set to false) or the setFocusable method, as shown in the first line of Example 10-10. A user changes which View has focus using D-pad keys or by tapping the screen when touch is supported.

When a widget is in focus, it usually renders itself with some kind of highlighting to provide feedback that it is the current target of keystrokes. For instance, when an EditText widget is in focus, it is drawn both highlighted and with a cursor at the text insert position.

To receive notification when a widget enters or leaves focus, install an OnFocusChange Listener. Example 10-12 shows the listener needed to add a focus-related feature to the demo program. It causes a randomly positioned black dot to be added automatically to the DotView every now and then, whenever it is in focus.

Example 10-12. Handling focus

```
dotView.setOnFocusChangeListener(new OnFocusChangeListener() {
    @Override public void onFocusChange(View v, boolean hasFocus) {
```

```
        if (!hasFocus && (null != dotGenerator)) {
            dotGenerator.done();
            dotGenerator = null;
        }
        else if (hasFocus && (null == dotGenerator)) {
            dotGenerator = new DotGenerator(dots, dotView, Color.BLACK);
            new Thread(dotGenerator).start();
        }
} });
```

There should be few surprises in the OnFocusChangeListener. When the DotView comes into focus, it creates the DotGenerator and spawns a thread to run it. When the widget leaves focus, the DotGenerator is stopped and freed. The new data member, dotGenerator (whose declaration is not shown in the example), is nonnull only when the DotView is in focus. There is an important and powerful new tool in the implementation of DotGenerator, and we'll return to it in a moment.

Focus is transferred to a particular widget by calling its View method, requestFocus. When requestFocus is called for a new target widget, the request is passed up the tree, parent by parent, to the tree root. The root remembers the widget that is in focus and passes subsequent key events to it directly.

This is exactly how the UI framework changes focus to a new widget in response to a D-pad keystroke. The framework identifies the widget that will be in focus next and calls that widget's requestFocus method. This causes the previously focused widget to lose focus and the target to gain it.

The process of identifying the widget that will gain focus is complicated. In order to do it, the navigation algorithm has to perform some tricky calculations that may depend on the locations of every other widget on the screen.

Consider, for instance, what happens when the right D-pad button is pressed and the framework attempts to transfer focus to the widget immediately to the right of the one that is currently in focus. When looking at the screen, it may be completely obvious which widget that is. In the View tree, however, it is not nearly so obvious. The target widget may be at another level in the tree and several branches away. Identifying it depends on the exact dimensions of widgets in yet other distant parts of the tree. Fortunately, despite the considerable complexity, the Android UI framework implementation usually just works as expected.

When it does not, there are four properties—set either by application method or by XML attribute—that can be used to force the desired focus navigation behavior: nextFocusDown, nextFocusLeft, nextFocusRight, and nextFocusUp. Setting one of these properties with a reference to a specific widget will ensure that D-pad navigation transfers focus directly to that widget when navigating in the respective direction.

Another complexity of the focus mechanism is the distinction that the Android UI framework makes between D-pad focus and touch focus, for devices with touch-sensitive screens. To understand why this is necessary, recall that on a screen that does not accept touch input, the only way to push a button is to focus on it, using D-pad navigation, and then to use the center D-pad key to generate a click. On a screen that does accept touch events, however, there is never any reason to focus on a button. Tapping the button clicks it, regardless of which widget happens to be in focus at the time. Even on a touch-sensitive screen, however, it is still necessary to be able to focus on a widget that accepts keystrokes—an EditText widget, for instance—in order to identify it as the target for subsequent key events. In order to handle both kinds of focus correctly, you will have to look into View's handling of FOCUSABLE_IN_TOUCH_MODE, and the View methods isFocusableInTouchMode and isInTouchMode.

In an application with multiple windows, there is at least one more twist in the focus mechanism: it is possible for a window to lose focus without notifying the currently in-focus widget that its focus has been lost. This makes sense when you think about it. If the out-of-focus window is brought back to the top, the widget that was in focus in that window will again be in focus, with no other action.

Consider entering a friend's phone number into an address book application. Suppose you momentarily switch back to a phone application to refresh your memory of the last few digits of his phone number. You'd be annoyed if, on returning to the address book, you had to focus again on the EditText box in which you'd been typing. You expect the state to be just as you left it.

On the other hand, this behavior can have surprising side effects. In particular, the implementation of the auto-dot feature presented in Example 10-12 continues to add dots to the DotView even when it is hidden by another window. If a background task should run only when a particular widget is visible, that task must be cleaned up when the widget loses focus, when the Window loses focus, and when the Activity is paused or stopped.

Most of the implementation of the focus mechanism is in the ViewGroup class, in methods such as requestFocus and requestChildFocus. Should it be necessary to implement an entirely new focus mechanism, you'll need to look carefully at these methods, and override them appropriately.

Leaving the subject of focus and returning to the implementation of the newly added auto-dot feature, Example 10-13 contains the implementation of DotGenerator.

Example 10-13. Enqueuing a task for the main thread

```
private final class DotGenerator implements Runnable {
    final Dots dots;
    final DotView view;
    final int color;

    private final Handler hdlr = new Handler();❶
    private final Runnable makeDots = new Runnable() {❷
        public void run() { makeDot(dots, view, color); }
    };

    private volatile boolean done;
```

```
    // Runs on the main thread
    DotGenerator(Dots dots, DotView view, int color) {❸
        this.dots = dots;
        this.view = view;
        this.color = color;
    }

    // Runs on the main thread
    public void done() { done = true; }

    // Runs on a different thread!
    public void run() {
        while (!done) {
            try { Thread.sleep(1000); }
            catch (InterruptedException e) { }
            hdlr.post(makeDots);❹
        }
    }
}
```

Here are some of the highlights of the code:

❶ Creates an `android.os.Handler` object, the new tool introduced in this section.

❷ Creates a new anonymous `Runnable` object. It is used to call `MakeDot` from the main thread in item 4.

❸ The Constructor for `DotGenerator`. The `DotGenerator` is created on the main thread.

❹ The dot generation loop generates a new dot about every second. This is the only part of the code that runs on a completely different thread.

A naïve implementation of `DotGenerator` would simply call `makeDot` directly within its run method. Doing this wouldn't be safe, however, unless `makeDot` was thread-safe—and the `Dots` and `DotView` classes were too, for that matter. This would be tricky to get correct and hard to maintain. In fact, the Android UI framework actually forbids access to a `View` from multiple threads. Running the naive implementation would cause the application to fail with an Android runtime error like this:

```
11-30 02:42:37.471: ERROR/AndroidRuntime(162):
android.view.ViewRoot$CalledFromWrongThreadException:
Only the original thread that created a view hierarchy can touch its views.
```

To get around this restriction, `DotGenerator` creates a `Handler` object within its constructor. A `Handler` object is associated with the thread on which it is created and provides safe, concurrent access to a canonical event queue for that thread.

Because `DotGenerator` creates a `Handler` during its own construction (which happens on the main thread), this `Handler` is associated with the main thread. Now `DotGenerator` can use the `Handler` to enqueue a `Runnable` that calls `makeDot` from the main thread. As you might guess, it turns out that the main-thread event queue on which the `Handler` enqueues the `Runnable` is exactly the same one that is used by the UI framework. The call to makeDot is dequeued and dispatched, like any other UI event, in its proper order. In this case, that causes its Runnable to be run. makeDot is called from the main thread and the UI stays single-threaded.

This is a very important pattern for coding with the Android UI framework. Whenever processing started on behalf of the user might take more than a few milliseconds to complete, doing that processing on the main thread might cause the entire UI to become sluggish or, worse, to freeze for a long time. If the main application thread does not service its event queue for a couple of seconds, the Android OS will kill the application for being unresponsive. The Handler class allows the programmer to avoid this danger by delegating slow or long-running tasks to other threads, so that the main thread can continue to service the UI. When a task completes, it uses a main-thread Handler to enqueue an update for the UI.

The demo application takes a slight shortcut here: it enqueues the creation of a new dot and its addition to the dot model on the main thread. A more complex application might pass a main thread Handler to the Model on creation, and provide a way for the UI to get a model-thread Handler from the model. The main thread would receive update events enqueued for it by the Model, using its main-thread Handler. The Model, running in its own thread, would use the Looper class to dequeue and dispatch incoming messages from the UI.

Passing events between the UI and long-running threads in this way dramatically reduces the constraints required to maintain thread safety. In particular, note that if an enqueuing thread retains no references to an enqueued object, or if that object is immutable, no additional synchronization is necessary.

The Menu

The final aspect of application control we'll cover in this chapter is the menu. Example 10-14 shows how to implement a simple menu by overriding two Activity methods.

Example 10-14. Implementing a menu

```
@Override public boolean onCreateOptionsMenu(Menu menu) {
    menu.add(Menu.NONE, CLEAR_MENU_ID, Menu.NONE, "Clear");
    return true;
}

@Override public boolean onOptionsItemSelected(MenuItem item) {
    switch (item.getItemId()) {
        case 1:
            dotModel.clearDots();
            return true;

        default: ;
    }
```

```
    return false;
}
```

When this code is added to the TouchMe class, clicking the device's Menu key will cause the application to present a menu (labeled "Clear" at the bottom of the screen), as shown in Figure 10-7.

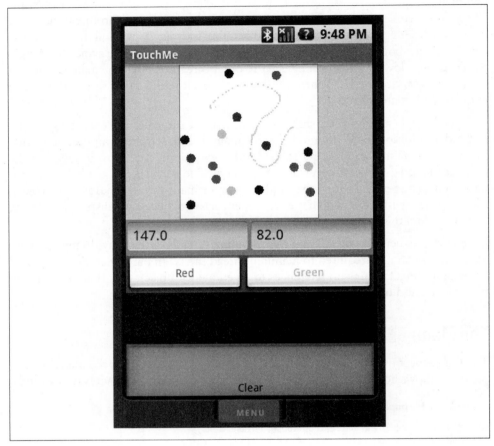

Figure 10-7. A simple menu

Clicking the Enter key or tapping the menu item again will clear the dot widget.

Interestingly, if you run this application, you will find that while the added menu item works most of the time, it does not work when the DotView is in focus. Can you guess why?

If you guessed that the problem is caused by the `OnKeyListener` installed in the `DotView`, you are correct! As implemented in Example 10-15, the listener swallows the menu key event by returning `true` when it is clicked. This prevents the standard `View` processing of the menu key keystroke. In order to make the menu work, the `OnKey Listener` needs a new case, shown in Example 10-15.

Example 10-15. Improved key handling

```
switch (keyCode) {
    case KeyEvent.KEYCODE_MENU:
        return false;
    // ...
```

The Android UI framework also supports contextual menus. A `ContextMenu` appears in response to a long click in a widget that supports it. The code required to add a contextual menu to an application is entirely analogous to that for the options menu shown earlier except that the respective methods are `onCreateContextMenu` and `onContextItemSelected`. Additionally, one more call is required. In order to support contextual menus, a widget must be assigned a `View.OnCreateContextMenuListener` by calling its `View` method, `setOnCreateContextMenuListener`. Fortunately, since `Activity` implements the `View.OnCreateContextMenuListener` interface, a common idiom looks like Example 10-16.

Example 10-16. Installing a ContextMenuListener

```
findViewById(R.id.ctxtMenuView).setOnCreateContextMenuListener(this);
```

Simply overriding the default, empty `Activity` implementations of the context menu listener methods will give your application a context menu.

This chapter has shown how the Android graphical interface works overall, and has given you the tools to manipulate its basic components: windows, Views, and events. The following chapter explains the most useful widgets Android makes available, and Chapter 12 shows you how to do your own graphics programming.

CHAPTER 11

A Widget Bestiary

As we have seen, there are three ways to implement a new behavior in an application. In increasing order of complexity, you can:

- Find a toolbox widget that already does nearly what you need and extend it.
- Use the handler mechanism demonstrated previously in Example 10-4.
- Override event receiver methods and implement them yourself.

Handling raw events across multiple platforms can be quite complicated. Different devices, for instance, may have radically different keypads: for instance, four-key versus five-key D-pads. Some devices still require triple-tapping to enter alphabetic information. This kind of diversity is a serious issue in the mobile environment and can be a nightmare for the developer who wants to keep her application portable.

When designing your application, it's clearly smart to let the framework do as much as possible. The best option is to find some toolbox widget that has nearly the behavior you require and extend it to meet your needs. The toolkit provides extensive tools for doing this: XML attributes, fine-grained and overridable methods, and so on.

If it isn't possible to customize an existing widget, you should consider the listener mechanism, demonstrated previously in Example 10-5. Only when it is necessary to change the existing behavior of a widget should you consider overriding event receiver methods.

User interface frameworks have different names for the components from which they're composed: the text boxes, buttons, canvases, and other components that you use to create your unique application user interface. Android generically calls them Views, and the documentation defines them simply as:

> View: An object that knows how to draw itself to the screen.

So any object that draws itself is a View, and Views that can contain or group other Views are appropriately called ViewGroups. Views are arranged and displayed on the screen according to a Layout, which gives Android hints about how you'd like to see the Views arranged. In the next few sections we'll look first at simple Views, then at

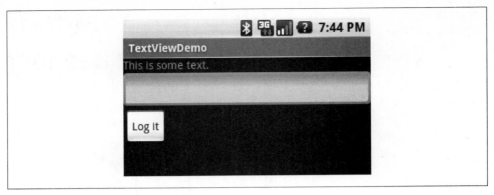

Figure 11-1. TextView, EditText, and Button

ViewGroups, and finally at Layouts. Since expandability is a core principle for Android, we will also look at what you need to do to define your own custom Views and Layouts.

As we've already seen, Views and Layouts both have attributes that can either be defined in Java source code or in the XML file associated with the Activity that uses the View or Layout. When the attributes are in an XML file, they are "inflated" at runtime, meaning that they are applied to their respective Views by the Android framework to determine how the Views look and operate.

There are so many attributes that it doesn't make sense to list them all in these examples. We describe the key ones, and the rest are explained in the documentation that comes with the Android SDK. A quick search for `android.widget.view_name` will give you the class definition for that View, including all the attributes available for it, and a description of each.

Android Views

The Views in the following section are the meat and potatoes of your application; essential widgets that you'll use over and over and that your users will be familiar with from other applications.

TextView and EditText

A TextView, as shown in the line "This is some text" in Figure 11-1, is just what you'd expect: a place to display a text string. The vanilla TextView is for display only, whereas EditText is a predefined subclass of TextView that includes rich editing capabilities.

Each TextView has the attributes you'd expect of such a component: you can change its height, width, font, text color, background color, and so forth. TextViews also have some useful unique attributes:

autoLink

If set (true), finds URLs in the displayed text and automatically converts them to clickable links.

autoText

If set (true), finds and corrects simple spelling errors in the text.

editable

If set (true), indicates that the program has defined an input method to receive input text (default is false for TextView, and true for EditText).

inputMethod

Identifies the input method (EditText defines one for generic text).

Example 11-1 shows how to use a TextView and an EditText with Buttons. (Buttons are covered in the next section.) It also shows the XML layout file (*main.xml*), which uses pretty standard and recommended layout parameters.

Example 11-1. Layout file for TextView and EditView example

```xml
<?xml version="1.0" encoding="utf-8"?>
<LinearLayout xmlns:android="http://schemas.android.com/apk/res/android"
    android:orientation="vertical"
    android:layout_width="fill_parent"
    android:layout_height="fill_parent"
    >
<TextView
    android:id="@+id/txtDemo"
    android:layout_width="fill_parent"
    android:layout_height="wrap_content"
    />
<EditText
    android:id="@+id/eTxtDemo"
    android:layout_width="fill_parent"
    android:layout_height="wrap_content"
    />
<Button
    android:id="@+id/btnDone"
    android:layout_width="wrap_content"
    android:layout_height="wrap_content"
    android:text="Log it"
    />
</LinearLayout>
```

Example 11-2 contains the accompanying Java source (*TextViewDemo.java*).

Example 11-2. Java for TextView and EditView: TextViewDemo.java

```java
package com.oreilly.demo;

import android.app.Activity;
import android.os.Bundle;
import android.util.Log;
import android.view.View;
import android.widget.Button;
```

```
import android.widget.EditText;
import android.widget.TextView;

public class TextViewDemo extends Activity {
    private static TextView txt1;
    private static EditText etxt1;
    private static Button btn1;

    // Create a button click listener for the Done button.
    private final Button.OnClickListener btnDoneOnClick = new Button.OnClickListener() {❶
        public void onClick(View v) {
          String input = etxt1.getText().toString();
          //Log the input string
          Log.v("TextViewDemo", input);
          etxt1.setText("");
        }
    };

    /** Called when the activity is first created. */
    @Override
    public void onCreate(Bundle savedInstanceState) {❷
        super.onCreate(savedInstanceState);
        setContentView(R.layout.main);❸

        //Get pointers to the Views defined in main.xml
        txt1 = (TextView) findViewById(R.id.txtDemo);❹
        etxt1 = (EditText) findViewById(R.id.eTxtDemo);
        btn1 = (Button) findViewById(R.id.btnDone);

        //Set the string displayed in TextView1
        txt1.setText("This is some text.");❺

        //Set the OnClickListener for the Done button
        btn1.setOnClickListener(btnDoneOnClick);❻
    }
}
```

Here are some of the highlights of the code:

❶ Defines a ClickListener that we'll attach to the "Log it" Button.

❷ Because onCreate is executed just once, as soon as Android instantiates this View, we put all the configuration we need here.

❸ Loads the XML layout file for the application by setting the ContentView to *main.xml*.

❹ Finds the Views that are defined in *main.xml*.

❺ Puts an initial string into the TextView. (We also could have done this in the XML file, as was done in the MicroJobs application in "Initialization in Micro-Jobs.java" on page 46.)

❻ Connects the Button with the ClickListener.

Now the user can enter and edit text in the EditText, and when he clicks on "Log it", the OnClickListener is called and the text is written to the logcat log. The string in the EditText is cleared out, and the widget is ready for another entry.

Button and ImageButton

The Button View is just a button, printed with some text to identify it, that the user can click to invoke some action. The previous section created a Button and connected it to an OnClickListener method that executes when the Button is clicked.

Android has a very visual, mobile-oriented user interface, so you might want to use a button with an image on it rather than one with text. Android provides the ImageButton View for just that purpose. You can adapt Example 11-2 to use an ImageButton by making one change in the XML file and another in the Java code:

1. In *main.xml*, replace the Button definition for btnDone with an ImageButton:

   ```
   ...
   <ImageButton
     android:id="@+id/btnDone"
     android:layout_width="wrap_content"
     android:layout_height="wrap_content"
     />
   ...
   ```

2. In *TextViewDemo.java*, redefine btn1 as an ImageButton and add a line to set the image to a PNG image in the *drawable* directory:

   ```
   ...
       private static ImageButton btn1;

   ...
       /** Called when the activity is first created. */
       @Override
       public void onCreate(Bundle savedInstanceState) {
           super.onCreate(savedInstanceState);
           setContentView(R.layout.main);

           //Get pointers to the Views defined in main.xml
           txt1 = (TextView) findViewById(R.id.txtDemo);
           etxt1 = (EditText) findViewById(R.id.eTxtDemo);
           btn1 = (ImageButton) findViewById(R.id.btnDone);
   ...
           //Set the image for the Done button
           btn1.setImageResource(R.drawable.log);
   ...
   ```

The button now appears as shown in Figure 11-2.

Figure 11-2. Text boxes with an ImageButton

Adapters and AdapterViews

Adapters and AdapterViews are an important and useful basis for several of the views discussed in the rest of this chapter. Using extensions to these classes, you can address an extremely wide variety of situations.

The AdapterView is a generic, list-oriented view of data. Any collection of data objects that can be ordered in some relatively stable way can be displayed through an AdapterView. An AdapterView is always associated with an Adapter, which acts as the bridge between it and the underlying data collection. The Adapter has two responsibilities:

- At the request of the AdapterView, the Adapter must be able to find the data object that corresponds to a particular index. It must, in other words, be able to find the data object that is visible in the AdapterView at a particular location.

- Inversely, the Adapter must be able to supply a view through which the data at a particular index can be displayed.

It takes only a moment's reflection to understand how the `AdapterView` works: It is a `ViewGroup` that contains all the machinery necessary to serve as both the View and Controller for a collection of generic widgets. It can lay them out on the display, pass in clicks and keystrokes, and so on. It need never concern itself with what the subviews actually display; it distinguishes them only by their indexes. Whenever it needs to perform either of the two operations that are not entirely generic—creating a new view or getting the data object attached to a particular view—it relies on the `Adapter` to convert an index into either a data object or the view of a data object.

The `AdapterView` requests new views from an implementation of the `Adapter` interface, as it needs them, for display. For instance, as a user scrolls though a list of contacts, the `AdapterView` requests a new view for each new contact that becomes visible. As an optimization, the `AdapterView` may offer a view that is no longer visible (in this case, one that has scrolled off the display) for reuse. This can dramatically reduce memory churn and speed up display.

When offered a recycled view, however, the `Adapter` must verify that it is the right kind of view through which to display the data object at the requested index. This is necessary because the `Adapter` is not limited to returning instances of a single view class in response to the request for a view. If the `Adapter` represents several kinds of objects, it might create several different types of views, each applicable to some subset of the data objects in the collection. A list of contacts, for instance, might have two entirely different view classes: one for displaying acquaintances that are currently online and another for those who are not. The latter might completely ignore clicks, whereas the former would open a new chat session when clicked.

Although `AdapterView` and `Adapter` are both abstract and cannot be directly instantiated, the UI toolkit includes several prebuilt `Adapters` and `AdapterViews` that can be used unmodified or further subclassed to provide your own customizations. `ListAdapter` and `SpinnerAdapter` are particularly useful `Adapters`, while `ListView`, `GridView`, `Spinner`, and `Gallery` are all handy subclasses of `AdapterView`. If you plan to create your own subclass of `AdapterView`, a quick look at the code for one of these classes will get you off to a running start.

A good example of the use of an `AdapterView` can be found in "Gallery and Grid-View" on page 198. The `Gallery` view in that section is a subclass of `AdapterView`, and uses a subclass of `Adapter` called `ImageAdapter`.

CheckBoxes, RadioButtons, and Spinners

The Views we present in this section are probably familiar to you from other user interfaces. Their purpose is to allow the user to choose from multiple options. CheckBoxes are typically used when you want to offer multiple selections with a yes/no or true/false choice for each. RadioButtons are used when only one choice is allowed at a time.

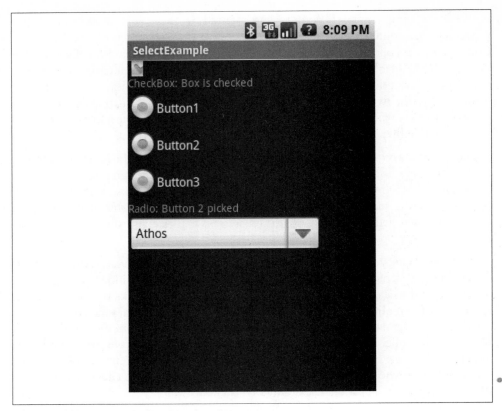

Figure 11-3. CheckBox, RadioButtons, and Spinner

Spinners are similar to combo boxes in some frameworks. A combo box typically displays the currently selected option, along with a pull-down list from which the user can click on another option to select it.

Android has adapted these familiar components to make them more useful in a touchscreen environment. Figure 11-3 shows the three types of multiple-choice Views laid out on an Android application, with the Spinner pulled down to show the options.

The layout XML file that created the screen in the figure looks like this:

```
<?xml version="1.0" encoding="utf-8"?>
<LinearLayout xmlns:android="http://schemas.android.com/apk/res/android"
    android:orientation="vertical"
    android:layout_width="fill_parent"
    android:layout_height="fill_parent"
    >
<CheckBox
    android:id="@+id/cbxBox1"
    android:layout_width="20dp"
    android:layout_height="20dp"
    android:checked="false"
    />
```

```
<TextView
  android:id="@+id/txtCheckBox"
    android:layout_width="fill_parent"
    android:layout_height="wrap_content"
    android:text="CheckBox: Not checked"
    />
<RadioGroup
  android:id="@+id/rgGroup1"
  android:layout_width="fill_parent"
  android:layout_height="wrap_content"
  android:orientation="vertical">
  <RadioButton android:id="@+id/RB1" android:text="Button1" />
  <RadioButton android:id="@+id/RB2" android:text="Button2" />
  <RadioButton android:id="@+id/RB3" android:text="Button3" />
  </RadioGroup>
<TextView
  android:id="@+id/txtRadio"
  android:layout_width="fill_parent"
  android:layout_height="wrap_content"
  android:text="RadioGroup: Nothing picked"
  />
<Spinner
  android:id="@+id/spnMusketeers"
  android:layout_width="250dp"
  android:layout_height="wrap_content"
  android:layout_centerHorizontal="true"
  android:layout_marginTop="2dp"
  />
</LinearLayout>
```

The file just lists each View we want on the screen along with the attributes we want. A RadioGroup is really a ViewGroup, so it contains the appropriate RadioButton Views. Example 11-3 shows the Java file that responds to user clicks.

Example 11-3. Java for CheckBox, RadioButtons, and Spinner

```
package com.oreilly.select;

import java.util.ArrayList;
import java.util.HashMap;
import java.util.List;

import com.google.android.maps.GeoPoint;

import android.app.Activity;
import android.os.Bundle;
import android.util.Log;
import android.view.View;
import android.widget.AdapterView;
import android.widget.ArrayAdapter;
import android.widget.CheckBox;
import android.widget.RadioButton;
import android.widget.RadioGroup;
import android.widget.Spinner;
import android.widget.TextView;
```

```
import android.widget.AdapterView.OnItemSelectedListener;

public class SelectExample extends Activity {

    private CheckBox checkBox;
    private TextView txtCheckBox, txtRadio;
    private RadioButton rb1, rb2, rb3;
    private Spinner spnMusketeers;

    /** Called when the activity is first created. */
    @Override
    public void onCreate(Bundle savedInstanceState) {
        super.onCreate(savedInstanceState);
        setContentView(R.layout.main);

        checkBox = (CheckBox) findViewById(R.id.cbxBox1);
        txtCheckBox = (TextView) findViewById(R.id.txtCheckBox);
        txtRadio = (TextView) findViewById(R.id.txtRadio);
        rb1 = (RadioButton) findViewById(R.id.RB1);
        rb2 = (RadioButton) findViewById(R.id.RB2);
        rb3 = (RadioButton) findViewById(R.id.RB3);
        spnMusketeers = (Spinner) findViewById(R.id.spnMusketeers);

        // React to events from the CheckBox
        checkBox.setOnClickListener(new CheckBox.OnClickListener() {
          public void onClick(View v){
                if (checkBox.isChecked()) {
                    txtCheckBox.setText("CheckBox: Box is checked");
                }
                else
                {
                  txtCheckBox.setText("CheckBox: Not checked");
                }
          }
        });

        // React to events from the RadioGroup
        rb1.setOnClickListener(new RadioGroup.OnClickListener() {
          public void onClick(View v){
            txtRadio.setText("Radio: Button 1 picked");
          }
        });

        rb2.setOnClickListener(new RadioGroup.OnClickListener() {
          public void onClick(View v){
            txtRadio.setText("Radio: Button 2 picked");
          }
        });

        rb3.setOnClickListener(new RadioGroup.OnClickListener() {
          public void onClick(View v){
            txtRadio.setText("Radio: Button 3 picked");
          }
        });
```

```
        // Set up the Spinner entries
        List<String> lsMusketeers = new ArrayList<String>();
        lsMusketeers.add("Athos");
        lsMusketeers.add("Porthos");
        lsMusketeers.add("Aramis");

        ArrayAdapter<String> aspnMusketeers =
          new ArrayAdapter<String>(this, android.R.layout.simple_spinner_item,
            lsMusketeers);
        aspnMusketeers.setDropDownViewResource
          (android.R.layout.simple_spinner_dropdown_item);
        spnMusketeers.setAdapter(aspnMusketeers);

    // Set up a callback for the spinner
    spnMusketeers.setOnItemSelectedListener(
        new OnItemSelectedListener() {
            public void onNothingSelected(AdapterView<?> arg0) { }

            public void onItemSelected(AdapterView<?> parent, View v,
              int position, long id)  {

              // Code that does something when the Spinner value changes
            }
        });
    }
}
```

The Views work as follows:

CheckBox

The CheckBox View takes care of flipping its state back and forth and displaying the appropriate checkmark when the state is true. All you have to do is create an "OnClickListener" to catch click events, and you can add whatever code you want to react.

RadioGroup

As mentioned earlier, the RadioGroup View is really a ViewGroup that contains any number of RadioButton Views. The user can select only one of the buttons at a time, and you capture the selections by setting OnClickListeners for each RadioButton. Note that clicking on one of the RadioButtons does *not* fire a click event for the RadioGroup.

Spinner

Spinners require the most work of these three Views, but can also provide the best use of scarce screen real estate. As shown, the Spinner is normally collapsed to the currently selected entry, and when you touch the down arrow on the right, it presents a drop-down list of the other choices. To make that happen, you must:

1. Create a list of the selections (which can be a dynamic list built and changed by your application).

2. Create an ArrayAdapter from the list that the Spinner can use for its drop-down list. Note that the formats shown for the ArrayAdapter (`simple_spinner_item`

and `simple_spinner_dropdown_item`) are defined by Android; they do not appear in your resource XML files.

3. Create an onItemSelectedListener for the Spinner to capture select events. The listener has to contain both an `onItemSelected` method and an `onNothingSelected` method.

ViewGroups

ViewGroups are Views that contain child Views. Each `ViewGroup` class embodies a different set of assumptions about how to display its child Views. All ViewGroups descend from the `android.view.ViewGroup` class. Layouts, which we'll discuss later in the chapter, are a subset of ViewGroups.

Gallery and GridView

The Gallery ViewGroup (Figure 11-4) displays multiple items in a horizontally scrolling list. The currently selected item is locked in the center of the screen. Any items that approach the edge of the screen begin to fade, giving the user the impression that there may be more items "around the corner." The user can scroll horizontally through the items within the gallery. This ViewGroup is useful when you want to present a large set of possible choices to the user without using too much screen real estate.

A GridView (Figure 11-5, shown later) is very similar to a Gallery. Like a Gallery, the GridView displays many child Views that the user can manipulate. But in contrast to a Gallery, which is a one-dimensional list that the user can scroll horizontally, a GridView is a two-dimensional array that the user can scroll vertically.

The `Gallery` and `GridView` classes both descend from the `AdapterView` class, so you need a subclass of Adapter to provide a standardized way to access the underlying data. Any class that implements the `Adapter` class must implement the following abstract functions from that class:

`int getCount`
Returns the number of items in the data set represented by the Adapter.

`Object getItem(int position)`
Returns the object in the Adapter function (Adapter class) at the given position.

`long getItem(int position)`
Returns the row ID within the Adapter of the object at the given position.

`View getView(int position, View convertView, ViewGroup parent)`
Returns a View object that will display the data in the given position in the data set.

The ApiDemos application's *views.Gallery1.java* file shows off the Gallery ViewGroup nicely. The demo displays a variety of images for the user to select, and when the user does select one, the image's index number briefly appears as toast.

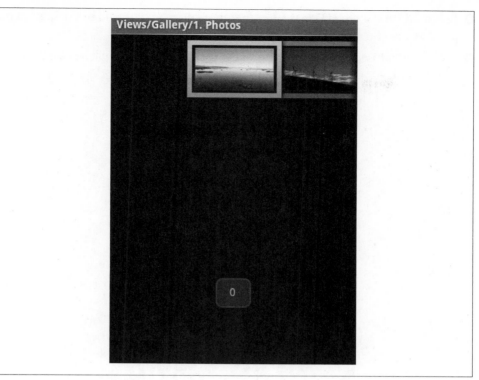

Figure 11-4. The Gallery ViewGroup

The ApiDemos application also includes two example GridView Activities that show how to use the GridView. We will not examine the GridView here, because the Gallery example is so similar.

Example 11-4 shows how to use a Gallery ViewGroup. Example 11-4 shows the XML layout file (*gallery_1.xml*).

Example 11-4. Layout file for Gallery example

```xml
<?xml version="1.0" encoding="utf-8"?>
<Gallery xmlns:android="http://schemas.android.com/apk/res/android"
    android:id="@+id/gallery"❶
      android:layout_width="fill_parent"❷
      android:layout_height="wrap_content"❸
/>
```

Here are some of the highlights of the layout code:

❶ The id for the Gallery View is gallery. As you have seen before, the id is used by the *findViewById* function to hook a Java Object to the XML object named in the layout file.

❷ layout_width is set to fill_parent so that the Gallery's width will be the same as the parent's.

❸ layout_height is set to wrap_content, meaning that the height will be as high as the tallest child.

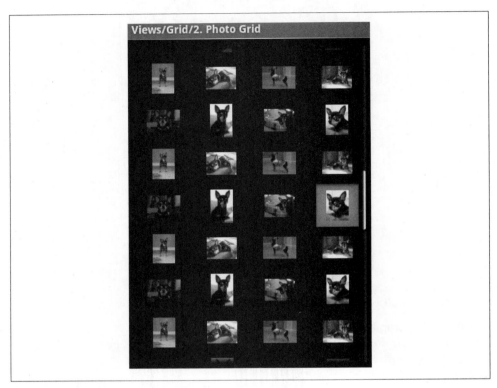

Figure 11-5. The GridView ViewGroup

Now we'll turn our attention to the Java implementation, *Gallery1.java*, shown in Example 11-5. We've modified the code from ApiDemos slightly to remove some features that do not add to our understanding of the Gallery ViewGroup.

Example 11-5. Java for Gallery: Gallery1.java

```java
public class Gallery1 extends Activity {

    @Override
    public void onCreate(Bundle savedInstanceState) {
        super.onCreate(savedInstanceState);
        setContentView(R.layout.gallery_1);

        // Reference the Gallery view
        Gallery g = (Gallery) findViewById(R.id.gallery);❶
        // Set the adapter to our custom adapter (below)
```

```
        g.setAdapter(new ImageAdapter(this));❷

        // Set a item click listener, and just Toast the clicked position
        g.setOnItemClickListener(new OnItemClickListener() {❸
            public void onItemClick(AdapterView parent, View v, int position, long id) {
                Toast.makeText(Gallery1.this, "" + position, Toast.LENGTH_SHORT).show();❹
            }
        });
    }
```

Here are some of the highlights of the code:

❶ In the Gallery's onCreate method, create a Gallery object hooked to the id named gallery from the XML layout.

❷ Display each user option using the custom adapter defined in Example 11-6 (shown next).

❸ Set up a click listener on the Gallery object.

❹ Display the the index (position) within the ImageAdapter of the photo the user clicked on as a Toast pop up.

In Example 11-5, the setAdapter function tells the Gallery object to use the ImageAdapter object as its Adapter. Example 11-6 defines our ImageAdapter class. This ImageAdapter implements all of the abstract functions required in its base class, BaseAdapter. For the simple case of this demo, picture resources represent the data that the Gallery view is displaying. An integer array, mImageIds, contains the resource IDs of the picture resources.

Example 11-6. Java for Gallery's Adapter

```
    public class ImageAdapter extends BaseAdapter {
        int mGalleryItemBackground;

        private Context mContext;

        private Integer[] mImageIds = {❶
                R.drawable.gallery_photo_1,
                R.drawable.gallery_photo_2,
                R.drawable.gallery_photo_3,
                R.drawable.gallery_photo_4,
                R.drawable.gallery_photo_5,
                R.drawable.gallery_photo_6,
                R.drawable.gallery_photo_7,
                R.drawable.gallery_photo_8
        };

        public ImageAdapter(Context c) {
            mContext = c;

            TypedArray a = obtainStyledAttributes(android.R.styleable.Theme);
            mGalleryItemBackground = a.getResourceId(
                    android.R.styleable.Theme_galleryItemBackground, 0);
```

```
        a.recycle();
    }

    public int getCount() {
        return mImageIds.length;
    }

    public Object getItem(int position) {
        return position;
    }

    public long getItemId(int position) {
        return position;
    }

    public View getView(int position, View convertView, ViewGroup parent) {
        ImageView i = new ImageView(mContext);

        i.setImageResource(mImageIds[position]);❷
        i.setScaleType(ImageView.ScaleType.FIT_XY);❸
        i.setLayoutParams(new Gallery.LayoutParams(136, 88));❹

        // The preferred Gallery item background
        i.setBackgroundResource(mGalleryItemBackground);

        return i;
    }
  }
}
```

Here are some of the highlights of the code:

❶ Defines the mImageIds array. Each element holds a resource reference to an image that appears in the Gallery, and each image resource name maps to the filename in the resources directory. Thus R.drawable.gallery_photo_1 maps directly to */res/drawable/gallery_photo_1.jpg* in the resource directory.

❷ Sets the image for this position in the Gallery to the image in the corresponding element of mImageIds.

❸ setScaleType controls how the image is resized to match the size of its container.

❹ This call to setLayoutParams sets the size of the ImageView container.

ListView and ListActivity

ListView is similar to Gallery, but uses a vertically scrolling list in place of Gallery's horizontally scrolling list. To create a ListView that takes up the entire screen, Android provides the ListActivity class (Figure 11-6).

The ApiDemos application includes many examples of ListActivity. The simplest is the List1 class, which displays a huge number of cheese names in a list. The cheese names are kept in a simple String array (who knew there were that many cheese varieties!):

```
public class List1 extends ListActivity {

    @Override
    public void onCreate(Bundle savedInstanceState) {
        super.onCreate(savedInstanceState);

        // Use an existing ListAdapter that will map an array
        // of strings to TextViews
        setListAdapter(new ArrayAdapter<String>(this,
                android.R.layout.simple_list_item_1, mStrings));
    }

    private String[] mStrings = {
            "Abbaye de Belloc", "Abbaye du Mont des Cats", "Abertam", "Abondance",
            "Ackawi",
            "Acorn", "Adelost", "Affidelice au Chablis", "Afuega'l Pitu", "Airag",
            "Airedale",
            ...
```

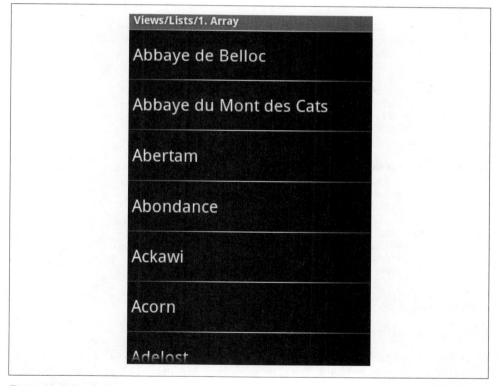

Figure 11-6. ListActivity

Filling the ListView in the ListActivity is a simple matter of calling **setListAdapter** and passing it an **ArrayAdapter** that contains a reference to the list of strings.

ScrollView

A ScrollView is a container for another View that lets the user scroll that View vertically (a scrollbar is optional). A ScrollView often contains a LinearLayout, which in turn contains the Views that make up the form.

Don't confuse ScrollView with ListView. Both Views present the user with a scrollable set of Views, but the ListView is designed to display a set of similar things, such as the cheeses in the previous section. The ScrollView, on the other hand, allows an arbitrary View to scroll vertically. The Android documentation warns that one should never house a ListView within a ScrollView, because that defeats the performance optimizations of a ListView.

A ScrollView is a FrameLayout, which means that it can have only one child View. The most popular View for this purpose is a LinearLayout.

The following layout code from ApiDemos, *scroll_view_2.xml*, shows how to set up a ScrollView. The XML layout resource is sufficient; this example includes no extra Java code:

```xml
<ScrollView xmlns:android="http://schemas.android.com/apk/res/android"
    android:layout_width="fill_parent"
    android:layout_height="wrap_content"
    android:scrollbars="none">❶
    <LinearLayout❷
        android:id="@+id/layout"
        android:orientation="vertical"
        android:layout_width="fill_parent"
        android:layout_height="wrap_content">

        <TextView❸
            android:layout_width="fill_parent"
            android:layout_height="wrap_content"
            android:text="@string/scroll_view_2_text_1"/>

        <Button
            android:layout_width="fill_parent"
            android:layout_height="wrap_content"
            android:text="@string/scroll_view_2_button_1"/>

    </LinearLayout>
</ScrollView>
```

Here are some of the highlights of the code:

❶ The unnamed ScrollView fills the width of the screen and is as tall as it needs to be to contain all of its contents. It has no scrollbars, but that's not a problem, because scrollbars act only as visual queues in Android; they're not as important in UIs that scroll by flicking as opposed to mousing.

❷ The child view is a LinearLayout.

❸ The XML layout file has two controls within the LinearLayout: a TextView and a Button. The Java code that uses this layout creates 63 more buttons, to ensure that the example LinearLayout will be larger than the screen device and big enough to scroll.

Figure 11-7. The first tab of a TabHost ViewGroup

Figure 11-8. The second tab of a TabHost ViewGroup

TabHost

Most modern UIs provide an interface element that lets the user flip through many pages of information quickly using tabs, with each "screen" of information available when its tab is pressed. Android's option is the TabHost View. Figures 11-7 through 11-10 show how it operates.

Android enables the developer to choose between three different approaches for setting the tab's content. The developer can:

- Set the content of a tab to an Intent. Figures 11-7 and 11-9 use this method.
- Use a TabContentFactory to create the tab's content on-the-fly. Figure 11-8 uses this method.
- Retrieve the content from an XML layout file, much like that of a regular Activity. Figure 11-10 uses this method.

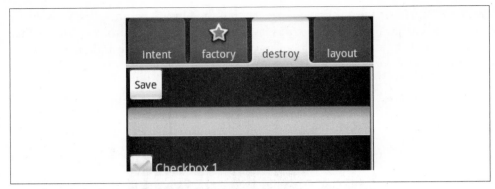

Figure 11-9. The third tab of a TabHost ViewGroup

Figure 11-10. The fourth tab of a TabHost ViewGroup

We'll examine each of these possibilities using a modified Activity from the ApiDemos application. The fourth tab is not part of the ApiDemos, but combines some other TabHost demonstration Activities in ApiDemos.

Let's start by looking at the *tabs4.xml* layout file (Example 11-7).

Example 11-7. Layout file for TabHost (tabs4.xml)

```
<FrameLayout xmlns:android="http://schemas.android.com/apk/res/android"
    android:layout_width="fill_parent"
    android:layout_height="fill_parent">

    <TextView android:id="@+id/view4"
        android:background="@drawable/green"❶
        android:layout_width="fill_parent"
        android:layout_height="fill_parent"
        android:text="@string/tabs_4_tab_4"/>❷

</FrameLayout>
```

Here are some of the highlights of the code:

❶ Defines a TextView view with an `id` of `view4`. We'll insert the TextView into a tab in our Java code. Notice the nice green background for this tab body.

❷ The referenced string is simply `tab4`.

And now we'll dissect the Java code that produces the tabs (Example 11-8).

Example 11-8. Java for TabHost

```java
public class Tabs4 extends TabActivity implements TabHost.TabContentFactory {❶

    protected void onCreate(Bundle savedInstanceState) {
        super.onCreate(savedInstanceState);

        final TabHost tabHost = getTabHost();❷

        LayoutInflater.from(this).inflate(R.layout.tabs4, tabHost.getTabContentView(),
            true);❸

        tabHost.addTab(tabHost.newTabSpec("tab1")
                .setIndicator("intent")❹
                .setContent(new Intent(this, List1.class)));❺

        tabHost.addTab(tabHost.newTabSpec("tab2")
                .setIndicator("factory",
                  getResources().getDrawable(R.drawable.star_big_on))❻
                .setContent(this));❼

        tabHost.addTab(tabHost.newTabSpec("tab3")
                .setIndicator("destroy")
                .setContent(new Intent(this, Controls2.class)❽
                    .addFlags(Intent.FLAG_ACTIVITY_CLEAR_TOP)));❾

        tabHost.addTab(tabHost.newTabSpec("tab4")
                .setIndicator("layout")
                .setContent(R.id.view4));❿
    }

    public View createTabContent(String tag) {⓫
        final TextView tv = new TextView(this);
        tv.setText("Content for tab with tag " + tag);
        return tv;
    }
}
```

Here are some of the highlights of the code:

❶ To implement tabs, you need to extend TabActivity instead of just Activity. This gives you all the tab functionality.

❷ The **tabHost** variable allows you to define the tabs and their contents.

❸ This basically says "using the LayoutInflater from my current Context, inflate the XML layout referenced by R.layout.tabs4 into the content section of the **tabHost**." Whew. As mentioned before, XML layout files are normally inflated automatically when **setContentView** runs. However, in this case the XML layout must be instantiated manually. Note that this XML layout is used only in the fourth tab.

❹ Sets up the first tab (Figure 11-7). The title is arbitrary, but we've called this tab **intent** as documentation that its contents are an Intent.

❺ Set the content of the first tab to the List1.class in this application. This simply brings up the referenced class in the tab. This is a slick way to make the contents of a regular application visible inside a tab.

❻ Now we're setting up the second tab (Figure 11-8). This is how you put an image on a tab face.

❼ This tab's contents are filled in by a factory method in this class. Notice that the class implements the TabHost.TabContentFactory interface.

❽ Set the content for the third tab (Figure 11-9) from an Intent. Using an Intent here is similar to navigating from one Activity in your application to another by using an intent. However, using tabs, the user can navigate back and forth between separate parts of your application quickly and easily.

❾ Adding this flag to the tabHost creates a new instance of the View each time it is displayed. In the case of the demo, all changes to the UI will be lost if you navigate away from the tab and then back to it.

❿ This tab displays the TextView from the XML layout item referenced by R.id.view4. The TextView was set up in item 1 of Example 11-7.

⓫ This is the factory method that creates the view for the second tab. The factory must return a view that the tab will use as its content. In this case, we create a very simple TextView that displays the tag associated with the tab.

Layouts

Layouts are Android's solution to the variety of screens that come on Android devices: they can have different pixel densities, different dimensions, and different aspect ratios. Typical Android devices, such as the HTC G1 mobile phone, even allow changing the screen orientation (portrait or landscape) while applications are running, so the layout infrastructure needs to be able to respond on the fly. Layouts are intended to give developers a way to express the physical relationship of Views as they are drawn on the screen. As Android inflates the Layout, it uses the developer requests to come up with a screen layout that best approximates what the developer has asked for.

Looking a little deeper, layouts in Android are in the form of a tree, with a single root and a hierarchy of Views. Look back at any of the XML Layout files in the previous section and you'll see that the XML tags create just such a hierarchy, with a screen Layout as the root of the tree. Each View in the tree is termed the *parent* of the Views it contains and the child of the View that contains it. Layout is a two-pass process:

Measure pass
> Traversing the tree from the root, each View in the layout records its dimensional request—in other words, how much vertical height and horizontal width it needs to display itself in the final display.

Layout pass

Again traversing the tree from the root, each parent View uses the available layout information to position its children as requested. If the requests can't be followed explicitly, Android does its best to make everything fit on the screen. If there are no requests given, it uses a default set of layout parameters. Each parent can pass layout information on to its children, telling them where they are positioned and what screen dimensions they have been granted (they might get less than they requested).

A Layout is a View itself, so there's nothing wrong with having multiple Layouts in a single layout XML file—they just have to be arranged in a hierarchy. So it's perfectly valid to have a vertical LinearLayout that includes a TableLayout as one of its rows. You'll learn a lot more about layouts in Chapter 12.

Frame Layout

The Frame Layout is sort of a null layout specification. It reserves space on the screen for a single View to be drawn, and the View is always located at the upper left of the space. There is no way to specify a different location for the View, and there can be only one View in the Layout. If more than one View is defined in the layout file, they are just drawn on top of each other, all pinned to the upper-left corner.

LinearLayout

LinearLayouts are used extensively in Android applications, and we used them in example code earlier. A LinearLayout asks that the contained Views be layed out as either a series of rows (vertical LinearLayout) or a series of columns (horizontal LinearLayout). In a vertical LinearLayout, all the rows are the same width (the width of the widest child). In a horizontal LinearLayout, there is one row of Views, all the same height (the height of the tallest child).

Figure 11-11 shows an example of a vertical LinearLayout, and Figure 11-12 is an example of a horizontal one. Both have EditText Views as children. Example 11-9 shows the XML resource file that produces the vertical layout, and Example 11-10 shows the file that created the horizontal one.

Example 11-9. Vertical LinearLayout resource file

```
<?xml version="1.0" encoding="utf-8"?>
<LinearLayout xmlns:android="http://schemas.android.com/apk/res/android"
    android:orientation="vertical"
    android:layout_width="fill_parent"
    android:layout_height="fill_parent"
    >
<EditText
    android:layout_width="fill_parent"
    android:layout_height="wrap_content"
    android:text="EditText1"
```

```
        />
<EditText
    android:layout_width="fill_parent"
    android:layout_height="wrap_content"
    android:text="EditText2"
    />
<EditText
    android:layout_width="fill_parent"
    android:layout_height="wrap_content"
    android:text="EditText3"
    />
<EditText
    android:layout_width="fill_parent"
    android:layout_height="wrap_content"
    android:text="EditText4"
    />
</LinearLayout>
```

Figure 11-11. Vertical LinearLayout

Example 11-10. Horizontal LinearLayout resource file

```
<?xml version="1.0" encoding="utf-8"?>
<LinearLayout xmlns:android="http://schemas.android.com/apk/res/android"
```

```
    android:orientation="horizontal"
    android:layout_width="fill_parent"
    android:layout_height="fill_parent"
    >
<EditText
    android:layout_width="wrap_content"
    android:layout_height="fill_parent"
    android:text="E1"
    />
<EditText
    android:layout_width="wrap_content"
    android:layout_height="fill_parent"
    android:text="E2"
    />
<EditText
    android:layout_width="wrap_content"
    android:layout_height="fill_parent"
    android:text="E3"
    />
<EditText
    android:layout_width="wrap_content"
    android:layout_height="fill_parent"
    android:text="E4"
    />
</LinearLayout>
```

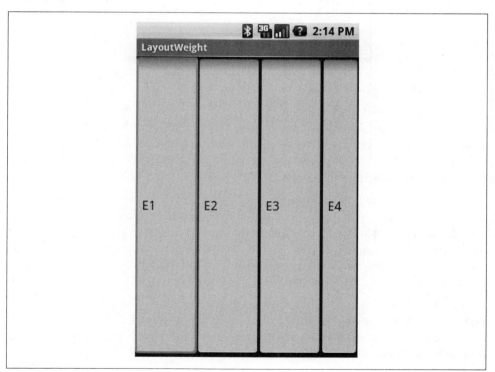

Figure 11-12. Horizontal LinearLayout

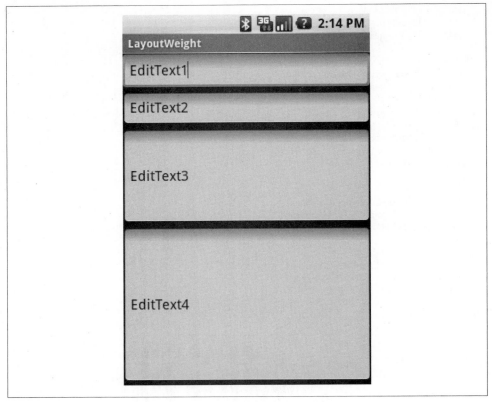

Figure 11-13. Weighted LinearLayout

The horizontal layout might not look exactly as you would think: how come E4 is narrower than the other three? The answer is that there is a default minimum width for an EditText. If you build and run the horizontal example and type something into EditText E1, you'll see that it expands in width as the line gets longer, which is just what we asked for with `android:layout_width="wrap_content"`.

In addition to the usual dimensional parameters for child Views (width, height, padding), you can include a weight for each child (attribute `android:layout_weight=;weight`). The weight tells the layout manager how you want to use unfilled space, and defaults to a value of 0. If you specify children with weights greater than zero, the layout manager will allocate unused space to each child in proportion to its weight.

Figure 11-13 shows an example of a LinearLayout containing four EditTexts. The first two have no weights assigned. EditText3 has a weight of 1 and EditText4 has a weight of 2. The effect is to make EditText4 twice as big as EditText3, while EditText1 and EditText2 just split whatever space the layout leaves over.

TableLayout

A TableLayout is just what you'd expect: it lays out the included Views in the form of a table (similar to an HTML table). We can create a table of TextViews to show how you would create that kind of screen for an application. Here's an example TableLayout XML file:

```xml
<?xml version="1.0" encoding="utf-8"?>
<TableLayout xmlns:android="http://schemas.android.com/apk/res/android"
    android:id="@+id/tblJobs"
    android:layout_width="fill_parent"
    android:layout_height="wrap_content"
    >
    <TableRow
        android:layout_width="fill_parent"
        android:layout_height="wrap_content">
        <Button android:text="Cell 11"
        android:id="@+id/btnCel11"
        android:layout_width="20dip"
        android:layout_height="wrap_content"
        />
    <TextView
    android:id="@+id/txtCell12"
    android:layout_width="20dip"
    android:layout_height="wrap_content"
    android:text="Cell 12"
    />
    <TextView
    android:id="@+id/txtCell13"
    android:layout_width="20dip"
    android:layout_height="wrap_content"
    android:text="Cell 13"
    />
    <TextView
    android:id="@+id/txtCell14"
    android:layout_width="20dip"
    android:layout_height="wrap_content"
    android:text="Cell 14"
    />
    </TableRow>
    <TableRow
        android:layout_width="fill_parent"
        android:layout_height="wrap_content">
        <Button android:text="Cell 21"
        android:id="@+id/btnCo21"
        android:layout_width="80dip"
        android:layout_height="wrap_content"
        />
    <TextView
    android:id="@+id/txtCell22"
    android:layout_width="80dip"
    android:layout_height="wrap_content"
    android:text="Cell 22"
    />
    <TextView
```

```
            android:id="@+id/txtCell23"
            android:layout_width="80dip"
            android:layout_height="wrap_content"
            android:text="Cell 23"
            />
        <TextView
            android:id="@+id/txtCell24"
            android:layout_width="80dip"
            android:layout_height="wrap_content"
            android:text="Cell 24"
            />
    </TableRow>
</TableLayout>
```

Figure 11-14 shows the resulting layout on the emulator screen.

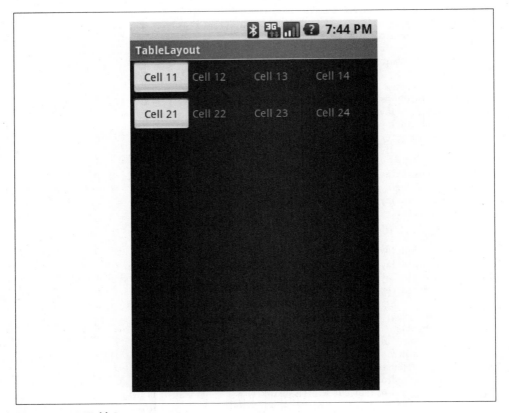

Figure 11-14. TableLayout

The structure of the XML file is pretty evident: the TableLayout tags contain a list of TableRows that in turn contain the Views you want to appear on each line of the table. Notice that the layout_width values are different in the two rows—all the widths in the first row are specified as 20dip, whereas the widths in the second row are specified as

28dip—yet the columns line up on the screen. To preserve the look of a table, Android makes each column as wide as the widest cell in that column.

Of course, the cells are addressable from your Java code, and you can add rows programmatically to the table, if that's what your application needs to do.

AbsoluteLayout

An AbsoluteLayout puts views on the screen wherever you tell it to. It doesn't try to resize anything, and it doesn't try to line anything up; it just puts things where it's told. You might think that it would be an easy type of layout to use, since you don't have to second-guess how the layout manager is going to rearrange things on your screen, but in practice the use of AbsoluteLayout is a bad idea for almost all applications. You usually want your application to run on as many Android devices as possible, and the strength of the Android layout manager is that it will automatically adapt your screen layout from device to device. AbsoluteLayout bypasses most of the layout manager, and while your application may look perfect on the device you used for development, the odds are very good that it will look terrible on other Android devices.

That warning aside, let's take a look at an AbsoluteLayout XML file:

```xml
<?xml version="1.0" encoding="utf-8"?>
<AbsoluteLayout xmlns:android="http://schemas.android.com/apk/res/android"
    android:orientation="vertical"
    android:layout_width="fill_parent"
    android:layout_height="fill_parent"
    >
<TextView
    android:layout_width="fill_parent"
    android:layout_height="wrap_content"
    android:text="Upper Left"
    android:layout_x="0.0px"
    android:layout_y="0.0px"
    />
<TextView
    android:layout_width="fill_parent"
    android:layout_height="wrap_content"
    android:text="Middle"
    android:layout_x="140.0px"
    android:layout_y="200.0px"
    />
<TextView
    android:layout_width="fill_parent"
    android:layout_height="wrap_content"
    android:text="Lower Right"
    android:layout_x="240.0px"
    android:layout_y="400.0px"
    />
</AbsoluteLayout>
```

As with any dimension in a layout file, the positions can be expressed in pixels (px), device-independent pixels (dp), scaled pixels (sp), inches (in), or millimeters (mm), and

Figure 11-15. AbsoluteLayout

the dimension has to be a floating-point number. (For more about expressing sizes, see "Dimensions in Android" on page 51 in Chapter 4.)

Figure 11-15 shows the resulting screen layout. Obviously, the position (0, 0) is the upper-left corner of the display, and the View is properly flush with the corner. The lower-right corner on the emulator is supposed to be (320, 480), but the View appears to be a little shy of that in both dimensions.

Just to caution against the use of AbsoluteLayout again, we suggest you try changing the emulator skin to show the screen in landscape mode (enter `emulator -skin HVGA-L` from a command or terminal window before you run the application), and you can see in Figure 11-16 that the application no longer looks right.

RelativeLayout

We've used RelativeLayout, often in combination with LinearLayout, throughout the MJAndroid application. The advantage of RelativeLayout is that you can express the

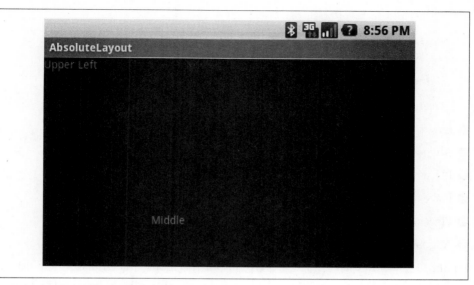

Figure 11-16. Same AbsoluteLayout in landscape mode

relative positioning of the Views in the screen, and the layout manager will do its best
to fit them all on the screen in the proper relations. An example follows:

```xml
<?xml version="1.0" encoding="utf-8"?>
<RelativeLayout xmlns:android="http://schemas.android.com/apk/res/android"
    android:orientation="vertical"
    android:layout_width="fill_parent"
    android:layout_height="fill_parent"
    >
  <TextView
    android:id="@+id/txtText1"
    android:layout_width="wrap_content"
    android:layout_height="wrap_content"
    android:text="Text1"
    android:gravity="top"❶
    android:layout_alignParentRight="true"❷
    />
  <TextView
    android:id="@+id/txtText2"
    android:layout_width="wrap_content"
    android:layout_height="wrap_content"
    android:text="Text2"
    android:layout_below="@+id/txtText1"❸
    />
  <Button
    android:id="@+id/btnButton1"
    android:layout_width="150dp"
    android:layout_height="wrap_content"
    android:text="Button1"
    android:layout_below="@+id/txtText2"❹
  />
```

```
<Button
  android:id="@+id/btnButton2"
  android:layout_width="150dp"
  android:layout_height="100dp"
  android:text="Button2"
  android:layout_toRightOf="@+id/btnButton1" ❺
  android:layout_alignTop="@+id/btnButton1" ❻
/>
</RelativeLayout>
```

❶ Lays out Text1 at the top of the screen.

❷ Aligns Text1 with the right side of its parent (which is the screen itself).

❸ Places Text2 below Text1.

❹ Places Button1 below Text2.

❺ Places Button2 just to the right of Button1.

❻ Aligns the tops of the two buttons.

Figure 11-17 shows what this looks like in portrait mode (the emulator default), and Figure 11-18 shows it in landscape mode. The layout manager has adjusted the arrangements in each case to match the layout hints we gave in the XML.

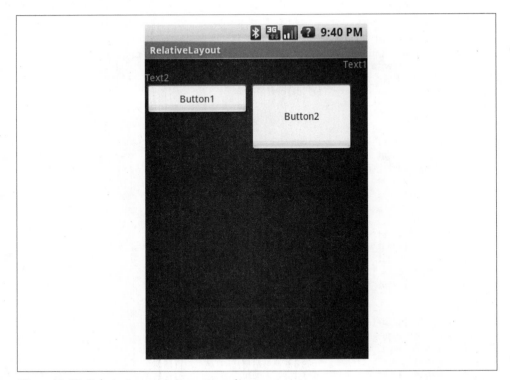

Figure 11-17. RelativeLayout in portrait mode

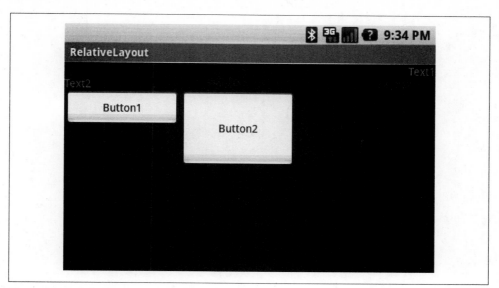

Figure 11-18. RelativeLayout in landscape mode

CHAPTER 12

Drawing 2D and 3D Graphics

The Android menagerie of widgets and the tools for assembling them are convenient, powerful, and cover a broad variety of needs. What happens, though, when none of the existing widgets offer what you need? Maybe your application needs to represent playing cards, phases of the moon, or the power diverted to the main thrusters of a rocket ship. In that case, you'll have to know how to roll your own.

This chapter is an overview of graphics and animation on Android. It's directed at programmers with some background in graphics, and goes into quite a bit of depth about ways to twist and turn the display. You will definitely need to supplement this chapter with Android documentation, particularly because the more advanced interfaces are still undergoing changes. But the techniques here will help you dazzle your users.

Rolling Your Own Widgets

As mentioned earlier, "widget" is a just convenient term for a subclass of `android.view.View`, typically for a leaf node in the view tree. Many views are just containers for other views and are used for layout; we don't consider them widgets, because they don't directly interact with the user, handle events, etc. So the term "widget," although informal, is useful for discussing the workhorse parts of the user interface that have the information and the behavior users care about.

You can accomplish a lot without creating a new widget. Chapter 11 constructed applications consisting entirely of existing widgets or simple subclasses of existing widgets. The code in that chapter demonstrated building trees of views, laying them out in code or in layout resources in XML files.

Similarly, the MicroJobs application has a view that contains a list of names corresponding to locations on a map. As additional locations are added to the map, new name-displaying widgets are added dynamically to the list. Even this dynamically changing layout is just a use of pre-existing widgets; it does not create new ones. The techniques in MicroJobs are, figuratively, adding or removing boxes from a tree like the one illustrated in Figure 10-3 in Chapter 10.

In contrast, this chapter shows you how to roll your own widget, which involves looking under the `View` hood.

The simplest customizations start with `TextView`, `Button`, `DatePicker`, or one of the many widgets presented in the previous chapter. For more extensive customization, you will implement your own widget as a direct subclass of `View`.

A very complex widget, perhaps used as an interface tool implemented in several places (even by multiple applications), might even be an entire package of classes, only one of which is a descendant of `View`.

This chapter is about graphics, and therefore about the View part of the Model-View-Controller pattern. Widgets also contain Controller code, which is good design because it keeps together all of the code relevant to a behavior and its representation on the screen. This part of this chapter discusses only the implementation of the View; the implementation of the Controller was discussed in Chapter 10.

Concentrating on graphics, then, we can break the tasks of this chapter into two essential parts: finding space on the screen and drawing in that space. The first task is known as *layout*. A leaf widget can assert its space needs by defining an `onMeasure` method that the Android framework will call at the right time. The second task, actually rendering the widget, is handled by the widget's `onDraw` method.

Layout

Most of the heavy lifting in the Android framework layout mechanism is implemented by *container views*. A container view is one that contains other views. It is an internal node in the view tree and subclasses of `ViewGroup` (which, in turn, subclasses `View`). The framework toolkit provides a variety of sophisticated container views that provide powerful and adaptable strategies for arranging a screen. `AbsoluteLayout` (see "AbsoluteLayout" on page 215), `LinearLayout` (see "LinearLayout" on page 209), and `RelativeLayout` (see "RelativeLayout" on page 216), to name some common ones, are container views that are both relatively easy to use and fairly hard to reimplement correctly. Since they are already available, fortunately you are unlikely to have to implement most of the algorithm discussed here. Understanding the big picture, though— how the framework manages the layout process—will help you build correct, robust widgets.

Example 12-1 shows a widget that is about as simple as it can be, while still working. If added to some Activity's view tree, this widget will fill in the space allocated to it with the color cyan. Not very interesting, but before we move on to create anything more complex, let's look carefully at how this example fulfills the two basic tasks of layout and drawing. We'll start with the layout process; drawing will be described later in the section "Canvas Drawing" on page 226.

Example 12-1. A trivial widget

```java
public class TrivialWidget extends View {

    public TrivialWidget(Context context) {
        super(context);
        setMinimumWidth(100);
        setMinimumHeight(20);
    }

    @Override
    protected void onMeasure(int widthMeasureSpec, int heightMeasureSpec) {
        setMeasuredDimension(
            getSuggestedMinimumWidth(),
            getSuggestedMinimumHeight());
    }

    @Override
    protected void onDraw(Canvas canvas) {
        canvas.drawColor(Color.CYAN);
    }
}
```

Dynamic layout is necessary because the space requirements for widgets change dynamically. Suppose, for instance, that a widget in a GPS-enabled application displays the name of the city in which you are currently driving. As you go from "Ely" to "Post Mills," the widget receives notification of the change in location. When it prepares to redraw the city name, though, it notices that it doesn't have enough room for the whole name of the new town. It needs to request that the screen be redrawn in a way that gives it more space, if that is possible.

Layout can be a surprisingly complex task and very difficult to get right. It is probably not very hard to make a particular leaf widget look right on a single device. On the other hand, it can be very tricky to get a widget that must arrange children to look right on multiple devices, even when the dimensions of the screen change.

Layout is initiated when the requestLayout method is invoked on some view in the view tree. Typically, a widget calls requestLayout on itself when it needs more space. The method could be invoked, though, from any place in an application, to indicate that some view in the current screen no longer has enough room to draw itself.

The requestLayout method causes the Android UI framework to enqueue an event on the UI event queue. When the event is processed, in order, the framework gives every container view an opportunity to ask each of its child widgets how much space each child would like for drawing. The process is separated into two phases: measuring the child views and then arranging them in their new positions. All views must implement the first phase, but the second is necessary only in the implementations of container views that must manage the layout of child views.

Measurement

The goal of the measurement phase is to provide each view with an opportunity to dynamically request the space it would ideally like for drawing. The UI framework starts the process by invoking the measure method of the view at the root of the view tree. Starting there, each container view asks each of its children how much space it would prefer. The call is propagated to all descendants, depth first, so that every child gets a chance to compute its size before its parent. The parent computes its own size based on the sizes of its children and reports that to its parent, and so on, up the tree.

In "Assembling a Graphical Interface" on page 161, for instance, the topmost LinearLayout asks each of the nested LinearLayout widgets for its preferred dimensions. They in turn ask the Buttons or EditText views they contain for theirs. Each child reports its desired size to its parent. The parents then add up the sizes of the children, along with any padding they insert themselves, and report the total to the topmost LinearLayout.

Because the framework must guarantee certain behaviors for all Views, during this process, the measure method is final and cannot be overridden. Instead, measure calls onMeasure, which widgets may override to claim their space. In other words, widgets cannot override measure, but they can override onMeasure.

The arguments to the onMeasure method describe the space the parent is willing to make available: a width specification and a height specification, measured in pixels. The framework assumes that no view will ever be smaller than 0 or bigger than 2^{30} pixels in size and, therefore, it uses the high-order bits of the passed int parameter to encode the *measurement specification mode*. It is as if onMeasure were actually called with four arguments: the width specification mode, the width, the height specification mode, and the height. Do not be tempted to do your own bit-shifting to separate the pairs of arguments! Instead, use the static methods MeasureSpec.getMode and MeasureSpec.getSize.

The specification modes describe how the container view wants the child to interpret the associated size. There are three of them:

MeasureSpec.EXACTLY
> The calling container view has already determined the exact size of the child view.

MeasureSpec.AT_MOST
> The calling container view has set a maximum size for this dimension, but the child is free to request less.

MeasureSpec.UNSPECIFIED
> The calling container view has not imposed any limits on the child, and so the child may request anything it chooses.

A widget is always responsible for telling its parent in the view tree how much space it needs. It does this by calling setMeasuredDimensions to set the properties that then become available to the parent, through the methods getMeasuredHeight and getMeasuredWidth. If your implementation overrides onMeasure but does not call setMeasuredDimensions, the measure method will throw IllegalStateException instead of completing normally.

The default implementation of onMeasure, inherited from View, calls set MeasuredDimensions with one of two values, in each direction. If the parent specifies MeasureSpec.UNSPECIFIED, it uses the default size of the view: the value supplied by either getSuggestedMinimumWidth or getSuggestedMinimumHeight. If the parent specifies either of the other two modes, the default implementation uses the size that was offered by the parent. This is a very reasonable strategy and allows a typical widget implementation to handle the measurement phase completely, simply by setting the values returned by getSuggestedMinimumWidth and getSuggestedMinimumHeight.

Your widget may not actually get the space it requests. Consider a view that is 100 pixels wide and has three children. It is probably obvious how the parent should arrange its children if the sum of the pixel widths requested by the children is 100 or less. If, however, each child requests 50 pixels, the parent container view is not going to be able to satisfy them all.

A container view has complete control of how it arranges its children. In the circumstance just described, it might decide to be "fair" and allocate 33 pixels to each child. Just as easily, it might decide to allocate 50 pixels to the leftmost child and 25 to each of the other two. In fact, it might decide to give one of the children the entire 100 pixels and nothing at all to the others. Whatever its method, though, in the end the parent determines a size and location for the bounding rectangle for each child.

Another example of a container view's control of the space allocated to a widget comes from the example widget shown previously in Example 12-1. It always requests the amount of space it prefers, regardless of what it is offered (unlike the default implementation). This strategy is handy to remember for widgets that will be added to the toolkit containers, notably LinearLayout, that implement *gravity*. Gravity is a property that some views use to specify the alignment of their subelements. The first time you use one of these containers, you may be surprised to find that, by default, only the first of your custom widgets gets drawn! You can fix this either by using the setGravity method to change the property to Gravity.FILL or by making your widgets insistent about the amount of space they request.

It is also important to note that a container view may call a child's measure method several times during a single measurement phase. As part of its implementation of onMeasure, a clever container view, attempting to lay out a horizontal row of widgets, might call each child widget's measure method with mode MEASURE_SPEC.UNSPECIFIED and a width of 0 to find out what size the widget would prefer. Once it has collected the preferred widths for each of its children, it could compare the sum to the actual width available (which was specified in its parent's call to its measure method). Now it might call each child widget's measure method again, this time with the mode MeasureSpec.AT_MOST and a width that is an appropriate proportion of the space actually available. Because `measure` may be called multiple times, an implementation of `onMeasure` must be idempotent and must not change the application state.

A container view's implementation of `onMeasure` is likely to be fairly complex. `ViewGroup`, the superclass of all container views, does not supply a default implementation. Each of the UI framework container views has its own. If you contemplate implementing a container view, you might consider basing it on one of them. If, instead, you implement measurement from scratch, you are still likely to need to call `measure` for each child and should consider using the `ViewGroup` helper methods: `measureChild`, `measureChildren`, and `measureChildWithMargins`. At the conclusion of the measurement phase, a container view, like any other widget, must report the space it needs by calling `setMeasuredDimensions`.

Arrangement

Once all the container views in the view tree have had a chance to negotiate the sizes of each of their children, the framework begins the second phase of layout, which consists of arranging the children. Again, unless you implement your own container view, you probably will never have to implement your own arrangement code. This section describes the underlying process so that you can better understand how it might affect your widgets. The default method, implemented in `View`, will work for typical leaf widgets, as demonstrated previously by Example 12-1.

Because a view's `onMeasure` method might be called several times, the framework must use a different method to signal that the measurement phase is complete and that container views must fix the final locations of their children. Like the measurement phase, the arrangement phase is implemented with two methods. The framework invokes a final method, `layout`, at the top of the view tree. The `layout` method performs processing common to all views and then delegates to `onLayout`, which custom widgets override to implement their own behaviors. A custom implementation of `onLayout` must at least calculate the bounding rectangle that it will supply to each child when it is drawn and, in turn, invoke the `layout` method for each child (because it might also be a parent to other widgets).

It is worth reiterating that a widget is not guaranteed to receive the space it requests. It must be prepared to draw itself in whatever space is actually allocated to it. If it attempts to draw outside the space allocated to it by its parent, the drawing will be clipped by the clip rectangle. To exert fine control—to fill exactly the space allocated to it, for instance—a widget must either implement `onLayout` and record the dimensions of the allocated space or inspect the clip rectangle of the `Canvas` that is the parameter to `onDraw`.

Canvas Drawing

Now that we've explored how widgets allocate the space on the screen in which they draw themselves, we can turn to coding some widgets that actually do some drawing.

The Android framework handles drawing in a way that should be familiar, now that you've read about measurement and arrangement. When some part of the application determines that the current screen drawing is stale because some state has changed, it calls the View method invalidate. This call causes a redraw event to be added to the event queue.

Eventually, when that event is processed, the framework calls the draw method at the top of the view tree. This time the call is propagated preorder, with each view drawing itself before it calls its children. This means that leaf views are drawn after their parents, which are, in turn, drawn after their parents. Views that are lower in the tree appear to be drawn on top of those nearer the root of the tree.

The draw method calls onDraw, which a subclass overrides to implement its custom rendering. When your widget's onDraw method is called, it must render itself according to the current application state and return. It turns out, by the way, that neither View.draw nor ViewGroup.dispatchDraw (responsible for the traversal of the view tree) is final! Override them at your peril!

In order to prevent extra painting, the framework maintains some state information about the view, called the *clip rectangle*. A key concept in the UI framework, the clip rectangle is part of the state passed in calls to a component's graphical rendering methods. It has a location and size that can be retrieved and adjusted through methods on the Canvas, and it acts like a stencil through which a component does all of its drawing. By correctly setting the size, shape, and location of the clip rectangle aperture, the framework can prevent a component from drawing outside its boundaries or redrawing regions that are already correctly drawn.

Before proceeding to the specifics of drawing, let's again put the discussion in the context of Android's single-threaded MVC design pattern. There are two essential rules:

- Drawing code should be inside the onDraw method. Your widget should draw itself completely, reflecting the program's current state, when onDraw is invoked.
- A widget should draw itself as quickly as possible when onDraw is invoked. The middle of the call to onDraw is no time to run a complex database query or to determine the status of some distant networked service. All the state you need to draw should be cached and ready for use at drawing time. Long-running tasks should use a separate thread and the Handler mechanism described in "Advanced Wiring: Focus and Threading" on page 179. The model state cached in the view is sometimes called the *view-model*.

The Android UI framework uses four main classes in drawing. If you are going to implement custom widgets and do your own drawing, you will want to become very familiar with them:

Canvas (a subclass of android.graphics.Canvas*)*
    The canvas has no complete analog in real-life materials. You might think of it as a complex easel that can orient, bend, and even crumple the paper on which you

are drawing in interesting ways. It maintains the clip rectangle, the stencil through which you paint. It can also scale drawings as they are drawn, like a photographic enlarger. It can even perform other transformations for which material analogs are more difficult to find: mapping colors and drawing text along paths.

Paint (a subclass of `android.graphics.Paint`*)*
> This is the medium with which you will draw. It controls the color, transparency, and brush size for objects painted on the canvas. It also controls font, size, and style when drawing text.

Bitmap (a subclass of `android.graphics.Bitmap`*)*
> This is the paper you are drawing on. It holds the actual pixels that you draw.

Drawables (likely a subclass of `android.graphics.drawable.Drawable`*)*
> This is the thing you want to draw: a rectangle or image. Although not all of the things that you draw are `Drawables` (text, for instance, is not), many, especially the more complex ones, are.

Example 12-1 used only the `Canvas`, passed as a parameter to `onDraw`, to do its drawing. In order to do anything more interesting, we will need `Paint`, at the very least. `Paint` provides control over the color and transparency (alpha) of the graphics drawn with it. `Paint` has many, many other capabilities, some of which are described in "Bling" on page 243. Example 12-2, however, is enough to get you started. Explore the class documentation for other useful attributes.

The graphic created by the code in the example is shown in Figure 12-1.

Example 12-2. Using Paint

```
@Override
protected void onDraw(Canvas canvas) {
    canvas.drawColor(Color.WHITE);

    Paint paint = new Paint();

    canvas.drawLine(33, 0, 33, 100, paint);

    paint.setColor(Color.RED);
    paint.setStrokeWidth(10);
    canvas.drawLine(56, 0, 56, 100, paint);

    paint.setColor(Color.GREEN);
    paint.setStrokeWidth(5);

    for (int y = 30, alpha = 255; alpha > 2; alpha >>= 1, y += 10) {
        paint.setAlpha(alpha);
        canvas.drawLine(0, y, 100, y, paint);
    }
}
```

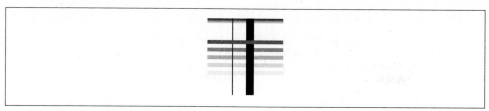

Figure 12-1. Using Paint

With the addition of `Paint`, we are prepared to understand most of the other tools necessary to create a useful widget. Example 12-3, for instance, is the widget used previously in Example 10-7. While still not very complex, it demonstrates all the pieces of a fully functional widget. It handles layout and highlighting, and reflects the state of the model to which it is attached.

Example 12-3. Dot widget

```
package com.oreilly.android.intro.view;

import android.content.Context;

import android.graphics.Canvas;
import android.graphics.Color;
import android.graphics.Paint;
import android.graphics.Paint.Style;

import android.view.View;

import com.oreilly.android.intro.model.Dot;
import com.oreilly.android.intro.model.Dots;


public class DotView extends View {
    private final Dots dots;

    /**
     * @param context the rest of the application
     * @param dots the dots we draw
     */
    public DotView(Context context, Dots dots) {
        super(context);
        this.dots = dots;
        setMinimumWidth(180);
        setMinimumHeight(200);
        setFocusable(true);
    }

    /** @see android.view.View#onMeasure(int, int) */
    @Override
    protected void onMeasure(int widthMeasureSpec, int heightMeasureSpec) {
        setMeasuredDimension(
            getSuggestedMinimumWidth(),
            getSuggestedMinimumHeight());
```

```
    }

    /** @see android.view.View#onDraw(android.graphics.Canvas) */
    @Override protected void onDraw(Canvas canvas) {
        canvas.drawColor(Color.WHITE);

        Paint paint = new Paint();
        paint.setStyle(Style.STROKE);
        paint.setColor(hasFocus() ? Color.BLUE : Color.GRAY);
        canvas.drawRect(0, 0, getWidth() - 1, getHeight() -1, paint);

        paint.setStyle(Style.FILL);
        for (Dot dot : dots.getDots()) {
            paint.setColor(dot.getColor());
            canvas.drawCircle(
                dot.getX(),
                dot.getY(),
                dot.getDiameter(),
                paint);
        }
    }
}
```

As with Paint, we have only enough space to begin an exploration of Canvas methods. There are two groups of functionality, however, that are worth special notice.

Drawing text

The most important Canvas methods are those used to draw text. Although some Canvas functionality is duplicated in other places, text-rendering capabilities are not. In order to put text in your widget, you will have to use the Canvas (or, of course, subclass some other widget that uses it).

Canvas methods for rendering text come in pairs: three sets of two signatures. Example 12-4 shows one of the pairs.

Example 12-4. A pair of text drawing methods

```
public void drawText(String text, float x, float y, Paint paint)
public void drawText(char[] text, int index, int count, float x, float y, Paint paint)
```

There are several pairs of methods. In each pair, the first of the two methods in the pair uses String, and the second uses three parameters to describe the text: an array of char, the index indicating the first character in that array to be drawn, and the number of total characters in the text to be rendered. In some cases, there are additional convenience methods.

Example 12-5 contains an onDraw method that demonstrates the use of the first style of each of the three pairs of text rendering methods. The output is shown in Figure 12-2.

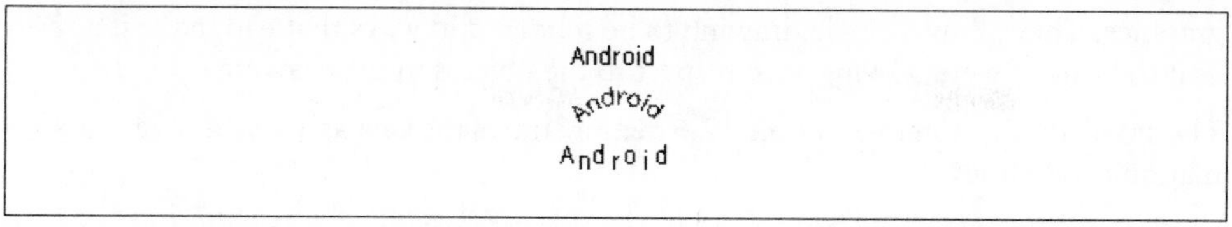

Android

Android

Android

Figure 12-2. Output from three ways of drawing text

Example 12-5. Three ways of drawing text

```
@Override
protected void onDraw(Canvas canvas) {
    canvas.drawColor(Color.WHITE);

    Paint paint = new Paint();

    paint.setColor(Color.RED);
    canvas.drawText("Android", 25, 30, paint);

    Path path = new Path();
    path.addArc(new RectF(10, 50, 90, 200), 240, 90);
    paint.setColor(Color.CYAN);
    canvas.drawTextOnPath("Android", path, 0, 0, paint);

    float[] pos = new float[] {
        20, 80,
        29, 83,
        36, 80,
        46, 83,
        52, 80,
        62, 83,
        68, 80
    };
    paint.setColor(Color.GREEN);
    canvas.drawPosText("Android", pos, paint);
}
```

As you can see, the most elementary of the pairs, drawText, simply draws text at the passed coordinates. With DrawTextOnPath, on the other hand, you can draw text along any Path. The example path is just an arc. It could just as easily have been a line drawing or a Bezier curve.

For those occasions on which even DrawTextOnPath is insufficient, Canvas offers DrawPosText, which lets you specify the exact position of each character in the text. Note that the character positions are specified by alternating array elements: x1,y1,x2,y2, and so on.

Matrix transformations

The second interesting group of Canvas methods are the Matrix transformations and their related convenience methods, rotate, scale, and skew. These methods transform what you draw in ways that will immediately be recognizable to those familiar with 3D graphics. They allow a single drawing to be rendered in ways that can make it appear as if the viewer were moving with respect to the objects in the drawing.

The small application in Example 12-6 demonstrates the **Canvas**'s coordinate transformation capabilities.

Example 12-6. Using a Canvas

```java
import android.app.Activity;

import android.content.Context;

import android.graphics.Canvas;
import android.graphics.Color;
import android.graphics.Paint;
import android.graphics.Rect;

import android.os.Bundle;

import android.view.View;

import android.widget.LinearLayout;


public class TranformationalActivity extends Activity {

    private interface Transformation {
        void transform(Canvas canvas);
        String describe();
    }

    private static class TransfomedViewWidget extends View {❶
        private final Transformation transformation;

        public TransfomedViewWidget(Context context, Transformation xform) {
            super(context);

            transformation = xform;❷

            setMinimumWidth(160);
            setMinimumHeight(105);
        }

        @Override
        protected void onMeasure(int widthMeasureSpec, int heightMeasureSpec) {
            setMeasuredDimension(
                getSuggestedMinimumWidth(),
                getSuggestedMinimumHeight());
        }

        @Override
        protected void onDraw(Canvas canvas) {❸
            canvas.drawColor(Color.WHITE);

            Paint paint = new Paint();
```

```
            canvas.save();❹
            transformation.transform(canvas);❺

            paint.setTextSize(12);
            paint.setColor(Color.GREEN);
            canvas.drawText("Hello", 40, 55, paint);

            paint.setTextSize(16);
            paint.setColor(Color.RED);
            canvas.drawText("Android", 35, 65, paint);

            canvas.restore();❻

            paint.setColor(Color.BLACK);
            paint.setStyle(Paint.Style.STROKE);
            Rect r = canvas.getClipBounds();
            canvas.drawRect(r, paint);

            paint.setTextSize(10);
            paint.setColor(Color.BLUE);
            canvas.drawText(transformation.describe(), 5, 100, paint);
        }

    }

    @Override
    public void onCreate(Bundle savedInstanceState) {❼
        super.onCreate(savedInstanceState);
        setContentView(R.layout.transformed);

        LinearLayout v1 = (LinearLayout) findViewById(R.id.v_left);❽
        v1.addView(new TransfomedViewWidget(❾
            this,
            new Transformation() {❿
                @Override public String describe() { return "identity"; }
                @Override public void transform(Canvas canvas) { }
            } ));
        v1.addView(new TransfomedViewWidget(❾
            this,
            new Transformation() {❿
                @Override public String describe() { return "rotate(-30)"; }
                @Override public void transform(Canvas canvas) {
                    canvas.rotate(-30.0F);
                } }));
        v1.addView(new TransfomedViewWidget(❾
            this,
            new Transformation() {❿
                @Override public String describe() { return "scale(.5,.8)"; }
                @Override public void transform(Canvas canvas) {
                    canvas.scale(0.5F, .8F);
                } }));
        v1.addView(new TransfomedViewWidget(❾
            this,
            new Transformation() {❿
```

```
            @Override public String describe() { return "skew(.1,.3)"; }
            @Override public void transform(Canvas canvas) {
                canvas.skew(0.1F, 0.3F);
            } }));

    LinearLayout v2 = (LinearLayout) findViewById(R.id.v_right);⓫
    v2.addView(new TransfomedViewWidget(⓬
        this,
        new Transformation() {⓾
            @Override public String describe() { return "translate(30,10)"; }
            @Override public void transform(Canvas canvas) {
                canvas.translate(30.0F, 10.0F);
            } }));
    v2.addView(new TransfomedViewWidget(⓬
        this,
        new Transformation() {⓾
            @Override public String describe()
                { return "translate(110,-20),rotate(85)"; }
            @Override public void transform(Canvas canvas) {
                canvas.translate(110.0F, -20.0F);
                canvas.rotate(85.0F);
            } }));
    v2.addView(new TransfomedViewWidget(⓬
        this,
        new Transformation() {⓾
            @Override public String describe()
                { return "translate(-50,-20),scale(2,1.2)"; }
            @Override public void transform(Canvas canvas) {
                canvas.translate(-50.0F, -20.0F);
                canvas.scale(2F, 1.2F);
            } }));
    v2.addView(new TransfomedViewWidget(⓬
        this,
        new Transformation() {⓾
            @Override public String describe() { return "complex"; }
            @Override public void transform(Canvas canvas) {
                canvas.translate(-100.0F, -100.0F);
                canvas.scale(2.5F, 2F);
                canvas.skew(0.1F, 0.3F);
            } }));
    }
}
```

The results of this protracted exercise are shown in Figure 12-3.

Here are some of the highlights of the code:

❶ Definition of the new widget, TransfomedViewWidget.

❷ Gets the actual transformation to perform from the second argument of the constructor.

❸ onDraw method of TransfomedViewWidget.

❹ Pushes the state on the stack through save before performing any transformation.

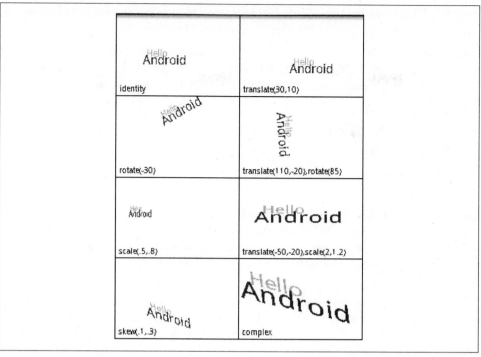

Figure 12-3. Transformed views

❺ Performs the transformation passed in item 2.

❻ Restores the old state saved in item 4, having finished the transformation.

❼ The Activity's `onCreate` method.

❽ Creates the first layout view.

❾ Instantiations of `TransfomedViewWidget`, added to layout view `v1`.

❿ Creates a transformation as part of the parameter list to the constructor of `TransfomedViewWidget`.

⓫ Creates the second layout view.

⓬ Instantiations of `TransfomedViewWidget`, added to layout view `v2`.

This small application introduces several new ideas and demonstrates the power of Android graphics for maintaining state and nesting changes.

The application defines a single widget, `TransformedViewWidget`, of which it creates eight instances. For layout, the application creates two views named `v1` and `v2`, retrieving their parameters from resources. It then adds four instances of `TransformedView Widget` to each `LinearLayout` view. This is an example of how applications combine resource-based and dynamic views. Note that the creation both of the layout views and the new widgets take place within the Activity's onCreate method.

This application also makes the new widget flexible through a sophisticated division of labor between the widget and its Transformation. Several simple objects are drawn directly within the definition of TransformedViewWidget, in its onDraw method:

- A white background
- The word "Hello" in 12-point green type
- The word "Android" in 16-point red type
- A black frame
- A blue label

In the middle of this, the onDraw method performs a transformation specified at its creation. The application defines its own interface, called Transformation, and the constructor for TransformedViewWidget accepts a Transformation as a parameter. We'll see in a moment how the caller actually codes a transformation.

It's important to see first how the widget onDraw preserves its own text from being affected by the Transformation. In this example, we want to make sure that the frame and label are drawn last, so that they are drawn over anything else drawn by the widget, even if they might overlap. On the other hand, we do not want the transformation applied earlier to affect them.

Fortunately, the Canvas maintains an internal stack onto which we can record and recover the translation matrix, clip rectangle, and many other elements of mutable state in the Canvas. Taking advantage of this stack, onDraw calls save to preserve its state before the transformation, and restore afterward to recover the saved state.

The rest of the application controls the transformation used in each of the eight instances of TransformedViewWidget. Each new instance of the widget is created with its own anonymous instance of Tranformation. The image in the area labeled "identity" has no translation applied. The other seven areas are labeled with the transformations they demonstrate.

The base methods for Canvas translation are setMatrix and concatMatrix. These two methods allow you to build any possible transformation. The getMatrix method allows you to recover a dynamically constructed matrix for later use. The methods introduced in the example—translate, rotate, scale, and skew—are convenience methods that compose specific, constrained matrixes into the current Canvas state.

Although it may not be obvious at first, these transformation functions can be tremendously useful. They allow your application to appear to change its point of view with respect to a 3D object. It doesn't take too much imagination, for instance, to see the scene in the square labeled "scale(.5,.8)" as the same as that seen in the square labeled "identity", but viewed from farther away. With a bit more imagination, the image in the box labeled "skew(.1,.3)" again could be the untransformed image, but this time viewed from above and slightly to the side. Scaling or translating an object can make it appear to a user as if the object has moved. Skewing and rotating can make it appear that the object has turned. We will make good use of this technique in animation.

When you consider that these transformation functions apply to everything drawn on a canvas—lines, text, and even images—their importance in applications becomes even more apparent. A view that displays thumbnails of photos could be implemented trivially, though perhaps not optimally, as a view that scales everything it displays to 10% of its actual size. An application that simulates what you see as you look to your left while driving down the street might be implemented in part by scaling and skewing a small number of images.

Drawables

A Drawable is an object that knows how to render itself on a Canvas. Because a Drawable has complete control during rendering, even a very complex rendering process can be encapsulated in a way that makes it fairly easy to use.

Examples 12-7 and 12-8 show the changes necessary to implement the previous example, Figure 12-3, using a Drawable. The code that draws the red and green text has been refactored into a HelloAndroidTextDrawable class, used in rendering by the widget's onDraw method.

Example 12-7. Using a TextDrawable

```
private static class HelloAndroidTextDrawable extends Drawable {
    private ColorFilter filter;
    private int opacity;

    public HelloAndroidTextDrawable() {}

    @Override
    public void draw(Canvas canvas) {
        Paint paint = new Paint();

        paint.setColorFilter(filter);
        paint.setAlpha(opacity);

        paint.setTextSize(12);
        paint.setColor(Color.GREEN);
        canvas.drawText("Hello", 40, 55, paint);

        paint.setTextSize(16);
        paint.setColor(Color.RED);
        canvas.drawText("Android", 35, 65, paint);
    }

    @Override
    public int getOpacity() { return PixelFormat.TRANSLUCENT; }

    @Override
```

```
    public void setAlpha(int alpha) { }

    @Override
    public void setColorFilter(ColorFilter cf) { }
}
```

Using the new `Drawable` implementation requires only a few small changes to the `onDraw` method.

Example 12-8. Using a Drawable widget

```
package com.oreilly.android.intro.widget;

import android.content.Context;
import android.graphics.Canvas;
import android.graphics.Color;
import android.graphics.Paint;
import android.graphics.Rect;
import android.graphics.drawable.Drawable;
import android.view.View;


/**A widget that renders a drawable with a transformation */
public class TransformedViewWidget extends View {

    /** A transformation */
    public interface Transformation {
        /** @param canvas */
        void transform(Canvas canvas);
        /** @return text descriptiont of the transform. */
        String describe();
    }

    private final Transformation transformation;
    private final Drawable drawable;

    /**
     * Render the passed drawable, transformed.
     *
     * @param context app context
     * @param draw the object to be drawn, in transform
     * @param xform the transformation
     */
    public TransformedViewWidget(
        Context context,
        Drawable draw,
        Transformation xform)
    {
        super(context);

        drawable = draw;
        transformation = xform;

        setMinimumWidth(160);
        setMinimumHeight(135);
```

```
        }

        /** @see android.view.View#onMeasure(int, int) */
        @Override
        protected void onMeasure(int widthMeasureSpec, int heightMeasureSpec) {
            setMeasuredDimension(
                getSuggestedMinimumWidth(),
                getSuggestedMinimumHeight());
        }

        /** @see android.view.View#onDraw(android.graphics.Canvas) */
        @Override
        protected void onDraw(Canvas canvas) {
            canvas.drawColor(Color.WHITE);

            canvas.save();
            transformation.transform(canvas);
            drawable.draw(canvas);
            canvas.restore();

            Paint paint = new Paint();
            paint.setColor(Color.BLACK);
            paint.setStyle(Paint.Style.STROKE);
            Rect r = canvas.getClipBounds();
            canvas.drawRect(r, paint);

            paint.setTextSize(10);
            paint.setColor(Color.BLUE);
            canvas.drawText(
                transformation.describe(),
                5,
                getMeasuredHeight() - 5,
                paint);
        }
}
```

This code begins to demonstrate the power of using a `Drawable`. This implementation of `TransformedViewWidget` will transform any `Drawable`, no matter what it happens to draw. It is no longer tied to rotating and scaling our original, hardcoded text. It can be reused to transform both the text from the previous example and a photo captured from the camera, as Figure 12-4 demonstrates. It could even be used to transform a `Drawable` animation.

The ability to encapsulate complex drawing tasks in a single object with a straightforward API is a valuable—and even necessary—tool in the Android toolkit. `Drawable`s make complex graphical techniques such as nine-patches and animation tractable. In addition, since they wrap the rendering process completely, `Drawable`s can be nested to decompose complex rendering into small reusable pieces.

Consider for a moment how we might extend the previous example to make each of the six images fade to white over a period of a minute. Certainly, we could just change

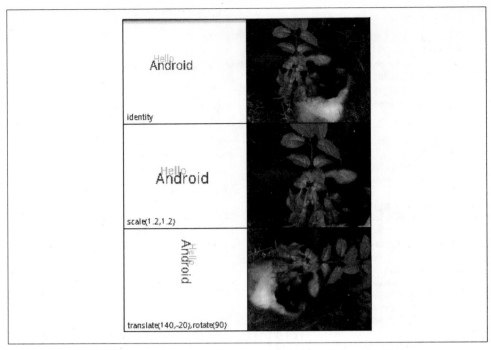

Figure 12-4. Transformed views with photos

the code in Example 12-8 to do the fade. A different—and very appealing—implementation involves writing one new `Drawable`.

This new `Drawable`, `FaderDrawable`, will take, in its constructor, a reference to its target, the `Drawable` that it will fade to white. In addition, it must have some notion of time, probably an integer—let's call it `t`—that is incremented by a timer. Whenever the `draw` method of `FaderDrawable` is called, it first calls the `draw` method of its target. Next, it paints over exactly the same area with the color white, using the value of `t` to determine the transparency (alpha value) of the paint (as demonstrated in Example 12-2). As time passes, `t` gets larger, the white gets more and more opaque, and the target `Drawable` fades to white.

This hypothetical `FaderDrawable` demonstrates some of the important features of `Drawables`. First, note that `FaderDrawable` is nicely reusable: it will fade just about any `Drawable`. Also note that, since `FaderDrawable` extends `Drawable`, we can use it anywhere that we would have used its target, the `Drawable` that it fades to white. Any code that uses a `Drawable` in its rendering process can use a `FaderDrawable` without change.

Of course, a `FaderDrawable` could itself be wrapped. In fact, it seems possible to achieve very complex effects, simply by building a chain of `Drawable` wrappers. The Android toolkit provides `Drawable` wrappers that support this strategy, including `ClipDrawable`, `RotateDrawable`, and `ScaleDrawable`.

At this point you may be mentally redesigning your entire UI in terms of `Drawable`s. Although a powerful tool, they are not a panacea. There are several issues to keep in mind when considering the use of `Drawable`s.

You may well have noticed that they share a lot of the functionality of the `View` class: location, dimensions, visibility, etc. It's not always easy to decide when a `View` should draw directly on the `Canvas`, when it should delegate to a subview, and when it should delegate to one or more `Drawable` objects. There is even a `DrawableContainer` class that allows grouping several child `Drawable`s within a parent. It is possible to build trees of `Drawable`s that parallel the trees of `View`s we've been using so far. In dealing with the Android framework, you just have to accept that sometimes there is more than one way to scale a cat.

One difference between the two choices is that `Drawable`s do not implement the `View` measure/layout protocol, which allows a container view to negotiate the layout of its components in response to changing view size. When a renderable object needs to add, remove, or lay out internal components, it's a pretty good indication that it should be a full-fledged `View` instead of a `Drawable`.

A second issue to consider is that `Drawable`s completely wrap the drawing process because they are not drawn like `String` or `Rect` objects. There are, for instance, no `Canvas` methods that will render a `Drawable` at specific coordinates. You may find yourself deliberating over whether, in order to render a certain image twice, a `View onDraw` method should use two different, immutable `Drawable`s or a single `Drawable` twice, resetting its coordinates.

Perhaps most important, though, is a more generic problem. The idea of a chain of `Drawable`s works because the `Drawable` interface contains no information about the internal implementation of the `Drawable`. When your code is passed a `Drawable`, there is no way for it to know whether it is something that will render a simple image or a complex chain of effects that rotates, flashes, and bounces. Clearly this can be a big advantage. But it can also be a problem.

Quite a bit of the drawing process is stateful. You set up `Paint` and then draw with it. You set up `Canvas` clip regions and transformations and then draw through them. When cooperating in a chain, if `Drawable`s change state, they must be very careful that those changes never collide. The problem is that, when constructing a `Drawable` chain, the possibility of collision cannot be explicit in the object's type by definition (they are all just `Drawable`s). A seemingly small change might have an effect that is not desirable and is difficult to debug.

To illustrate the problem, consider two `Drawable` wrapper classes, one that is meant to shrink its contents and another that is meant to rotate them by 90 degrees. If either is implemented by setting the transformation matrix to a specific value (instead of composing its transformation with any that already exist), composing the two `Drawable`s may not have the desired effect. Worse, it might work perfectly if A wraps B, but not if B wraps A! Careful documentation of how a `Drawable` is implemented is essential.

Bitmaps

The `Bitmap` is the last member of the four essentials for drawing: something to draw (a `String`, `Rect`, etc.), `Paint` with which to draw, a `Canvas` on which to draw, and the `Bitmap` to hold the bits. Most of the time, you don't have to deal directly with a `Bitmap`, because the `Canvas` provided as an argument to the `onDraw` method already has one behind it. However, there are circumstances under which you may want to use a `Bitmap` directly.

A common use for a `Bitmap` is as a way to cache a drawing that is time-consuming to draw but unlikely to change frequently. Consider, for example, a drawing program that allows the user to draw in multiple layers. The layers act as transparent overlays on a base image, and the user turns them off and on at will. It might be very expensive to actually draw each individual layer every time `onDraw` gets called. Instead, it might be faster to render the entire drawing with all visible layers once, and only update it when the user changes which are visible.

The implementation of such an application might look something like Example 12-9.

Example 12-9. Bitmap caching

```
private class CachingWidget extends View {
    private Bitmap cache;

    public CachingWidget(Context context) {
        super(context);
        setMinimumWidth(200);
        setMinimumHeight(200);
    }

    public void invalidateCache() {
        cache = null;
        invalidate();
    }

    @Override
    protected void onDraw(Canvas canvas) {
        if (null == cache) {
            cache = Bitmap.createBitmap(
                getMeasuredWidth(),
                getMeasuredHeight(),
                Bitmap.Config.ARGB_8888);

            drawCachedBitmap(new Canvas(cache));
        }

        canvas.drawBitmap(cache, 0, 0, new Paint());
    }


    // ... definition of drawCachedBitmap
}
```

This widget normally just copies the cached `Bitmap`, `cache`, to the `Canvas` passed to `onDraw`. If the cache is marked stale (by calling `invalidateCache`), only then will `drawCachedBitmap` be called to actually render the widget.

The most common way to encounter a `Bitmap` is as the programmatic representation of a graphics resource. `Resources.getDrawable` returns a `BitmapDrawable` when the resource is an image.

Combining these two ideas—caching an image and wrapping it in a `Drawable`—opens yet another interesting window. It means that anything that can be drawn can also be postprocessed. An application that used all of the techniques demonstrated in this chapter could allow a user to draw furniture in a room (creating a bitmap) and then to walk around it (using the matrix transforms).

Bling

The Android UI framework is a lot more than a just an intelligent, well-put-together GUI toolkit. When it takes off its glasses and shakes out its hair, it can be downright sexy! The tools mentioned here certainly do not make an exhaustive catalog. They might get you started, though, on the path to making your application Filthy Rich.

Several of the techniques discussed in this section are close to the edges of the Android landscape. As such, they are less well established: the documentation is not as thorough, some of the features are clearly in transition, and you may even find bugs. If you run into problems, the Google Group "Android Developers" is an invaluable resource. Questions about a particular aspect of the toolkit have sometimes been answered by the very person responsible for implementing that aspect.

Be careful about checking the dates on solutions you find by searching the Web. Some of these features are changing rapidly, and code that worked as recently as six months ago may not work now. A corollary, of course, is that any application that gets wide distribution is likely to be run on platforms that have differing implementations of the features discussed here. By using these techniques, you may limit the lifetime of your application and the number of devices that it will support.

The rest of this section considers a single application, much like the one used in Example 12-6: a couple of `LinearLayout`s that contain multiple instances of a single widget, each demonstrating a different graphics effect. Example 12-10 contains the key parts of the widget, with code discussed previously elided for brevity. The widget simply draws a few graphical objects and defines an interface through which various graphics effects can be applied to the rendering.

Example 12-10. Effects widget

```
public class EffectsWidget extends View {

    /** The effect to apply to the drawing */
    public interface PaintEffect { void setEffect(Paint paint); }

    // ...

    // PaintWidget's widget rendering method
    protected void onDraw(Canvas canvas) {
        Paint paint = new Paint();
        paint.setAntiAlias(true);

        effect.setEffect(paint);
        paint.setColor(Color.DKGRAY);

        paint.setStrokeWidth(5);
        canvas.drawLine(10, 10, 140, 20, paint);

        paint.setTextSize(26);
        canvas.drawText("Android", 40, 50, paint);

        paint = new Paint();
        paint.setColor(Color.BLACK);
        canvas.drawText(String.valueOf(id), 2.0F, 12.0F, paint);
        paint.setStyle(Paint.Style.STROKE);
        paint.setStrokeWidth(2);
        canvas.drawRect(canvas.getClipBounds(), paint);
    }
}
```

The application that uses this widget, shown in Example 12-11, should also feel familiar. It creates several copies of the EffectsWidget, each with its own effect. There are two special widgets: the bottom widget in the right column is animated, and the bottom widget in the left column uses OpenGL animation.

Example 12-11. Effects application

```
private void buildView() {
    setContentView(R.layout.main);

    LinearLayout view = (LinearLayout) findViewById(R.id.v_left);
    view.addView(new EffectsWidget(
        this,
        1,
        new EffectsWidget.PaintEffect() {
            @Override public void setEffect(Paint paint) {
                paint.setShadowLayer(1, 3, 4, Color.BLUE);
            } }));
    view.addView(new EffectsWidget(
        this,
        3,
        new EffectsWidget.PaintEffect() {
            @Override public void setEffect(Paint paint) {
```

```
                paint.setShader(
                    new LinearGradient(
                        0.0F,
                        0.0F,
                        160.0F,
                        80.0F,
                        new int[] { Color.BLACK, Color.RED, Color.YELLOW },
                        new float[] { 0.2F, 0.3F, 0.2F },
                        Shader.TileMode.REPEAT));
            } }));
    view.addView(new EffectsWidget(
        this,
        5,
        new EffectsWidget.PaintEffect() {
            @Override public void setEffect(Paint paint) {
                paint.setMaskFilter(
                    new BlurMaskFilter(2, BlurMaskFilter.Blur.NORMAL));
            } }));

    // Not and EffectsWidget: this is the OpenGL Anamation widget.
    glWidget = new GLDemoWidget(this);
    view.addView(glWidget);


    view = (LinearLayout) findViewById(R.id.v_right);
    view.addView(new EffectsWidget(
        this,
        2,
        new EffectsWidget.PaintEffect() {
            @Override public void setEffect(Paint paint) {
                paint.setShadowLayer(3, -8, 7, Color.GREEN);
            } }));
    view.addView(new EffectsWidget(
        this,
        4,
        new EffectsWidget.PaintEffect() {
            @Override public void setEffect(Paint paint) {
                paint.setShader(
                    new LinearGradient(
                        0.0F,
                        40.0F,
                        15.0F,
                        40.0F,
                        Color.BLUE,
                        Color.GREEN,
                        Shader.TileMode.MIRROR));
            } }));

    // A widget with an animated background
    View w = new EffectsWidget(
        this,
        6,
        new EffectsWidget.PaintEffect() {
            @Override public void setEffect(Paint paint) { }
        });
```

```
        view.addView(w);
        w.setBackgroundResource(R.drawable.throbber);

        // This is, alas, necessary until Cupcake.
        w.setOnClickListener(new OnClickListener() {
            @Override public void onClick(View v) {
                ((AnimationDrawable) v.getBackground()).start();
            } });
    }
```

Figure 12-5 shows what the code looks like when run. The bottom two widgets are animated: the green checkerboard moves from left to right across the widget, and the bottom-right widget has a throbbing red background.

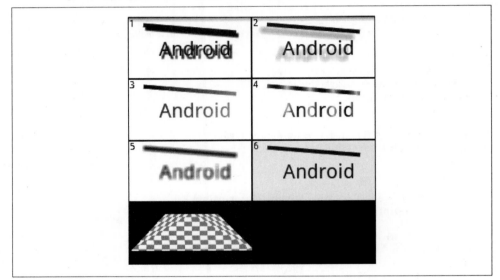

Figure 12-5. Graphics effects

Shadows, Gradients, and Filters

PathEffect, MaskFilter, ColorFilter, Shader, and ShadowLayer are all attributes of Paint. Anything drawn with Paint can be drawn under the influence of one or more of these transformations. The top several widgets in Figure 12-5 give examples of some of these effects.

Widgets 1 and 2 demonstrate shadows. Shadows are currently controlled by the setShadowLayer method. The arguments, a blur radius and X and Y displacements, control the apparent distance and position of the light source that creates the shadow, with respect to the shadowed object. Although this is a very neat feature, the documentation explicitly warns that it is a temporary API. However, it seems unlikely that the setShadowLayer method will completely disappear or even that future implementations will be backward-incompatible.

The Android toolkit contains several prebuilt shaders. Widgets 3 and 4 demonstrate one of them, the `LinearGradient` shader. A gradient is a regular transition between colors that might be used, for example, to give a page background a bit more life, without resorting to expensive bitmap resources.

A `LinearGradient` is specified with a vector that determines the direction and rate of the color transition, an array of colors through which to transition, and a mode. The final argument, the mode, determines what happens when a single complete transition through the gradient is insufficient to cover the entire painted object. For instance, in widget 4, the transition is only 15 pixels long, whereas the drawing is more than 100 pixels wide. Using the mode `Shader.TileMode.Mirror` causes the transition to repeat, alternating direction across the drawing. In the example, the gradient transitions from blue to green in 15 pixels, then from green to blue in the next 15, and so on across the canvas.

Animation

The Android UI toolkit offers several different animation tools. Transition animations—which the Google documentation calls *tweened animations*—are subclasses of `android.view.animation.Animation`: `RotateAnimation`, `TranslateAnimation`, `ScaleAnimation`, etc. These animations are used as transitions between pairs of views. A second type of animation, subclasses of `android.graphics.drawable.Animation Drawable`, can be put into the background of any widget to provide a wide variety of effects. Finally, there is full-on animation, on top of a `SurfaceView` that gives you full control to do your own seat-of-the-pants animation.

Because both of the first two types of animation, transition and background, are supported by `View`—the base class for all widgets—every widget, toolkit, and custom will potentially support them.

Transition animation

A transition animation is started by calling the `View` method `startAnimation` with an instance of `Animation` (or, of course, your own subclass). Once installed, the animation runs to completion: transition animations have no pause state.

The heart of the animation is its `applyTransformation` method. This method is called to produce successive frames of the animation. Example 12-12 shows the implementation of one transformation. As you can see, it does not actually generate entire graphical frames for the animation. Instead, it generates successive transformations to be applied to a single image being animated. You will recall, from the section "Matrix transformations" on page 231, that matrix transformations can be used to make an object appear to move. Transition animations depend on exactly this trick.

Example 12-12. Transition animation

```
@Override
protected void applyTransformation(float t, Transformation xf) {
    Matrix xform = xf.getMatrix();

    float z = ((dir > 0) ? 0.0f : -Z_MAX) - (dir * t * Z_MAX);

    camera.save();
    camera.rotateZ(t * 360);
    camera.translate(0.0F, 0.0F, z);
    camera.getMatrix(xform);
    camera.restore();

    xform.preTranslate(-xCenter, -yCenter);
    xform.postTranslate(xCenter, yCenter);
}
```

This particular implementation makes its target appear to spin in the screen plane (the rotate method call), and at the same time, to shrink into the distance (the translate method call). The matrix that will be applied to the target image is obtained from the Transformation object passed in that call.

This implementation uses camera, an instance of the utility class Camera. The Camera class—not to be confused with the camera in the phone—is a utility that makes it possible to record rendering state. It is used here to compose the rotation and translations transformations into a single matrix, which is then stored as the animation transformation.

The first parameter to applyTransformation, named t, is effectively the frame number. It is passed as a floating-point number between 0.0 and 1.0, and might also be understood as the percent of the animation that is complete. This example uses t to increase the apparent distance along the Z-axis (a line perpendicular to the plane of the screen) of the image being animated, and to set the proportion of one complete rotation through which the image has passed. As t increases, the animated image appears to rotate further and further counter-clockwise and to move farther and farther away, along the Z-axis, into the distance.

The preTranslate and postTranslate operations are necessary in order to translate the image around its center. By default, matrix operations transform their target around the origin. If we did not perform these bracketing translations, the target image would appear to rotate around its upper-left corner. preTranslate effectively moves the origin to the center of the animation target for the translation, and postTranslate causes the default to be restored after the translation.

If you consider what a transition animation must do, you'll realize that it is likely to compose two animations: the previous screen must be animated out and the next one animated in. Example 12-12 supports this using the remaining, unexplained variable dir. Its value is either 1 or –1, and it controls whether the animated image seems to shrink into the distance or grow into the foreground. We need only find a way to compose a shrink and a grow animation.

This is done using the familiar Listener pattern. The Animation class defines a listener named Animation.AnimationListener. Any instance of Animation that has a nonnull listener calls that listener once when it starts, once when it stops, and once for each iteration in between. Creating a listener that notices when the shrinking animation completes and spawns a new growing animation will create exactly the effect we desire. Example 12-13 shows the rest of the implementation of the animation.

Example 12-13. Transition animation composition

```
public void runAnimation() {
    animateOnce(new AccelerateInterpolator(), this);
}

@Override
public void onAnimationEnd(Animation animation) {
    root.post(new Runnable() {
        public void run() {
            curView.setVisibility(View.GONE);
            nextView.setVisibility(View.VISIBLE);
            nextView.requestFocus();
            new RotationTransitionAnimation(-1, root, nextView, null)
                .animateOnce(new DecelerateInterpolator(), null);
        } });
}

void animateOnce(
    Interpolator interpolator,
    Animation.AnimationListener listener)
{
    setDuration(700);
    setInterpolator(interpolator);
    setAnimationListener(listener);
    root.startAnimation(this);
}
```

The runAnimation method starts the transition. The overridden AnimationListener method, onAnimationEnd, spawns the second half. Called when the target image appears to be far in the distance, it hides the image being animated out (the curView) and replaces it with the newly visible image, nextView. It then creates a new animation that, running in reverse, spins and grows the new image into the foreground.

The Interpolater class represents a nifty attention to detail. The values for t, passed to applyTransformation, need not be linearly distributed over time. In this implementation the animation appears to speed up as it recedes, and then to slow again as the new image advances. This is accomplished by using the two interpolators: AccelerateInterpolator for the first half of the animation and DecelerateInterpolator for the second. Without the interpolator, the difference between successive values of t, passed to applyTransformation, would be constant. This would make the animation appear to have a constant speed. The `AccelerateInterpolator` converts those equally spaced values of t into values that are close together at the beginning of the animation and much further apart toward the end. This makes the animation appear to speed up. `DecelerateInterpolator` has exactly the opposite effect. Android also provides a `CycleInterpolator` and `LinearInterpolator`, for use as appropriate.

Animation composition is actually built into the toolkit, using the (perhaps confusingly named) `AnimationSet` class. This class provides a convenient way to specify a list of animations to be played, in order (fortunately *not* a `Set`: it is ordered and may refer to a given animation more than once). In addition, the toolkit provides several standard transitions: `AlphaAnimation`, `RotateAnimation`, `ScaleAnimation`, and `TranslateAnimation`. Certainly, there is no need for these transitional animations to be symmetric, as they are in the previous implementation. A new image might alpha fade in as the old one shrinks into a corner or slide up from the bottom as the old one fades out. The possibilities are endless.

Background animation

Frame-by-frame animation, as it is called in the Google documentation, is completely straightforward: a set of frames, played in order at regular intervals. This kind of animation is implemented by subclasses of `AnimationDrawable`.

As subclasses of `Drawable`, `AnimationDrawable` objects can be used in any context that any other `Drawable` is used. The mechanism that animates them, however, is not a part of the `Drawable` itself. In order to animate, an `AnimationDrawable` relies on an external service provider—an implementation of the `Drawable.Callback` interface—to animate it.

The `View` class implements this interface and can be used to animate an `Animation Drawable`. Unfortunately, it will supply animation services *only* to the one `Drawable` object that is installed as its background with one of the two methods `setBackground Drawable` or `setBackgroundResource`.

The good news, however, is that this is probably sufficient. A background animation has access to the entire widget canvas. Everything it draws will appear to be behind anything drawn by the `View.onDraw` method, so it would be hard to use the background to implement full-fledged sprites (animation integrated into a static scene). Still, with clever use of the `DrawableContainer` class (which allows you to animate several different animations simultaneously) and because the background can be changed at any time, it is possible to accomplish quite a bit without resorting to implementing your own animation framework.

An `AnimationDrawable` in a view background is entirely sufficient to do anything from, say, indicating that some long-running activity is taking place—maybe winged packets flying across the screen from a phone to a tower—to simply making a button's background pulse.

The pulsing button example is illustrative and surprisingly easy to implement. Examples 12-14 and 12-15 show all you need. The animation is defined as a resource, and code applies it to the button.

Example 12-14. Frame-by-frame animation (resource)

```
<animation-list
    xmlns:android="http://schemas.android.com/apk/res/android"
    android:oneshot="false">
  <item android:drawable="@drawable/throbber_f0" android:duration="70" />
  <item android:drawable="@drawable/throbber_f1" android:duration="70" />
  <item android:drawable="@drawable/throbber_f2" android:duration="70" />
  <item android:drawable="@drawable/throbber_f3" android:duration="70" />
  <item android:drawable="@drawable/throbber_f4" android:duration="70" />
  <item android:drawable="@drawable/throbber_f5" android:duration="70" />
  <item android:drawable="@drawable/throbber_f6" android:duration="70" />
</animation-list>
```

Example 12-15. Frame-by-frame animation (code)

```
// w is a button that will "throb"
button.setBackgroundResource(R.drawable.throbber);

//!!! This is necessary, but should not be so in Cupcake
button.setOnClickListener(new OnClickListener() {
    @Override public void onClick(View v) {
        AnimationDrawable animation
            = (AnimationDrawable) v.getBackground();
        if (animation.isRunning()) { animation.stop(); }
        else { animation.start(); }
        // button action.
    } });
```

There are several gotchas here, though. First of all, as of this writing, the `animation-list` example in the Google documentation does not quite work. There is a problem with the way it identifies the `animation-list` resource. To make it work, don't define an `android:id` in that resource. Instead, simply refer to the object by its filename (*R.drawable.throbber*), as Example 12-15 demonstrates.

The second issue is that a bug in the V1_r2 release of the toolkit prevents a background animation from being started in the `Activity.onCreate` method. If your application's background should be animated whenever it is visible, you'll have to use trickery to start it. The example implementation uses an `onClick` handler. There are suggestions on the Web that the animation can also be started successfully from a thread that pauses briefly before calling `AnimationDrawable.start`. The Android development team has a fix for this problem, so the constraint should be relaxed with the release of Cupcake.

Finally, if you have worked with other UI frameworks, especially Mobile UI frameworks, you may be accustomed to painting the view background in the first couple of lines of the `onDraw` method (or equivalent). If you do that in Android, however, you will paint over your animation. It is, in general, a good idea to get into the habit of using `setBackground` to control the `View` background, whether it is a solid color, a gradient, an image, or an animation.

Specifying an `AnimationDrawable` by resource is very flexible. You can specify a list of drawable resources—any images you like—that comprise the animation. If your animation needs to be dynamic, `AnimationDrawable` is a straightforward recipe for creating a dynamic drawable that can be animated in the background of a `View`.

Surface view animation

Full-on animation requires a `SurfaceView`. The `SurfaceView` provides a node in the view tree (and, therefore, space on the display) on which any process at all can draw. The `SurfaceView` node is laid out, sized, and receives clicks and updates, just like any other widget. Instead of drawing, however, it simply reserves space on the screen, preventing other widgets from affecting any of the pixels within its frame.

Drawing on a `SurfaceView` requires implementing the `SurfaceHolder.Callback` interface. The two methods `surfaceCreated` and `surfaceDestroyed` inform the implementor that the drawing surface is available for drawing and that it has become unavailable, respectively. The argument to both of the calls is an instance of yet a third class, `SurfaceHolder`. In the interval between these two calls, a drawing routine can call the `SurfaceView` methods `lockCanvas` and `unlockCanvasAndPost` to edit the pixels there.

If this seems complex, even alongside some of the elaborate animation discussed previously...well, it is. As usual, concurrency increases the likelihood of nasty, hard-to-find bugs. The client of a `SurfaceView` must be sure that access to any state shared across threads is properly synchronized, and also that it never touches the `SurfaceView`, `Surface`, or `Canvas` except in the interval between the calls to `surfaceCreated` and `surfaceDestroyed`. The toolkit could clearly benefit from a more complete framework support for `SurfaceView` animation.

If you are considering `SurfaceView` animation, you are probably also considering OpenGL graphics. As we'll see, there is an extension available for OpenGL animation on a `SurfaceView`. It will turn up in a somewhat out-of-the-way place, though.

OpenGL Graphics

The Android platform supports OpenGL graphics in roughly the same way that a silk hat supports rabbits. Although this is certainly among the most exciting technologies in Android, it is definitely at the edge of the map. It also appears that just before the final beta release, the interface underwent major changes. Much of the code and many of the suggestions found on the Web are obsolete and no longer work.

The API V1_r2 release is an implementation of OpenGL ES 1.0 and much of ES 1.1. It is, essentially, a domain-specific language embedded in Java. Someone who has been doing gaming UIs for a while is likely to be much more comfortable developing Android

OpenGL programs than a Java programmer, even a programmer who is a Java UI expert.

Before discussing the OpenGL graphics library itself, we should take a minute to consider exactly how pixels drawn with OpenGL appear on the display. The rest of this chapter has discussed the intricate View framework that Android uses to organize and represent objects on the screen. OpenGL is a language in which an application describes an entire scene that will be rendered by an engine that is not only outside the JVM, but possibly running on another processor altogether (the Graphics Processing Unit, or GPU). Coordinating the two processors' views of the screen is tricky.

The SurfaceView, discussed earlier, is nearly the right thing. Its purpose is to create a surface on which a thread other than the UI graphics thread can draw. The tool we'd like is an extension of SurfaceView that has a bit more support for concurrency, combined with support for OpenGL.

It turns out that there is exactly such a tool. All of the demo applications in the Android SDK distribution that do OpenGL animation depend on the utility class GLSurface View. Since the demo applications written by the creators of Android use this class, considering it for other applications seems advisable.

GLSurfaceView defines an interface, GLSurfaceView.Renderer, which dramatically simplifies the otherwise overwhelming complexity of using OpenGL and GLSurfaceView. GLSurfaceView calls the renderer method getConfigSpec to get its OpenGL configuration information. Two other methods, sizeChanged and surfaceCreated, are called by the GLSurfaceView to inform the renderer that its size has changed or that it should prepare to draw, respectively. Finally, drawFrame, the heart of the interface, is called to render a new OpenGL frame.

Example 12-16 shows the important methods from the implementation of an OpenGL renderer.

Example 12-16. Frame-by-frame animation with OpenGL

```
// ... some state set up in the constructor

@Override
public void surfaceCreated(GL10 gl) {
    // set up the surface
    gl.glDisable(GL10.GL_DITHER);

    gl.glHint(
        GL10.GL_PERSPECTIVE_CORRECTION_HINT,
        GL10.GL_FASTEST);

    gl.glClearColor(0.4f, 0.2f, 0.2f, 0.5f);
    gl.glShadeModel(GL10.GL_SMOOTH);
    gl.glEnable(GL10.GL_DEPTH_TEST);

    // fetch the checker-board
    initImage(gl);
```

```
    }

    @Override
    public void drawFrame(GL10 gl) {
        gl.glClear(GL10.GL_COLOR_BUFFER_BIT | GL10.GL_DEPTH_BUFFER_BIT);

        gl.glMatrixMode(GL10.GL_MODELVIEW);
        gl.glLoadIdentity();

        GLU.gluLookAt(gl, 0, 0, -5, 0f, 0f, 0f, 0f, 1.0f, 0.0f);

        gl.glEnableClientState(GL10.GL_VERTEX_ARRAY);
        gl.glEnableClientState(GL10.GL_TEXTURE_COORD_ARRAY);

        // apply the checker-board to the shape
        gl.glActiveTexture(GL10.GL_TEXTURE0);

        gl.glTexEnvx(
            GL10.GL_TEXTURE_ENV,
            GL10.GL_TEXTURE_ENV_MODE,
            GL10.GL_MODULATE);
        gl.glTexParameterx(
            GL10.GL_TEXTURE_2D,
            GL10.GL_TEXTURE_WRAP_S,
            GL10.GL_REPEAT);
        gl.glTexParameterx(
            GL10.GL_TEXTURE_2D,
            GL10.GL_TEXTURE_WRAP_T,
            GL10.GL_REPEAT);

        // animation
        int t = (int) (SystemClock.uptimeMillis() % (10 * 1000L));
        gl.glTranslatef(6.0f - (0.0013f * t), 0, 0);

        // draw
        gl.glFrontFace(GL10.GL_CCW);
        gl.glVertexPointer(3, GL10.GL_FLOAT, 0, vertexBuf);
        gl.glEnable(GL10.GL_TEXTURE_2D);
        gl.glTexCoordPointer(2, GL10.GL_FLOAT, 0, textureBuf);
        gl.glDrawElements(
            GL10.GL_TRIANGLE_STRIP,
            5,
            GL10.GL_UNSIGNED_SHORT, indexBuf);
    }

    private void initImage(GL10 gl) {
        int[] textures = new int[1];
        gl.glGenTextures(1, textures, 0);
        gl.glBindTexture(GL10.GL_TEXTURE_2D, textures[0]);

        gl.glTexParameterf(
            GL10.GL_TEXTURE_2D,
            GL10.GL_TEXTURE_MIN_FILTER,
            GL10.GL_NEAREST);
        gl.glTexParameterf(
```

```
        GL10.GL_TEXTURE_2D,
        GL10.GL_TEXTURE_MAG_FILTER,
        GL10.GL_LINEAR);
    gl.glTexParameterf(
        GL10.GL_TEXTURE_2D,
        GL10.GL_TEXTURE_WRAP_S,
        GL10.GL_CLAMP_TO_EDGE);
    gl.glTexParameterf(
        GL10.GL_TEXTURE_2D,
        GL10.GL_TEXTURE_WRAP_T,
        GL10.GL_CLAMP_TO_EDGE);
    gl.glTexEnvf(
        GL10.GL_TEXTURE_ENV,
        GL10.GL_TEXTURE_ENV_MODE,
        GL10.GL_REPLACE);

    InputStream in
        = context.getResources().openRawResource(R.drawable.cb);
    Bitmap image;
    try { image = BitmapFactory.decodeStream(in); }
    finally {
        try { in.close(); } catch(IOException e) {  }
    }

    GLUtils.texImage2D(GL10.GL_TEXTURE_2D, 0, image, 0);

    image.recycle();
}
```

The surfaceCreated method prepares the scene. It sets several OpenGL attributes that
need to be initialized only when the widget gets a new drawing surface. In addition, it
calls initImage, which reads in a bitmap resource and stores it as a 2D texture. Finally,
when drawFrame is called, everything is ready for drawing. The texture is applied to a
plane whose vertices were set up in vertexBuf by the constructor, the animation phase
is chosen, and the scene is redrawn.

CHAPTER 13

Inter-Process Communication

Android is designed to host a variety of applications and to maximize user choice. The platform is intended to eliminate the duplication of functionality in different applications, to allow functionality to be discovered and invoked on the fly, and to let users replace applications with others that offer similar functionality. Applications must have as few dependencies as possible, and must be able to contract out operations to other applications that may change at the user's discretion.

Inter-process communication (IPC) is thus the basis of key features of the Android programming model. The techniques we'll look at in this chapter are:

Intents

> These enable an application to select an Activity based on the action you want to invoke and the data on which they operate. In other words, you don't need a hard-coded path to an application to use its functions and exchange data with it. Data can be passed in both directions using Intent objects, and this enables a convenient, high-level system of inter-process communication.

Remote methods

> This feature resembles the remote procedure calls (RPCs) offered by other systems: it makes APIs accessible remotely. Remote objects allow you to make method calls that look "local" but are executed in another process. They involve the use of Android's interface definition language (AIDL).

In this chapter, we will see how these features work and how they can be used in applications.

Android applications could avoid inter-process communication and provide functions in packages loaded by the applications that need them. If applications had to exchange data, they could use the filesystem or other traditional Unix/Linux IPC mechanisms (sockets, shared memory, etc.). But these practices are error prone and hard to maintain. In particular, some of the problems include:

- Libraries are difficult to share among multiple Java processes. Java was designed to have threads, not processes, share common code resources.

- Sharing address space easily leads to errors and inappropriate access to private data.

Consequently, modern programming environments have moved on to more robust component-like systems. Intents and remote methods fit the bill excellently for Android.

Intents: Simple, Low-Overhead IPC

The Android system uses Intent objects to enable applications to specify an Activity or Service. Intent objects also deliver data from one application to another, providing a simple and convenient form of IPC.

The Intent class, the Activity class, and Android's Intent-based inter-process communication solve one of the user interface problems of smartphone platforms that support multiple separate applications: they feel like a collection of separate programs. You don't have the simplicity of navigating a hierarchical user interface, as in simpler feature phones, and you don't have multiple windows, as on a PC user interface. The way Activities work together on Android makes it possible to make a seamless user interface out of multiple applications, and inter-process communication can enhance cooperation among applications.

Intent Objects Used in Inter-Process Communication

We'll start with how the client makes a request. Several classes are involved:

Activity and Context
> We've seen Activity objects used throughout this book. The Context class, a parent class of Activity and Service, contains the methods for sending Intent objects from one Activity object to another, whether in the same process or a different one. So every place you have an Activity subclass— which is nearly every place in your application that needs to display a UI—you have the methods for slinging Intent objects around to other Activity instances elsewhere in the Android system.

Intent
> Intent objects are passed from process to process, using methods such as startActivity and startActivityForResult.
>
> The Intent class itself provides constructors, accessors, and other utilities for handling the content of an Intent object, but no methods for moving Intent objects.
>
> An important set of accessors are those named putExtra. Several methods with this name and different arguments—hence different signatures—let you attach "extra" data to an Intent. This data can be used for general-purpose inter-process communication. The first examples in this chapter will use this kind of simple inter-process communication.

Activity Objects and Navigating the User Interface Hierarchy

Most mobile handset user interfaces consist of a linked web, or hierarchy, of "screens"—user interface views that occupy the whole screen, except for areas where titles and indicator icons are displayed and where soft-key labels (if any) are displayed. Usually, these hierarchies are implemented by a single program that manages a "stack" of screens backward from the current screen (and sometimes forward, as well, as in an iPod-like UI). Intent and Activity objects work together, using inter-process communication, to link different parts of different applications' user interfaces into a coherent user experience with navigation that is unified and seamless when moving between applications. In this section we'll show how UI navigation and inter-process communication go hand-in-hand.

Example: An Intent to Pick How We Say "Hello World"

Almost everyone writes "Hello World" programs. So there is a nearly universal need to augment these programs and prevent them from getting dull by providing a choice of greetings. That is what Example 13-1 does.

Example 13-1. An Intent that chooses alternate "Hello World" strings

```
package example.sayhello;

import example.sayhello.R;

import android.os.Bundle;
import android.app.Activity;
import android.content.Intent;
import android.view.View;
import android.view.View.OnClickListener;
import android.widget.Button;


/**
 * An activity returning a result
 */
public class SayHello extends Activity
{
        protected void onCreate(Bundle savedInstanceState)
    {
        // Call the parent class
        super.onCreate(savedInstanceState);

        // Put up the view for acquiring some input from the user
        setContentView(R.layout.main);

        // Set up the listeners for the buttons
        ((Button)findViewById(R.id.hello)).setOnClickListener(helloListener);
        ((Button)findViewById(R.id.goaway)).setOnClickListener(goAwayListener);
    }
```

```
    private OnClickListener helloListener = new OnClickListener()
    {
        public void onClick(View v)
        {
            returnResult("Hello, other Android!");
        }
    };

    private OnClickListener goAwayListener = new OnClickListener()
    {
        public void onClick(View v)
        {
                returnResult("Get off my lawn, damn kids!");
        }
    };

    // Put a result in an Intent object and set the result for this activity
    void returnResult(String greeting) {

    // Create the Intent object
    Intent i = new Intent();

    // Put an extra named "result" in the intent
    i.putextra("result", greeting);

    // Make this Intent the result for this activity
    setResult(RESULT_OK, i);

    // End this activity
        finish();
    }
}
```

Example 13-2 shows the layout file that specifies the user interface provided by this activity.

Example 13-2. Resource for alternate "Hello World" strings

```xml
<?xml version="1.0" encoding="utf-8"?>
<LinearLayout xmlns:android="http://schemas.android.com/apk/res/android"
  android:orientation="vertical" android:padding="4dip"
    android:gravity="center_horizontal"
    android:layout_width="fill_parent" android:layout_height="fill_parent">

    <TextView
        android:layout_width="fill_parent" android:layout_height="wrap_content"
        android:layout_weight="0"
        android:paddingBottom="8dip"
        android:text="Say hello, or not"/>

    <Button android:id="@+id/hello"
        android:layout_width="fill_parent" android:layout_height="wrap_content"
        android:text="Hello">
        <requestFocus />
    </Button>
```

```
<Button android:id="@+id/goaway"
    android:layout_width="fill_parent" android:layout_height="wrap_content"
    android:text="Go away">
</Button>

</LinearLayout>
```

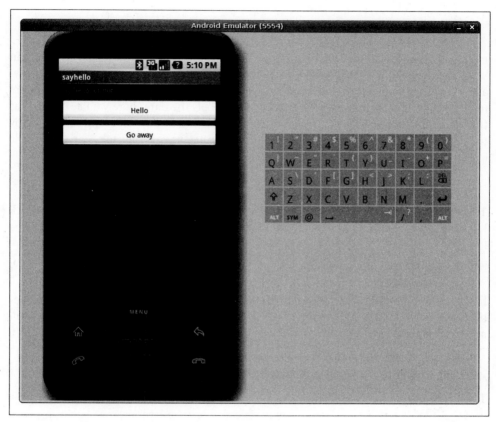

Figure 13-1. Output of simple "Hello World" program

This layout describes a screen with two buttons. The listeners for these buttons are called HelloListener and GoAwayListener. In the Java code in Example 13-1, the listener methods call returnResult, passing the string that will be returned.

You can try this program as a standalone application. Create a new Android project with the package named example.sayhello and an activity named SayHello. Use Example 13-1 for the SayHello class and Example 13-2 for the *main.xml* layout file. When run, the application will display Figure 13-1.

When you click on or press one of the buttons, the program finishes and disappears from the screen. It also creates an Intent object used as a "result" for the activity.

Let's take a closer look at how it does that. You may want to run the program under the debugger and set a breakpoint on the first line of the returnResult method, where we create an Intent object, and follow along using the "step over" command in the debugger.

First, an Intent object is created. This is what gets moved from this process to the process that started this Activity:

```
// Create the Intent object
Intent i = new Intent();
```

Here we will see how Intent objects facilitate inter-process communications: you can label and associate several types of data with an Intent object and send these "stow-aways" with the object from one process to another. Here we call putExtra to add data to the Intent. Its first argument is a String that labels the data; here we use "result" as the label. The second argument, the actual payload, can be any data type supported by the different putExtra methods (which differ in the arguments they take); in our simple example, we use a String for the payload as well:

```
// Put an extra named "result" in the intent
i.putExtra("result", greeting);
```

The returnResult method "returns" the result, not to the method that calls this method, but through an Intent object to the code that started this instance of SayHello. The following line sets the result:

```
// Make this Intent the result for this activity
setResult(RESULT_OK, i);
```

In this example, however, nothing happens to our result. Nobody expects it, and nobody uses it. Next we will change that, and see how one application can use a result produced by another.

Getting a Result via Inter-Process Communication

This section modifies the "Hello World" application from an earlier chapter to show how Android can make separate Activity objects in separate programs seem of-a-piece. This version uses one Activity to enable the user to choose which greeting to put on the screen in another Activity. A copy of the data put into the Intent object in the previous section ends up in an Intent object in the HelloWorldActivity Activity.

To enable a client to find the Intent, the server assigns it a label called an *action*. In this case, we'll call our action PICK, shown here in Example 13-3.

Example 13-3. HelloWorldActivity.java

```
package example.helloworld;

import android.app.Activity;
import android.content.Intent;
import android.os.Bundle;
```

```
import android.widget.TextView;

public class HelloWorldActivity extends Activity {
    TextView helloView;

    @Override
    public void onCreate(Bundle savedInstanceState) {
        super.onCreate(savedInstanceState);

        // Make a text view and set it to be the content view
        helloView = new TextView(this);
        setContentView(helloView);

        // Make an Intent instance to fill in
        Intent helloIntent = new Intent();

        // Set the action, and type
        helloIntent.setAction("android.intent.action.PICK");
        helloIntent.setType("vnd.example.greeting/vnd.example.greeting-text");

        // Ask an activity that matches our Intent object
        startActivityForResult(helloIntent, 0);
    }

    @Override
        protected void onActivityResult(int requestCode, int resultCode, Intent result)
        {
        if (resultCode == RESULT_OK) {
                String greeting = result.getStringExtra("result");

            helloView.setText(greeting);
        }
    }
}
```

The changes we made will start an Activity in a separate application and a separate process to provide the user interface for selecting a greeting. After that greeting is returned by the other Activity, this one uses it to say hello.

Run the program. You will see the user interface presented by the SayHello program, just as in Figure 13-1. But this time, when you press one of the two buttons, the screen will display the greeting you selected (Figure 13-2).

Let's take a closer look at how it's done. Here, again, you may want to follow along using the debugger.

 Did you run the SayHello program yet? You need to do that before you run our modified HelloWorldActivity program. The Android emulator installs programs the first time you run them, so once you run SayHello it will stay around as long as the emulator is running. But if the program hasn't been run yet, the startActivityForResult call in the current example will fail, because Android cannot find SayHello.

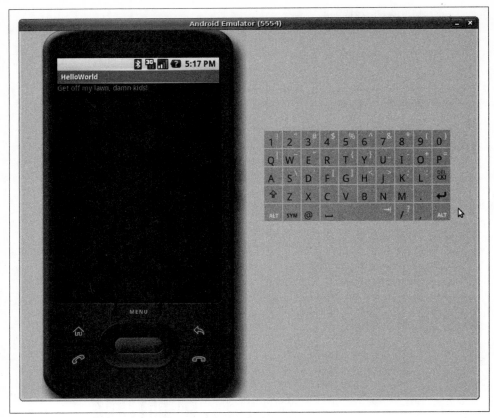

Figure 13-2. Output of "Hello World" program after user selection

First, we need to start our helper application, which we do using an **Intent** object:

```
// Make an Intent instance to fill in
Intent helloIntent = new Intent();
```

Then, we need to specify an Activity that is neither a part of our application nor part of an Activity in any of the programs that come with Android:

```
// Set the action, and type
helloIntent.setAction("android.intent.action.PICK");
helloIntent.setType("vnd.example.greeting/vnd.example.greeting-text");
```

The **setType** method requires a MIME type. We will use a vendor-specific MIME type unique to our purpose (by vendor here, I mean us). As a result, our **SayHello** activity is launched because it has an Intent filter that matches the parameters we have set in this **Intent** object.

Now we call the **startActivityForResult** method, passing the **Intent** object we created to hold the information that tells the Android framework to find an Activity matching the specifications in our Intent: the **PICK** action and the requested MIME type. We don't explicitly request the `SayHello` Activity—we might want to replace it with something else at some point—but for now, that activity is what Android will find:

```
// Ask an activity that matches our Intent object
startActivityForResult(helloIntent, 0);
```

The `startActivityForResult` method navigates to a UI that obtains information and returns it. This is a good illustration of using IPC for a task that could otherwise have required redundant code in all applications that need similar information.

Now `SayHello` should run and display its user interface for selecting a greeting. When you have selected a greeting and the `setResult` method is called, Android's inter-process communication system will move the result to this process, and the `OnActivityResult` method will be called. We've defined it as follows:

```
protected void onActivityResult(int requestCode, int resultCode, Intent result) {
    if (resultCode == RESULT_OK) {
        String greeting = result.getStringExtra("result");

        helloView.setText(greeting);
    }
}
```

The method calls `getStringExtra` to access the greeting we have chosen. It uses the `setText` method of the `TextView` class to display our selected greeting.

To summarize, in this example one program (`SayHello`) acquires some information and supplies it to another program (`HelloWorldActivity`). We have successfully used inter-process communication.

Android includes a component system based on remote objects and methods, which we'll examine in the next section. This is a powerful feature with many uses, but remote method calls are overkill in many cases. As you design your programs, first consider whether your inter-process communications needs fit what Intents and the `Context` class's Intent-related methods can do. Particularly when you're using inter-process communication to provide a user interface in an Activity, this high-level form of IPC is easy to use and appropriate to the task.

Remote Methods and AIDL

This section describes how one program can provide other programs with access to its methods. A number of important Android APIs use this feature. For instance, the `TelephonyManager` introduced in Chapter 15 uses a remote object interface in order to manage and share the phone hardware in an Android device.

There are three steps to creating and using remote methods in Android:

1. Define the interface in the AIDL.
2. Implement the interface. That is, write methods that match the signatures in the interface and that perform the operations you want in the program that provides the desired services.

---

3. Invoke the methods where you want to use them.

Android Interface Definition Language

To communicate from one process to another, data stored in memory has to be moved across process boundaries. That means the data has to be "marshalled"—packaged for transport—and "unmarshalled"—put into the right member variables after the data has been moved across the process boundary. (Some Android documentation uses the word "flattened," with the connotation of taking a data stored in several objects and turning it into a "flat" array of bytes that can be sent between processes.)

Java's basic types, such as String, are easy to marshall, but complex types, such as multidimensional arrays, are much harder. Marshalling data spread in an object that holds references to other objects requires following every reference and marshalling all the data that it references.

Usually, marshalling and unmarshalling is performed on the parameters in a remote method call, to let you pass data from one application to another and return results.

Marshalling and unmarshalling data is tedious, and you would find it hard to understand code that had to carry out the task every place it uses inter-process communication. Therefore, most implementations of remote objects or components use an interface definition language that generates calls to marshalling methods. The syntax of the interface definition language resembles the main language in use (Java in this case), so that a remote procedure call closely resembles a normal method call. However, the interface definition language really is a separate language.

AIDL syntax is identical to Java interface definition syntax, except that in AIDL you can label the parameters for remote method calls as in, out, or inout. Any parameter labeled in will be transferred to the remote method, whereas any parameter labeled out will be returned to the caller from the remote method. In the example, from the ApiDemos application we use here, the keywords indicating in and out parameters are not used. The defaults apply: all parameters are in, the return value is used for returning data from the remote method, and any parameter labeled inout will transfer data to the remote method and refer to a value transferred from the remote method when it returns. In the example, the AIDL code is therefore completely compatible, in syntax, to Java code.

When you save your AIDL file in Eclipse, the Android Eclipse plug-in compiles it. Both the calling and implementing side of a remote method interface share the information in the AIDL file.

For the examples in this section, we're excerpting code from the *ISecondary.aidl* file in the ApiDemos application.

This is how you specify an interface to a remote object:

```
interface ISecondary {
    /**
```

```
 * Request the PID of this service, to do evil things with it.
 */
int getPid();

/**
 * This demonstrates the basic types that you can use as parameters
 * and return values in AIDL.
 */
void basicTypes(int anInt, long aLong, boolean aBoolean, float aFloat,
        double aDouble, String aString);
}
```

This looks like Java code, but it isn't. It looks like an interface definition. There are two method signatures, and no implementation of the methods. That is all AIDL needs to create code that moves the parameters between applications. Next we will take a look at the code generated by AIDL to see exactly how the parameters are moved from one process to another, and to see how to implement the API defined in this AIDL definition.

The Android SDK plug-in for Eclipse automatically compiles this code to Java, resulting in the following set of Java definitions. Normally this code is not formatted for readability, so what you see here looks different from the file you see in the ApiDemos project in your Eclipse IDE. But it is the same Java code:

```
package com.example.android.apis.app;

import java.lang.String;
import android.os.RemoteException;
import android.os.IBinder;
import android.os.IInterface;
import android.os.Binder;
import android.os.Parcel;

/**
 * Example of a secondary interface associated with a service.  (Note that
 * the interface itself doesn't impact, it is just a matter of how you
 * retrieve it from the service.)
 */
public interface ISecondary extends android.os.IInterface {

    /** Local-side IPC implementation stub class. */
    public static abstract class Stub extends android.os.Binder
      implements com.example.android.apis.app.ISecondary {

        private static final java.lang.String DESCRIPTOR =
          "com.example.android.apis.app.ISecondary";

        /** Construct the stub at attach it to the interface. */
        public Stub() {
            this.attachInterface(this, DESCRIPTOR);
        }

        /**
         * Cast an IBinder object into an ISecondary interface,
         * generating a proxy if needed.
```

```
    */
    public static
      com.example.android.apis.app.ISecondary asInterface(android.os.IBinder obj) {
        if ((obj == null)) {
            return null;
        }
        android.os.IInterface iin =
          (android.os.IInterface) obj.queryLocalInterface(DESCRIPTOR);
        if (((iin != null) &&
          (iin instanceof com.example.android.apis.app.ISecondary))) {
            return ((com.example.android.apis.app.ISecondary) iin);
        }
        return new com.example.android.apis.app.ISecondary.Stub.Proxy(obj);
    }

    public android.os.IBinder asBinder() {
        return this;
    }

    public boolean onTransact(int code, android.os.Parcel data, android.os.Parcel
     reply,
      int flags) throws android.os.RemoteException {
        switch (code) {
            case INTERFACE_TRANSACTION: {
                reply.writeString(DESCRIPTOR);
                return true;
            }
            case TRANSACTION_getPid: {
                data.enforceInterface(DESCRIPTOR);
                int _result = this.getPid();
                reply.writeNoException();
                reply.writeInt(_result);
                return true;
            }
            case TRANSACTION_basicTypes: {
                data.enforceInterface(DESCRIPTOR);
                int _arg0;
                _arg0 = data.readInt();
                long _arg1;
                _arg1 = data.readLong();
                boolean _arg2;
                _arg2 = (0 != data.readInt());
                float _arg3;
                _arg3 = data.readFloat();
                double _arg4;
                _arg4 = data.readDouble();
                java.lang.String _arg5;
                _arg5 = data.readString();
                this.basicTypes(_arg0, _arg1, _arg2, _arg3, _arg4, _arg5);
                reply.writeNoException();
                return true;
            }
        }
        return super.onTransact(code, data, reply, flags);
    }
```

```
private static class Proxy implements
  com.example.android.apis.app.ISecondary {

    private android.os.IBinder mRemote;

    Proxy(android.os.IBinder remote) {
        mRemote = remote;
    }

    public android.os.IBinder asBinder() {
        return mRemote;
    }

    public java.lang.String getInterfaceDescriptor() {
        return DESCRIPTOR;
    }

    /**
     * Request the PID of this service, to do evil things with it.
     */
    public int getPid() throws android.os.RemoteException {
        android.os.Parcel _data = android.os.Parcel.obtain();
        android.os.Parcel _reply = android.os.Parcel.obtain();
        int _result;
        try {
            _data.writeInterfaceToken(DESCRIPTOR);
            mRemote.transact(Stub.TRANSACTION_getPid, _data, _reply, 0);
            _reply.readException();
            _result = _reply.readInt();
        } finally {
            _reply.recycle();
            _data.recycle();
        }
        return _result;
    }

    /**
     * This demonstrates the basic types that you can use as parameters
     * and return values in AIDL.
     */
    public void basicTypes(int anInt, long aLong, boolean aBoolean,
      float aFloat,
        double aDouble, java.lang.String aString)
          throws android.os.RemoteException {
          android.os.Parcel _data = android.os.Parcel.obtain();
          android.os.Parcel _reply = android.os.Parcel.obtain();
          try {
              _data.writeInterfaceToken(DESCRIPTOR);
              _data.writeInt(anInt);
              _data.writeLong(aLong);
              _data.writeInt(((aBoolean) ? (1) : (0)));
              _data.writeFloat(aFloat);
              _data.writeDouble(aDouble);
              _data.writeString(aString);
```

```
                mRemote.transact(Stub.TRANSACTION_basicTypes, _data, _reply, 0);
                _reply.readException();
            } finally {
                _reply.recycle();
                _data.recycle();
            }
        }
    }
    static final int TRANSACTION_getPid = (IBinder.FIRST_CALL_TRANSACTION + 0);
    static final int TRANSACTION_basicTypes = (IBinder.FIRST_CALL_TRANSACTION
        + 1);
}

/**
 * Request the PID of this service, to do evil things with it.
 */
public int getPid() throws android.os.RemoteException;

/**
 * This demonstrates the basic types that you can use as parameters
 * and return values in AIDL.
 */
public void basicTypes(int anInt, long aLong, boolean aBoolean, float aFloat,
    double aDouble, java.lang.String aString) throws android.os.RemoteException;
}
```

That's a lot of code! Now you can appreciate the value of AIDL instead of building a remote object interface by hand. After we see what is going on inside the AIDL-generated code, we will take a look at the other two steps to creating and using a remote object interface: implementing the methods and invoking them.

Classes Underlying AIDL-Generated Interfaces

Now let's take a look at the android.os.IInterface class. It's a base type on which all the interfaces created by AIDL are built, so they can be referenced through references of the same type. ISecondary extends IInterface.

Most of the code in the ISecondary interface is part of the definition of an abstract class called Stub. You implement remote methods by extending the Stub class. Every remote interface has this class, but because it is inside the interface created by AIDL particular to your remote methods, there is no name conflict.

The word "stub" was chosen to refer to this class because remote method systems work by creating a method on the client with the same name as the method that runs on the server. The client method is considered a "stub" because it doesn't actually carry out the operation requested; it just marshalls the data, sends it to the server, and unmarshalls the return value. We'll show some details later in this chapter.

Implementing the Stub interface

So how do you write the code that actually implements these remote method calls? In this case, the implementation is in the class RemoteService of the ApiDemos application, and the following excerpt shows the method definitions. The first line extends the abstract class and makes a new instance of it:

```
private final ISecondary.Stub mSecondaryBinder = new ISecondary.Stub() {
    public int getPid() {
        return Process.myPid();
    }
    public void basicTypes(int anInt, long aLong, boolean aBoolean,
            float aFloat, double aDouble, String aString) {
    }
};
```

This is all you need to do to turn a method in your application into a remote method. The rest of the work of invoking the method in the other application, passing the parameters, and responding with a return value from the remote method is performed by code generated by AIDL in the Stub abstract class.

So, for a remote interface generated by AIDL, the code takes the abstract Stub class and implements the method code that will actually be used. But how does data from another process get to these methods? That is where the onTransact method comes in.

The onTransact method (see the AIDL-generated code shown earlier) is called when data in a Parcel object is delivered to a remote interface in an Android program. This method is generated by AIDL for each remote interface. In this case, it reads each argument to the method from a Parcel object, makes the method call, and writes the result to another Parcel object used for the return value of a remote method.

Parcel objects are what Java applications in Android pass to the Android IPC mechanism for moving between processes. In the simple IPC example earlier in this chapter, underlying the Context method calls used to move Intent objects between applications, the Intent object and the "extras" data associated with it are marshalled, or "flattened," into a Parcel object to be moved from one process to another and reconstituted into an Intent object with the same extras in the other process.

Basic types such as long and int are marshalled and unmarshalled by methods in the Parcel class. Other classes in the Android base classes, such as Intent and String, implement the Parcelable interface. As the name suggests, this provides an interface for the Parcel class to marshall those objects. And on top of that, implementing the Parcelable interface in your classes enables them to be marshalled, unmarshalled, and moved from one application to another.

Getting an instance of the remote Proxy object

There is one more part to this story: how does a different application find out about the interface called ISecondary, and how does the caller of the remote method actually call these methods? The answer is in the asInterface method of the Stub class, and the

Proxy class nested within Stub. And that means that any application that wants to make a remote method call must share the interface definition with the application that implements the interface. In practical terms, that means that the calling application and the application that implements the remote interface have to be compiled with the same AIDL files.

Now let's take a look at how the remote interface gets called. In the ApiDemos code we are using as an example here, this happens in the RemoteServiceBinding class, where the asInterface method is called:

```
mSecondaryService =
        ISecondary.Stub.asInterface(service);
```

The parameter named service here is a reference to an IBinder interface. The Binder abstract class implements IBinder, and the Stub class (the guts of what AIDL has generated) extends Binder. Let's see how this parameter is used in the asInterface method:

```
public static com.example.android.apis.app.ISecondary asInterface(android.os.IBinder
  obj) {
    if ((obj == null)) {
        return null;
    }
    android.os.IInterface iin = (android.os.IInterface)
      obj.queryLocalInterface(DESCRIPTOR);
    if (((iin != null) && (iin instanceof com.example.android.apis.app.ISecondary))) {
        return ((com.example.android.apis.app.ISecondary) iin);
    }
    return new com.example.android.apis.app.ISecondary.Stub.Proxy(obj);
}
```

Here the parameter is named obj, and first it is tested to see whether it is null. Then, asInterface checks to see whether there is an instance of ISecondary with the correct name. What that means is that the "remote" interface we were looking for is actually in the same application as the code calling it. And that means no inter-process communication is necessary. Otherwise, if it isn't a local interface, an instance of the Proxy object is created. Remember that this code is executing in the context of the application that wants to call the remote interface.

The Proxy class is the counterpart of the Stub abstract class. It may seem a little mind-bending that the Proxy class, which implements ISecondary, is defined inside the Stub class, which is itself inside the ISecondary interface, but it turns out to be convenient. Otherwise, more class files would have to be created by AIDL, and somehow uses of those classes managed.

Looking inside the Proxy class, we see that it has methods that have the same signature as the remote methods defined in the AIDL file. Here, unlike in the abstract class Stub, the methods are implemented, and the implementations create Parcel objects and fill them with the "flattened" parameters in exactly the right order for the onTransact method to "unflatten" them and call the remote *methods*.

That means an application calls a remote method by getting an instance of the Proxy class and calling the remote methods as if they were local. You can see this here, excerpted from the RemoteServiceBinding class:

```
int pid = mSecondaryService.getPid();
```

Recall that mSecondaryService is returned from the ISecondary.Stub.asInterface method. Because the caller gets a Proxy object and the remote methods are implemented in a Stub object, and because both Proxy and Stub implement ISecondary, it all looks like a local method call, but the implementations of the methods are completely different in the calling application and the application that implements the remote methods.

To review:

- You define remote interfaces in AIDL. They look like Java interfaces, but are not.
- AIDL turns your remote interface definition into a Java interface with Stub and Proxy classes nested inside.
- Both the application that calls the remote method and the application that implements it use the same AIDL file and the same generated interface.

The application calling the remote interface gets an instance of the Proxy class that implements the very same interface it is defined inside of. The instance also implements "proxy" methods with the same signature as the remote methods, but they package up their parameters into a Parcel object and send them off to the application that implements the remote methods and unpackages and returns the results.

In the remote application, a concrete class extending Stub has implementations of the remote methods. The onTransact method "unflattens" data in a Parcel object, calls the remote methods and "flattens" the result, writes it into a Parcel, and sends that Parcel object back to the calling application.

However, if both the calling application and the remote service are not, in fact, remote from one another, an instance of the concrete class that implements the not-so-remote methods is used instead, cutting out the inter-process communication if it is not needed.

Publishing an Interface

The server *publishes* an interface to make it possible for other activities to find it. Publishing is accomplished by overriding the onBind method of the Service class (described in "Android Service Lifecycle" on page 10).

A client calls the bindService method of the Context class, causing a call to the server's onBind method. The bindService and onBind methods are the "handshake" required to start using a remote interface in a specific Service object in a specific process running in the Android environment. Here is the example of an onBind implementation from the the class RemoteService in the ApiDemos application:

```java
@Override
public IBinder onBind(Intent intent) {
    // Select the interface to return.  If your service only implements
    // a single interface, you can just return it here without checking
    // the Intent.
    if (IRemoteService.class.getName().equals(intent.getAction())) {
        return mBinder;
    }
    if (ISecondary.class.getName().equals(intent.getAction())) {
        return mSecondaryBinder;
    }
    return null;
}
```

mBinder and mSecondaryBinder refer to objects implementing the Stub interface. You will see the implementation of mSecondaryBinder in the next section, where implementation of the Stub interface is explained. Let's take a look at this method in detail. First, the interface requested depends on matching the name of the interface, which is passed in the action parameter of the Intent object:

```java
if
(IRemoteService.class.getName().equals(intent.getAction())) {
        return mBinder;
    }
```

In the client application looking for this interface, the contents of the Intent object were specified in a call to the bindService method of the Context class. That means that a program publishing a remote method interface must be a subclass of Service. But a program using a remote method interface can be any subclass of Context, including Activity and Service.

The Intent object is used to specify the interface. The class name of the interface is the action parameter of the Intent.

If the interface matches, the onBind method returns an IBinder instance, an instance of the Stub interface in the remote interface.

Android IPC Compared with Java Native Interface (JNI)

Remote procedure calls (RPC) using Android's inter-process communications largely replace the use of the Java Native Interface (JNI) in Android. In almost all cases, a remote procedure call is efficient enough to make it a superior alternative to loading a library—especially one that dynamically allocates a significant amount of memory—into the Java virtual machine's address space. And if a process exposing an RPC interface fails, it is less likely to bring down the Android UI with it.

Android inter-process communication behaves a lot like JNI: the caller's thread is blocked until the result is returned. Marshalling data across the IPC boundary is about the same amount of work as data conversions in JNI. But Binder-based remote procedure calls have a significant advantage over JNI: if non-Java code crashes or runs out of memory, the caller of a remote procedure call gets an error that must be handled, but the Java application does not crash. Remote procedure calls are a more robust way to call "external" libraries and subject the Java application to fewer risks in the form of clashing memory management strategies and other differences between Java applications and libraries implemented in languages other than Java.

What Binder Doesn't Do

There are at least three things Binder doesn't do, compared with other systems capable of providing similar functionality:

- Binder does not manage version information.
- Binder does not traverse networks.
- It does not enable applications to discover interfaces.

Some inter-process communications systems enable the two sides of an inter-process API to negotiate version compatibility. Binder, along with the higher-level mechanisms built on Binder, does not do this. This means APIs built on Binder should remain compatible with older versions if the APIs are open for other applications to use, and it means that consumers of remote APIs should be resilient to failures caused by incompatibilities. Make sure to handle those exceptions!

Binder-based inter-process communication is also limited to a single node: it won't take you across the network to other Android systems. This is a limitation, to be sure, but it is appropriate to a mobile handset, where endpoint-to-endpoint data connections are rarely used and often blocked by the routing in a mobile data network.

Binder and Linux

Binder is not a widely used IPC mechanism in Linux. D-BUS is the most widely used IPC mechanism, and has become commonly used in both server and desktop Linux distributions and in numerous applications and daemons. In contrast, Binder was developed by Palm, abandoned, open-sourced as OpenBinder, and subsequently adopted by Google for Android.

Binder may not be the choice of most other Linux distributions, but it isn't a bad choice: Binder is used throughout Android, including performance-critical parts of Android, such as the Surface Flinger, Android's system for sharing the screen among multiple processes. Binder is simple and performant. It is also an example of the ways in which Android diverges from the typical use of Linux in mobile handsets and other small devices.

Android is not a shrunken desktop Linux. The use of Binder, the way Linux user IDs are used to "sandbox" applications, the unique 2D graphics library, and other design decisions are all in the service of making Android an ideal platform for running Android applications. It is debatable whether every design decision that diverges from standards was worth it, and developers who have started porting and extending Android actively debate these issues, but some things are certain:

- Android performs well. None of the unique design decisions that went into Android were to the detriment of performance. Android performance is good enough to allow multitasking—something Apple abjures in iPhone so as not to risk the multimedia user experience.

- Android is not attempting to set a general direction for Linux, or even for embedded Linux. Android has, of course, charted a radically different course for application development. Android is consciously different and optimized for a range of smartphone hardware: big and powerful enough to run a browser, but not encroaching on the laptop format enough to need a multiwindow user interface. Android, as a whole, is meant to be just right for its intended purpose.

CHAPTER 14

Simple Phone Calls

Android provides the user with several ways of starting phone calls: from the contact list, from the call history, using a dialer that displays a 12-key dialpad on the screen, etc. All of these software modules use the same application to start a phone call. Your program can initiate a phone call in the same way: by using an `Intent` object to ask Android's specialized telephony application to make the call. We'll cover that technique in this chapter, and take a look behind the scenes at how the process works.

In Chapter 15, we'll introduce Android classes that give you more information about telephony, such as tracking the state of the call you made.

Quick and Easy Phone Calls

Android includes an application called PhoneApp that embodies the functions of a mobile phone. Through the use of `Intent` objects, Android enables applications to tell other applications to perform certain operations, such as initiating a phone call. To enable your application to initiate a phone call, a method like the one in Example 14-1 will do the job.

Example 14-1. How to make a phone call

```
private void call() {
    try {
        Intent callIntent = new Intent(Intent.ACTION_CALL);
        callIntent.setData(Uri.parse("tel:9785551212"));
        startActivity(callIntent);
    } catch (ActivityNotFoundException activityException) {
        Log.e("dialing-example", "Call failed", activityException);
    }
}
```

What happens when you start a phone call depends, in part, on the telephone network. The number may be incorrect. The network may be busy or otherwise unavailable. The call can be interrupted. Here, however, you see no error-handling logic, except for catching and logging exceptions that can be thrown if Android's system encounters a problem when finding applications that can process Intent objects. Instead, the PhoneApp application, which already has code for interpreting and remediating errors, handles the job from the time the phone call is started.

When an application just wants to start phone calls, making it handle all these contingencies is a large burden. Systems that provide a telephony API place that burden on application authors when, in most cases, all an application needs is to start a phone call—not to manage the lifecycle of a phone call.

Starting a phone call is a multistep operation. Here we'll take a detailed look at each step in the execution of the call method shown in Example 14-1. Along the way, we'll see how it uses Android's system of Intent objects and Intent filters.

Creating an Example Application to Run the call Method

To test the method in Example 14-1, create a new Android project in Eclipse by selecting File → New → Project → Other…. When the "Select a Wizard" dialog appears, select Android → Android Project. When you see the new project dialog, fill it in as shown in Figure 14-1.

Press Finish to create a project named dialing-example in your Eclipse workspace. (The complete code for this example is also on the book's website.) You will see this project in the Package Explorer pane of your Eclipse IDE. Expand the project to see a set of folders, including one named *src*. Expand this folder to see a package named *example.dialing*. Expand that package and you will see two Java source files, one of which is named *dialing.java*. This file contains the code in Example 14-2.

Example 14-2. Setting up an application to make phone calls

```
package example.dialing;

import android.app.Activity;
import android.content.ActivityNotFoundException;
import android.content.Intent;
import android.net.Uri;
import android.os.Bundle;
import android.util.Log;

public class dialing extends Activity {
    /** Called when the activity is first created. */
    @Override
    public void onCreate(Bundle savedInstanceState) {
        super.onCreate(savedInstanceState);
        setContentView(R.layout.main);
    }
}
```

This is where you will put the code that invokes our `call` method.

Figure 14-1. Creating a phone project in Eclipse

Embedding the Code Snippet in a Simple Application

Now that you have created a simple Android application, you can use it to isolate and observe operations, such as starting a phone call.

Copy the method we created in "Creating an Example Application to Run the call Method" on page 278 to the `dialing` class in the *dialing.java* file. Then, add a line to the `onCreate` method that calls the `call` method. The results should look something like Example 14-3.

Example 14-3. The dialing class with call method and its invocation

```
package example.dialing;

import android.app.Activity;
import android.content.ActivityNotFoundException;
import android.content.Intent;
import android.net.Uri;
import android.os.Bundle;
import android.util.Log;

public class dialing extends Activity {
    /** Called when the activity is first created. */
    @Override
    public void onCreate(Bundle savedInstanceState) {
        super.onCreate(savedInstanceState);
        setContentView(R.layout.main);
        call();
    }

private void call() {
    try {
        Intent callIntent = new Intent(Intent.ACTION_CALL);
        callIntent.setData(Uri.parse("tel:9785551212"));
        startActivity(callIntent);
    } catch (ActivityNotFoundException activityException) {
        Log.e("dialing-example", "Call failed", activityException);
    }
}
}
```

Make sure your program compiles and runs. To run the program, select the Run →
Run command. When the Run As dialog appears, select Android Application. If you
have followed the steps in this chapter, the result should be displayed in the Android
emulator window (Figure 14-2).

You can use the red "end" button on the phone depicted in the emulator to let the user
end the simulated phone call.

Exploring the Phone Code Through the Debugger

We will use the Eclipse debugger, set breakpoints, and inspect class members in the
running application to observe what is going on inside this example. The use of the
debugger with Android is described in Chapter 5. If you have not used a debugger
before, don't worry: we will use a limited set of debugging capabilities here to observe
a program that works correctly. Just follow the steps in this section and let the debugger
show you what is happening.

First, we will set a breakpoint where we want to start observing what is happening
inside the application. To set a breakpoint, double-click on the left margin of the view
that shows the program code in Eclipse. A blue dot will appear. If you change your

Figure 14-2. Dialer starts

mind and decide not to insert a breakpoint, double-click again on the blue dot, and it will disappear.

All we want is to stop execution of the program at the point where we want to start inspecting what happens to the members of this instance of the `dialing` class. To do this, set a breakpoint on line 21 of the program. You can tell which line you are on by clicking a line in the program. In the status bar at the bottom of the Eclipse window, you will see two numbers separated by a colon. The first number is the line number where you just clicked, and the second number is the character position on that line where the insertion point is right now.

Start the application with the debugger by selecting Run → Debug, and when the "Debug as" dialog appears, select Android Application.

The program will stop at the breakpoint, after the Android emulator appears on your screen but before the appearance of the dialer shown in Figure 14-2. Eclipse will switch to a *debug perspective*: a set of views configured for debugging a program instead of editing it. Eclipse will ask if you want to switch perspectives the first time you run the

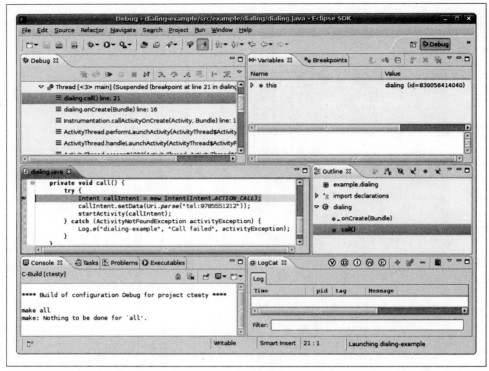

Figure 14-3. Eclipse debugger stopped in call method

debugger; you can save your answer if you want Eclipse to do the same thing each time you start debugging.

In the debug perspective, the view displaying the program code will show a small arrow overlapping the blue dot in the left margin. This line of code will be highlighted. The program has stopped before executing the Java bytecodes corresponding to the Java source code on this line of the program.

Figure 14-3 shows the Eclipse window in debug perspective with contents similar to those that should appear on your screen. The main information to look for is that the program stopped executing on the line where you set the breakpoint.

Creating an Instance of an Intent

The line of code where the program stopped in the previous section looks like this:

```
Intent callIntent = new Intent(Intent.ACTION_CALL);
```

This creates an instance of the Intent class. Use the "step over" command to execute this line, by selecting the Run → Step Over option from the menu or any of the shortcuts available in Eclipse.

"Step over" does not mean "skip." Instead, it tells the debugger to run the entire line of code and all the method calls it contains (the Intent constructor, in this case) instead of entering the method calls and going through them line by line. It isn't useful to see the internals of the Intent constructor. So "step over" creates the Intent and presents you with the next line of your own code.

The debugger also has commands for "stepping into" methods and "stepping out" of the method currently being executed. These commands are more convenient than setting more breakpoints and using the Resume command.

Now that we have used the new operator and the Intent constructor with an argument that specifies we want to initialize the Intent with the Intent.ACTION_CALL constant, we have an instance of the Intent class. The action we use, ACTION_CALL, will enable Android to find PhoneApp or any other program the user may install that offers the ACTION_CALL action.

Let's take a look inside by entering the Variables view in Eclipse. You will see two columns in this view. The first column shows the names of the variables, and the second column shows their values. In our case, the names refer to instances of classes, and the values consist of the class name and the ID of the instance.

That's not very informative! Let's look inside these instances and see what they contain. Click on the triangle icon in the left margin next to the variable named callIntent. Now you see all the members of the Intent class and the values for this instance of the Intent class. The only member that has a nondefault value is mAction. Its value is the string "android.intent.action.CALL". This is the result of calling the Intent class's constructor with the argument we used.

Adding Data to an Instance of an Intent

So far, our instance of the Intent class has enough information to tell the Android system we want to start a phone call, but not enough to tell it what number to call.

After creating the Intent instance with the information that means "we want to call a number," in the next line we will add to it the number to call:

```
callIntent.setData(Uri.parse("tel:9785551212"));
```

Two things happen on this line of code: an instance of a Uri is created, and we use that instance as an argument to the setData method of the Intent class. Step over this line of code, and then let's see what happens to the variables we are inspecting.

Look at the Variable view in Eclipse and you will see that the mData member of this instance of the Intent now refers to the instance of Uri that was returned from the parse method of the Uri class. And if you click on the triangle icon next to "mData", you will see the members of the Uri class, including the uriString member that refers to the string `tel:9785551212`. Now our instance of the `Intent` class contains all the information we need to start a phone call.

Why use a URI? All mobile numbers conform to the E.164 standard, so why not use a `String` object containing a valid E.164 number? A URI has the advantage of generality. All parts of Android are replaceable and the components of Android that handle this particular `Intent` object could be augmented or replaced by a module that can also connect VoIP calls with SIP URIs or Gmail addresses.

Initiating a Phone Call

The next line in our program looks like this:

```
startActivity(callIntent);
```

This looks like we want to start an Activity, using the `Intent` object we created. But why don't we need to specify an instance, or even a class, when we call `startActivity`? Because our program is an instance of the `Activity` class. We are calling a method of the class this object is an instance of. We could have used the following instead:

```
this.startActivity(callIntent);
```

Our program is already an Activity, but we now want to start a new instance of the `Activity` class—one that can handle the `Intent` instance we created. The Android framework handles the call by searching for an Intent that matches our request for `ACTION_CALL`. Let's step over this line and see what happens.

Now the arrow in the left margin of the code view points to the last line of the call method, just before the method returns. The emulator window shows the Android call status application displaying the number we specified. It should look like Figure 14-2, shown earlier in this chapter.

The fact that we stepped over this line of code and can now continue executing our program means that making a phone call this way is asynchronous: it allows our program to continue running while the dialer program makes the phone call.

Android is a collection of applications, and the application you are debugging places no restrictions on other applications that can be running at the same time.

Exception Handling

What if something goes wrong? The code in the call method that starts the dialer is wrapped in a try/catch block. The `catch` statement contains a line of code that logs an error if the `startActivity` method throws an exception of the type `ActivityNotFoundException`. If a method can throw an exception that indicates an error, the call to that method should be in a try/catch block that catches that type of exception. In this case, we use Android's logging facility to record the error.

We do not catch all exceptions, because unexpected exceptions indicate failures a program cannot, in general, recover from.

Let's make an exception happen. We can do this by removing part of the data needed to have the `startActivity` method call work correctly. Comment out line 22 of the code, as shown:

```
// callIntent.setData(Uri.parse("tel:9785551212"));
```

Now make some changes to breakpoints. Clear the breakpoint on line 21, and set a breakpoint on line 25, where, in the catch clause, the method of the `Log` class is called to log the caught exception. Use the Run → Debug command again to start the program.

This time you will see execution stop at the new breakpoint you set. You will also see that an exception has been thrown. The Debug view in Eclipse shows a *stack backtrace*, a list of all the methods called when the exception was thrown. The Variables view shows that `activityException` now refers to the exception that was thrown. Look at the members of the exception to see the information this exception provides.

If you examine the exception that was thrown (you can do this by hovering your mouse over `activityException`) you will see that the explanation for the exception reads "No activity found to handle intent." That is, in the case of an `Intent` object created with `Intent.ACTION_CALL` as the argument to the constructor, it also needs the data of the Intent to be set correctly in order to find an activity to process that Intent.

Android Application-Level Modularity and Telephony

Getting modularity right is difficult. In the case of Android, the problem is especially difficult: mobile phones were not designed to have replaceable software components, but Android is all about replaceable, modular parts. Every part of the Android application environment, even core components that handle phone calls and talk to the mobile radio, can be replaced by code you can write.

How do you avoid perplexing program authors with too much complexity managing the interfaces and the versions of the interfaces between modules? The mobile radio in a handset has a particularly complex interface. In addition to the obvious functionality for starting and ending phone calls and reporting state and error conditions, it also encompasses critical functions such as emergency calls, and obscure functions such as "MMI codes" that enable users to access features of the phone and mobile network through special dialing strings.

Android provides a practical, usable, and flexible system for modularity for telephony applications. It uses the Android system of `Intent` objects and activities that listen for `Intent` objects that indicate they should handle a particular request. In this case, we see that the `Intent` class and the activities and data you need to specify when making a phone call are easy to use. We also see that application-level modularity is a boon to practicality: because you don't need to track the inner workings of a phone call—PhoneApp does it for you.

Android does all of this without replacing, modifying, or adding requirements to the modularity tools provided by Java. You still have class libraries, reflection, and other tools for making and using existing Java software modules.

In the next chapter, you will see what happens inside of Android's telephony software, all the way down to how the mobile radio is commanded to start a phone call.

CHAPTER 15

Telephony State Information and Android Telephony Classes

The previous chapter showed how to use Android's built-in PhoneApp application, which simplifies the task of placing of phone calls. This chapter shows you how to get more information about telephone service and the actual calls you make.

After an example that puts one of the telephony features to use, we'll present a short guide to PhoneApp internals.

 We use the term "telephony" to refer to the parts of the Android system that depend on a radio communicating with the public land mobile network (PLMN) to provide communication and location functions. Sharing the use of this radio among multiple applications is a key goal for Android's telephony modules.

Operations Offered by the android.telephony Package

The `android.telephony` package contains a set of classes that can be used by any application in the Android environment to monitor the state of Android's mobile network connection. It also contains classes for locating a device using the mobile network. Finally, it offers utility classes for parsing, formatting, and otherwise managing phone numbers, although there is no architectural benefit to locating those classes in this package.

The telephony package does not allow you to place, end, or otherwise meddle in phone calls; it focuses on retrieving information and giving users an interface to edit telephone numbers. We'll explain later why Android reserves the actual control over phone calls to PhoneApp.

Package Summary

The `android.telephony` package contains the following packages:

`CellLocation`
> Methods to request location information.

`PhoneNumberFormattingTextWatcher`
> Callback methods that notify an application about changes to phone numbers themselves. When used with a `TextView` object, it formats the text as a phone number using methods in the `PhoneNumberUtils` class.

`PhoneNumberUtils`
> A utility class that contains methods for processing strings containing phone numbers.

`PhoneStateListener`
> Callback methods that track changes in the state of the mobile network connection, the call, or other telephony objects.

`ServiceState`
> Methods that return information about the current mobile network service provider and the availability of service.

`TelephonyManager`
> Methods that provide information about the state of mobile service, the call state, the SIM, the network, the subscriber to the mobile service, voicemail, and other related information.

Because these classes don't control hardware or change state information about phone calls, they don't have any access control.

Limitations on What Applications Can Do with the Phone

Some readers may be disappointed to see that the `android.telephony` package limits their access to getting information, and does not provide direct control over the dialer or the state of a call. There are good reasons for this. Essentially, providing a low-level telephony API that can be shared among multiple applications is perilous.

A mobile handset is a state machine that keeps track of the mobile radio reports, provides audible call state indications to the user, and enables the user to provide inputs that modify that state. Even if you could design an API that would, hypothetically, share a mobile radio among multiple applications on a per-call basis, the user interface and ergonomic design that would go along with shared control among multiple applications would be difficult and probably even intractable. A phone is not like a PC with a desktop user interface: you can't share control over the parts of a device that constitute the phone the way you can share the screen of a PC.

Android provides a workable solution that keeps telephony usable while making as much of the system open to your applications as is practicable. As we saw in the previous chapter, PhoneApp exposes an Intent that lets other applications initiate phone calls, while enabling a single application to control the mobile radio in an Android handset. The `android.telephony` package further exposes information about telephone service and the calls made by an application.

It's useful to think of telephony on Android as an interface that keeps critical functions private while providing public APIs for functions where it is safe to do so. This is a good example of a successful Android design strategy.

Example: Determining the State of a Call

This section shows how to track the state of a phone call. It adds some of the classes described in the previous section to the application shown in "Creating an Example Application to Run the call Method" on page 278, which finds and uses PhoneApp to start and control a phone call. Here, in addition to starting a phone call and letting PhoneApp control it, the application gets some information about the call as it is happening.

In order to get this information, we need to extend the `PhoneStateListener` class, make an instance of our subclass, and pass that instance to the `TelephonyManager.listen` method. Example 15-1 shows the code for our subclass of the `PhoneStateListener` class.

Example 15-1. Defining a Listener for telephone call state

```
private class ListenToPhoneState extends PhoneStateListener {

    public void onCallStateChanged(int state, String incomingNumber) {❶
        Log.i("telephony-example", "State changed: " + stateName(state));❷
    }

    String stateName(int state) {❸
        switch (state) {
            case TelephonyManager.CALL_STATE_IDLE: return "Idle";
            case TelephonyManager.CALL_STATE_OFFHOOK: return "Off hook";
            case TelephonyManager.CALL_STATE_RINGING: return "Ringing";
        }
        return Integer.toString(state);
    }
}
```

The lines we've highlighted are:

❶ Overrides the `onCallStateChanged` method of the `PhoneStateListener` class.

❷ Adds a message to Android's log whenever the state changes.

❸ Chooses meaningful strings to represent call states.

In this subclass of the `PhoneStateListener` class, we override the `onCallStateChanged` method, which Android calls when a call's state changes. We use the `Log` class, a static class with utility methods for logging information, to log the changes as Android passes them to us.

Finally, our `stateName` method decodes the states that correspond to the constants defined in the `TelephonyManager` class to make the log more readable.

Returning to our main application from "Creating an Example Application to Run the call Method" on page 278, we have to change it by creating a Listener and assigning our subclass of `PhoneStateListener` to it. Here is the code for the entire modified example application, which now tracks and logs state transitions:

```
package example.telephony;

import android.app.Activity;
import android.content.ActivityNotFoundException;
import android.content.Context;
import android.content.Intent;
import android.net.Uri;
import android.os.Bundle;
import android.telephony.PhoneStateListener;❶
import android.telephony.TelephonyManager;❶
import android.util.Log;

public class telephonyExplorer extends Activity {
ListenToPhoneState listener;❷

    /** Called when the activity is first created. */
    @Override
    public void onCreate(Bundle savedInstanceState) {
        super.onCreate(savedInstanceState);
        setContentView(R.layout.main);
        call();
    }

    private void call() {
        try {
            Intent callIntent = new Intent(Intent.ACTION_CALL);
            callIntent.setData(Uri.parse("tel:9785551212"));
            startActivity(callIntent);

            TelephonyManager tManager = (TelephonyManager)
                getSystemService(Context.TELEPHONY_SERVICE);❸
            listener = new ListenToPhoneState();❹
            tManager.listen(listener, PhoneStateListener.LISTEN_CALL_STATE);
        } catch (ActivityNotFoundException activityException) {
            Log.e("telephony-example", "Call failed", activityException);
        }
    }

    private class ListenToPhoneState extends PhoneStateListener {❺

        public void onCallStateChanged(int state, String incomingNumber) {
            Log.i("telephony-example", "State changed: " + stateName(state));
        }
```

```
        String stateName(int state) {
            switch (state) {
                case TelephonyManager.CALL_STATE_IDLE: return "Idle";
                case TelephonyManager.CALL_STATE_OFFHOOK: return "Off hook";
                case TelephonyManager.CALL_STATE_RINGING: return "Ringing";
            }
            return Integer.toString(state);
        }
    }
}
```

The lines we've highlighted are:

❶ New classes that must be imported to add a Listener for the telephone call state.

❷ Adds a definition for the Listener.

❸ Connects to Android's telephone call manager.

❹ Assigns our extended Listener class (defined at item 5) to the variable defined in item 2.

❺ Code from Example 15-1, defining our Listener.

Running this application results in output to the log window in Eclipse that should look something like this:

```
11-19 01:47:03.704: INFO/telephony-example(159): State changed: Idle
11-19 01:47:04.774: INFO/telephony-example(159): State changed: Off hook
```

Android Telephony Internals

The rest of this chapter covers telephony-related classes in the internals package that only PhoneApp uses, android.internal.telephony. This package is layered over an implementation of telephony internals for a particular telephony technology, such as GSM or CDMA. That layer, in turn, communicates with a Radio Interface Layer (RIL) that is implemented as a daemon in Android.

Figure 15-1 shows the architecture of the Android telephony system. PhoneApp supports an Intent that enables other applications to start phone calls. The Telephony Manager is available through Listeners, as shown in the previous section.

Inter-Process Communication and AIDL in the android.internal.telephony Package

Many of the internal packages use the remote methods feature discussed in "Remote Methods and AIDL" on page 265. The TelephonyManager and PhoneStateListener classes rely on this to communicate with PhoneApp. The ServiceManager class is also used.

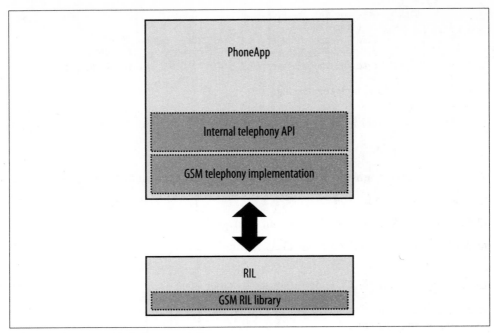

Figure 15-1. Layers of telephony packages

To marshall data for remote methods, the package includes AIDL files. For instance, the following AIDL comes from *IPhoneStateListener.aidl*:

```
oneway interface IPhoneStateListener {
    void onServiceStateChanged(in ServiceState serviceState);
    void onSignalStrengthChanged(int asu);
    void onMessageWaitingIndicatorChanged(boolean mwi);
    void onCallForwardingIndicatorChanged(boolean cfi);

    // we use bundle here instead of CellLocation so it can get the right subclass
    void onCellLocationChanged(in Bundle location);
    void onCallStateChanged(int state, String incomingNumber);
    void onDataConnectionStateChanged(int state);
    void onDataActivity(int direction);
}
```

The android.internal.telephony Package

This package contains the classes and interfaces PhoneApp uses to provide services to other applications that want to start phone calls, and classes that define an API to the RIL.

PhoneApp, like all parts of Android, is theoretically replaceable. If your application needs to modify the classes used by PhoneApp, your application will probably have to replace or modify PhoneApp, and should provide the same services to other applications, using the classes in this package.

The description of these classes should help you understand how Android interfaces to a mobile radio, and the capabilities that are exposed—and not exposed—by PhoneApp to other applications. This is a large and complex package, and a complete understanding will require reading the Android source code. These descriptions will help you find where to start for your purposes:

ATParseEx

Extends RuntimeException and is thrown by methods of the `ATResponseParser` class.

ATResponseParser

This class parses part of the AT command syntax used to communicate with the mobile radio hardware in a mobile handset. This is, in fact, a command syntax very much like the AT command syntax used by modems, a standard described in the 3GPP document number TS 27.007 and related specifications. This protocol for controlling mobile radios is widely used.

Call

This class is an abstract base class. Other classes use it as a basis for objects that represent phone calls and the state of those calls.

CallerInfo

This class holds information about the party that originated an incoming call. This class starts with caller ID information from the mobile network interface and looks up other information about a caller in the database of contacts.

CallerInfoAsyncQuery

This class enables asynchronous database queries for information that could be found about a caller based on the caller ID information.

CallStateException

The class extends Exception and is thrown by methods that maintain call state in cases where state is inconsistent.

Connection

This class is an abstract base class used by other classes, and is a basis for objects that represent connections on the mobile network and the state of these connections. `Connection` objects can be associated with a `Call` object, but they can also exist independently. The data in a `Connection` object can be especially useful in diagnosing the reason a call failed.

DefaultPhoneNotifier

This class implements the PhoneNotifier interface in order to receive notifications from a `Phone` object. It then uses the Android service system to communicate state to Activity instances that have registered to receive those notifications. See the `Handler` and `Mailbox` classes for information on how to receive notifications.

IPhoneStateListener

This interface defines the signatures of methods an application implements to receive notification of call state change, and changes to forwarding and message-waiting states.

IPhoneSubInfo

This interface is used to obtain subscriber information.

ITelephony

This interface defines the inter-process interface used in TelephonyManager to enable applications to communicate with PhoneApp.

ITelephonyRegistry

This interface is the callback interface from the RIL daemon.

MmiCode

This interface defines callbacks related to "MMI codes." These are special numbers a user can dial and key sequences that a user can enter during a call to access, control, and administer supplementary services, such as call waiting, call hold, etc. MMI codes and related functionality are described in the 3GPP document number TS 22.030.

Phone

This interface includes callbacks and methods for accessing the state of a mobile phone.

PhoneBase

This class is an abstract base class that implements the Phone interface.

PhoneFactory

This class contains methods used to create instances of the GSMPhone class, a subclass of the Phone class.

PhoneNotifier

This interface specifies the API a telephony implementation uses to notify a phone state listener of state changes.

PhoneStateIntentReceiver

This class handles Intent objects that have intent types specified in the TelephonyIntents class. This class enables Android applications to use the Intents system to obtain phone state information.

PhoneSubInfo

This class contains methods for obtaining information about a mobile service subscriber, such as the unique identifying number for the handset (IMEI), the unique identifying number for the subscriber (IMSI), the serial number of the SIM card, etc.

SimCard

This interface defines the API for accessing the SIM card.

TelephonyIntents

> This class defines constants for broadcast intents that have similar functionality to the TelephonyManager API.

TelephonyProperties

> This class defines the constants used with the SystemProperties class for setting and getting telephony-related properties.

These classes are not documented in the Android SDK documentation, but the descriptions here should give you some understanding of the source code for these classes.

The android.internal.telephony.gsm Package

Many of the classes and interfaces in the previous section are typical of a Java API that can have multiple implementations. The implementations of the API defined in the telephony.internal package correspond to a library used in the RIL. To better understand this API, we will look at one implementation here that supports GSM.

Thus, this section delves further into the telephony internals of Android, looking especially at how the interfaces and abstract base classes are implemented and subclassed to enable access to the functionality of GSM telephony. Although it may seem that specifications such as TS 27.007 cover mobile telephony in general, this layer of Android actually has to accommodate variations in mobile telephony standards. In CDMA telephony, for instance, the SIM card is an optional part of the standard and is rarely present in CDMA handsets. In this case, the package described in this section would be replaced by a CDMA-oriented package with a similar architectural relationship to the higher-level classes described in the previous section. The RIL code is also specific to the type of telephony in the handset.

At the RIL layer, the differences between GSM and CDMA are mainly outside the core functionality of making phone calls, so you may be wondering why all these layers and APIs are necessary. But, as the description of the classes specific to communicating with a GSM RIL will show, there are plenty of differences in detail, such as SIM cards, the type of mobile data network, etc. These make it impractical to design a universal interface to mobile radios, despite the use of a standard protocol for communicating with them:

AdnRecord

> This class is used to load and store Abbreviated Dialing Numbers (ADNs) to and from the SIM card. ADNs are short numbers used for information calls, emergency calls, etc.

AdnRecordCache

> This class caches and enables access to ADNs.

ApnSetting

This class holds data specifying the access point name (APN) and other parameters for connecting to General Packet Radio Service (GPRS) and 3G mobile data networks. This mobile data technology is specific to GSM networks.

BaseCommands

This class implements the CommandsInterface interface, which is used throughout the GSM telephony classes to communicate with the GSM radio.

CallFailCause

This interface defines constants for decoding failure cause codes.

CallForwardInfo

This class holds data that corresponds to the parameters of a call-forwarding command to the RIL.

CallTracker

This class maps information from the RIL to state transitions for the GSMCall class.

CommandException

This class is an exception thrown when the RIL reports an error from a command.

CommandsInterface

This interface defines the API to the GSM RIL. This interface is implemented by the BaseCommands class.

DataConnectionTracker

This tracks the state of GPRS packet data protocol (PDP) connections. This type of connection is specific to GSM mobile data.

DataLink

This class implements the DataLinkInterface interface and is used in the PPPLink class, which manages point to point protocol (PPP) links in GPRS networking.

DataLinkInterface

This class defines the API for connecting and disconnecting PPP links.

DriverCall

This class parses information, in AT command syntax, from the mobile radio, and turns it into call state information.

EncodeException

This class is an exception thrown by methods of the GSM alphabet class, which encodes UTF-16 (as used in Java) into the 7-bit SMS character set.

GSMAlphabet

This class is a utility class containing static methods for encoding UTF-16 to the 7-bit SMS character set.

GSMCall

This class extends the Call class, and implements the abstract methods of that class, thereby implementing parts of the Android telephony internals API. This class models calls in GSM telephony.

GSMConnection

This class extends the `Connection` class, and like the `GSMCall` class, implements the abstract methods of the `Connection` class. This class models connections in GSM telephony.

GSMPhone

This class extends the `Phone` class and, as with both the `GSMCall` and `GSMConnection` classes, implements the abstract methods of the `Phone` class.

GsmMmiCode

This class implements the MmiCode interface and the part of the telephony API defined in that interface.

GsmSimCard

This class implements the SimCard interface, another part of the implementation of the telephony internals API. This class enables access to data in the SIM card.

ISimPhoneBook

This interface defines an API for accessing ADN records stored in the SIM card.

ISms

This interface defines the API for sending SMS messages.

MccTable

This class is a utility class that contains a table of Mobile Country Codes (MCCs). In principle, these codes are not specific to a GSM RIL, but they are specific to this implementation of a GSM RIL.

NetworkInfo

This class is a container for network state information.

PDPContextState

This contains data about a PDP session, including the IP address.

PdpConnection

This class contains information about the data connection associated with a PDP context.

PppLink

This class extends DataLink and implements DataLinkInterface to provide an implementation of this part of the RIL interface.

RIL

This class extends the `BaseCommands` class and also implements the CommandsInterface interface, forming a complete implementation of the interface for sending commands to the RIL. This is where communication with the RIL takes place. An instance of the `RIL` class is created in the `PhoneFactory` class, in the course of creating an instance of the `GSMPhone` class.

RILConstants

This interface defines constants used in the `RIL` class.

ServiceStateTracker

This class polls the RIL daemon for signal strength and tracks other aspects of the state of mobile service.

SIMFileHandler

This enables access to the SIM filesystem.

SIMRecords

This class enables access to specific files in the SIM filesystem containing information such as the subscriber's IMSI.

SimConstants

This interface contains constants used in other classes accessing data in the SIM.

SimException

This class extends Exception and is used in other classes to throw an exception related to errors accessing data in the SIM.

SimFileNotFound

This class extends `SimException` and is used in the `SimIoResult` class in specific error conditions.

SimPhoneBookInterfaceManager

This class extends `ISimPhoneBook` and provides a service interface for accessing ADN records in the SIM.

SimProvider

This class extends `ContentProvider` and creates a content provider interface to SIM ADN/SDN/FDN records in the SIM.

SimSmsInterfaceManager

This class extends ISms and creates a service interface for accessing SMS messages stored in the SIM.

SimTlv

This class is an object interface for accessing tag-length-value records in the SIM, and is used in the `SIMRecords` class.

SimUtils

This class contains static utility methods for manipulating data encoded in binary-coded decimal and other encodings encountered in SIM data.

SMSDispatcher

This class implements the sending of SMS messages and notifies applications that use the Handler interface to this class regarding the status of SMS messages.

SmsHeader

This class contains constants and methods for decoding SMS headers.

SmsRawData

This class implements Parcelable and is used in implementing service interfaces for accessing SIM data.

SmsResponse
> This class associates a message reference with an acknowledgment.

SuppServiceNotification
> This class contains constants for decoding information about supplementary services.

VoiceMailConstants
> This class parses information in the *etc/voicemail-conf.xml file.*

There is another package organized hierarchically under the `internal.telephony.gsm` package: the `stk` package, which contains classes for accessing the SIM. This package is not exposed outside the `internal.telephony.gsm` package and is beyond the scope of this chapter.

Exploring Android Telephony Internals

A lot of code lies between creating an `ACTION_CALL` `Intent` object and dialing a call. Here we will go even deeper into Android's telephony system to see what Android is telling the mobile radio, and match that up with what we have done in the example application earlier in this chapter.

To see how, and when, Android actually commands the hardware to dial a number, we can use Android's logging system. To access the log buffer for information about the traffic between Android software and the mobile radio, we will also have to use the Android Debug Bridge, **adb**. We will start a shell that can run commands in the emulator, and we will use the logcat utility to display logging information as it becomes available.

First, set a breakpoint in the example application on line 25, where the `Intent` object is created and before the call to the `startActivity` method.

Then, start the application with the debugger: Select Run → Debug. When the "Debug as" dialog appears, select Android Application.

The application will run and stop at the breakpoint.

Now look at the log. Open a command-line window and change your working directory to the directory where you have put the Android SDK. There you should see a directory named *tools*. Change your working directory to *tools*. You should see a program there named *adb*.

Next, use **adb** to find the name of the emulator that is running as a result of starting the application with the debugger. Type the following:

```
./adb devices
```

adb will list all the emulators running, which should be just one. The output will look something like this:

```
...
emulator-5554 device
```

Now use **adb** to start a shell that can run programs in the emulator (if **adb** finds an emulator with a different name on your system, use that name instead of "emulator-5554"):

```
./adb -s emulator-5554 shell
```

This will result in a shell prompt:

```
#
```

The shell you are now typing commands into is executing those commands in the emulator. Now use the **logcat** command to show the log of traffic between the mobile radio and the RIL:

```
# logcat -b radio
```

This will result in a lengthy listing of AT commands and responses. For the most part, they are asking for and reporting the signal strength. This is what the RIL and the mobile radio are doing when nothing else is going on.

The lines tagged D/AT are the verbatim AT commands exchanged between the mobile radio and the RIL. The ones labeled AT> are from the RIL to the mobile radio, and the ones labeled AT< are from the mobile radio to the RIL. The other lines in the log are a more-readable decoding of the information in the AT commands. You can see the part of the RIL interface in Java logging requests sent to the RIL daemon, RILD, and the RIL code in RILD logging as it sends the appropriate AT commands to the mobile radio and decodes the results.

Now use the Eclipse debugger to step over the line where the Intent object is created. Looking at the log output, you see that nothing interesting has happened yet: the RIL and the mobile radio (really, an emulation of a mobile radio) are polling the signal strength. Step over the next line, where the phone number is added to the Intent object and, similarly, nothing has happened yet.

Now step over the next line, which should look like this:

```
startActivity(callIntent);
```

Here we get quite a bit of interesting output from the logger. It should look something like this:

```
D/GSM ( 85): [GSMConn] update: parent=DIALING, hasNewParent=false,
  wasConnectingInOrOut=true, wasHolding=false, isConnectingInOrOut=true,changed=false
D/RILJ ( 85): [0161]> SET_MUTE false
D/RIL ( 22): onRequest: SET_MUTE
D/RILJ ( 85): [0161]< SET_MUTE error:
  com.android.internal.telephony.gsm.CommandException: REQUEST_NOT_SUPPORTED
D/RILJ ( 85): [UNSL]< CALL_STATE_CHANGED
D/RILJ ( 85): [0162]> GET_CURRENT_CALLS
D/RIL ( 22): onRequest: GET_CURRENT_CALLS
D/AT ( 22): AT> AT+CLCC
```

```
D/AT  ( 22): AT< +CLCC: 1,0,2,0,0,"9785551212",129
D/AT  ( 22): AT< OK
D/RILJ ( 85): [0162]< GET_CURRENT_CALLS [id=1,mo,DIALING,voice,norm,129,0]
D/GSM  ( 85): [GSMConn] update: parent=DIALING, hasNewParent=false,
  wasConnectingInOrOut=true, wasHolding=false, isConnectingInOrOut=true, changed=false
D/AT  ( 22): AT< RING
D/RILJ ( 85): [UNSL]< CALL_STATE_CHANGED
D/RILJ ( 85): [0163]> GET_CURRENT_CALLS
D/RIL  ( 22): onRequest: GET_CURRENT_CALLS
D/AT  ( 22): AT> AT+CLCC
D/AT  ( 22): AT< +CLCC: 1,0,3,0,0,"9785551212",129
D/AT  ( 22): AT< OK
D/RILJ ( 85): [0163]< GET_CURRENT_CALLS [id=1,mo,ALERTING,voice,norm,129,0]
D/GSM  ( 85): [GSMConn] update: parent=ALERTING, hasNewParent=false,
  wasConnectingInOrOut=true, wasHolding=false, isConnectingInOrOut=true, changed=true
D/RILJ ( 85): [0164]> SET_MUTE false
D/RIL  ( 22): onRequest: SET_MUTE
D/RILJ ( 85): [0164]< SET_MUTE error:
  com.android.internal.telephony.gsm.CommandException:
  REQUEST_NOT_SUPPORTED
D/RILJ ( 85): [UNSL]< CALL_STATE_CHANGED
D/RILJ ( 85): [0165]> GET_CURRENT_CALLS
D/RIL  ( 22): onRequest: GET_CURRENT_CALLS
D/AT  ( 22): AT> AT+CLCC
D/AT  ( 22): AT< +CLCC: 1,0,3,0,0,"9785551212",129
D/AT  ( 22): AT< OK
D/RILJ ( 85): [0165]< GET_CURRENT_CALLS [id=1,mo,ALERTING,voice,norm,129,0]
D/GSM  ( 85): [GSMConn] update: parent=ALERTING, hasNewParent=false,
  wasConnectingInOrOut=true,
  wasHolding=false, isConnectingInOrOut=true, changed=false
D/RILJ ( 85): [UNSL]< CALL_STATE_CHANGED
D/RILJ ( 85): [0166]> GET_CURRENT_CALLS
D/RIL  ( 22): onRequest: GET_CURRENT_CALLS
D/AT  ( 22): AT> AT+CLCC
D/AT  ( 22): AT< +CLCC: 1,0,3,0,0,"9785551212",129
D/AT  ( 22): AT< OK
D/RILJ ( 85): [0166]< GET_CURRENT_CALLS [id=1,mo,ALERTING,voice,norm,129,0]
D/GSM  ( 85): [GSMConn] update: parent=ALERTING, hasNewParent=false,
  wasConnectingInOrOut=true,
  wasHolding=false, isConnectingInOrOut=true, changed=false
D/RILJ ( 85): [UNSL]< CALL_STATE_CHANGED
D/RILJ ( 85): [0167]> GET_CURRENT_CALLS
D/RIL  ( 22): onRequest: GET_CURRENT_CALLS
D/AT  ( 22): AT> AT+CLCC
D/AT  ( 22): AT< RING
D/AT  ( 22): AT< +CLCC: 1,0,0,0,0,"9785551212",129
D/AT  ( 22): AT< OK
D/RILJ ( 85): [UNSL]< CALL_STATE_CHANGED
D/RILJ ( 85): [0167]< GET_CURRENT_CALLS [id=1,mo,ACTIVE,voice,norm,129,0]
D/RILJ ( 85): [0168]> GET_CURRENT_CALLS
D/RIL  ( 22): onRequest: GET_CURRENT_CALLS
D/AT  ( 22): AT> AT+CLCC
D/AT  ( 22): AT< +CLCC: 1,0,0,0,0,"9785551212",129
D/AT  ( 22): AT< OK
D/RILJ ( 85): [0168]< GET_CURRENT_CALLS [id=1,mo,ACTIVE,voice,norm,129,0]
```

```
D/GSM ( 85): [GSMConn] update: parent=ACTIVE, hasNewParent=false,
  wasConnectingInOrOut=true,
  wasHolding=false, isConnectingInOrOut=false, changed=true
D/GSM ( 85): [GSMConn] onConnectedInOrOut: connectTime=1225978001674
D/RILJ ( 85): [UNSL]< CALL_STATE_CHANGED
D/RILJ ( 85): [0169]> SET_MUTE false
D/RIL ( 22): onRequest: SET_MUTE
D/RILJ ( 85): [0169]< SET_MUTE error:
 com.android.internal.telephony.gsm.CommandException:
 REQUEST_NOT_SUPPORTED
D/RILJ ( 85): [0170]> GET_CURRENT_CALLS
D/RIL ( 22): onRequest: GET_CURRENT_CALLS
D/AT ( 22): AT> AT+CLCC
D/AT ( 22): AT< +CLCC: 1,0,0,0,0,"9785551212",129
D/AT ( 22): AT< OK
D/RILJ ( 85): [0170]< GET_CURRENT_CALLS [id=1,mo,ACTIVE,voice,norm,129,0]
D/GSM ( 85): [GSMConn] update: parent=ACTIVE, hasNewParent=false,
  wasConnectingInOrOut=false,
  wasHolding=false, isConnectingInOrOut=false, changed=false
```

What you are seeing here is a mobile call being started. The call goes through three states: "dialing," "alerting," and "active." Take a look at how the mobile radio reports the state of a call. Here the call is in the "dialing" state:

```
+CLCC: 1,0,2,0,0,"9785551212",129
```

Here the call is in the "alerting" state:

```
+CLCC: 1,0,3,0,0,"9785551212",129
```

Here the call is in the "active" state:

```
+CLCC: 1,0,0,0,0,"9785551212",129
```

The third number in the list of parameters in the AT command response indicates the state of this call. The classes that model the connection, call, and network state in PhoneApp and the TelephonyManager API keep track of what RILD is telling the mobile radio and what the mobile radio is telling RILD, and this is where that information comes from.

Now press the red End button (the one with the picture of a telephone receiver) to end the call. Look for the AT commands that read the state change from the mobile radio, and at the corresponding TelephonyManager method call that notifies the application of the change.

Android and VoIP

You may have come to the end of this description of Android telephony surprised, and perhaps disappointed, to find no mention of Voice over IP (VoIP). After all, GoogleTalk supports voice calls from PC to PC. Why was this capability omitted from the core telephony functionality of Android?

Android was not designed to treat VoIP calls and mobile calls similarly or, from a programmer's perspective, through the same APIs. What you see described in this chapter is an abstraction for mobile telephony, not telephony in general. AT commands that are nearly universal in mobile telephony—and that are not used outside mobile telephony—pervade the APIs described here all the way up to the PhoneApp application. The inter-process interfaces are designed around capabilities of mobile telephony, mobile messaging, and mobile data.

As a result, designers of VoIP technologies for Android are left with some design decisions. The current direction treats VoIP as a separate application and makes it possible in the future to provide a very high-level integration with other parts of the system—for example, supporting the `ACTION_CALL` call in `Intent` objects. This development would give the user a choice between Android's built-in mobile telephony and an add-on for VoIP telephony.

A deeper integration of mobile telephony and VoIP can be implemented in Android, but it would require extending the functionality of PhoneApp to encompass both IP and conventional mobile telephony, while providing a compatible interface to applications written to Android's TelephonyManager API.

Wireless Protocols

If you're new to mobile development, the plethora of wireless telephony acronyms can be confusing at first. The good news is that, for the most part, you can ignore them because you don't know exactly which environment your application will run in. The bad news is that your application should be prepared to run in *all* of the environments.

To help you follow the debates, standards, and discussions that inevitably arise when discussing cellular and wireless technologies, this appendix introduces the main protocols in historical order.

Prehistory

When mobile phones were first invented in the 1940s, they were just analog radios driven from a car battery. The system was aptly named Mobile Telephone System (MTS), and it was woefully inadequate. In spite of the high cost of service, waiting lists to obtain the service were long because MTS offered only a few channels in any geography. An "improved" version called IMTS, introduced in the 1960s, helped some, but was still far short of the demand.

The first analog cellular radio mobile phone systems started to appear in 1969 and the early 1970s—with phones still the size of a briefcase. The various cellular technologies in North America converged around the Advanced Mobile Phone Service (AMPS) standard, still analog technology but now based on cellular radios that could reuse the frequency spectrum and were standardized across manufacturers. At this time Europe had no less than nine different analog mobile phone technology standards, one for each major region and country in the continent.

The Dawn of Second Generation (2G) Digital Cellular

Roaming in Europe was obviously impossible. Partly to alleviate this problem, the European operators decided to standardize the next generation of mobile phones by forming the European Telecommunications Standards Institute (ETSI). In the early

1980s, ETSI developed a digital mobile phone standard known as GSM (originally *Groupe Special Mobile*, later Global System for Mobile Communications). The GSM standard included something termed Short Message Service (SMS), which used spare bandwidth on the control channel to send and receive short 160-byte messages.

The GSM system and some other digital cellular standards (such as the digital successor to AMPS in North America, D-AMPS, or IS-54) multiplex different voice callers on a common radio frequency by using time division multiplexing (Time Division Multiple Access, or TDMA). Essentially, the signal from each user is rapidly sampled, and samples from different users are interleaved and broadcast in an assigned time slot. The sampled speech is reassembled at the receiving end of the signal, and in this way multiple users can share a single radio channel.

The cellular protocols are actually quite a bit more complex than this simple explanation would imply. At the same time the radio signal is being sampled and desampled, it is also hopping around to a preset sequence of frequencies, and samples are being reordered in time, all in order to reduce mobile effects such as interference, jitter, dropouts, and multipath distortion.

In the very late 1980s, Qualcomm introduced a new digital system in the U.S. termed CDMA, for Code Division Multiple Access (later also called IS-95 and still later cdmaOne). Instead of dividing each voice signal into time-based divisions, CDMA transmitted all of the signals on multiple radio frequencies at the same time.

But how to keep the signals from interfering with each other? In CDMA, the signals make use of orthogonal "codes" that define which of the frequencies are used for which signal. The signal is transmitted on a number of frequencies defined by the code, and can be extracted on the receiving end by sampling only those frequencies assigned to this particular code. The other signals on those same frequencies are averaged out as noise because they don't appear consistently in most of the frequencies. CDMA proved to be much more efficient at spectrum use than TDMA, but GSM had already taken hold, and was the more popular standard worldwide.

The 2G mobile protocols were mainly designed for voice, but also provided the first real channels for data. At first the data rates were slow, the coverage spotty, and the technology inefficient in its use of the available bandwidth because it was based on circuit switching. The optimistically named High Speed Circuit Switched Data (HSCSD) system used multiple GSM channels and was rated at 28.8 to 64 kilobits per second, though it rarely achieved even a fraction of that speed. In the 1990s, HSCSD was replaced with the General Packet Radio System (GPRS) standard, the first packet-switched technology for GSM.

Improved Digital Cellular (2.5G)

In the late 1990s, operators could see that demand for voice phones was saturating. They could foresee the day when everybody who wanted a mobile phone would have one. At the same time, the Internet was becoming ubiquitous, and users were starting to demand better data access from their mobile phones. Operators looked for ways to expand the data capacity of their mobile networks while taking advantage of their existing infrastructure investments. GSM operators expanded their GSM/GPRS networks to a new standard called Enhanced Data for GSM Evolution (EDGE), which further improved available data rates and made efficient use of GSM equipment the operators already had installed. CDMA operators capitalized on similar improvements in that domain, with standards such as CDMA2000 1X. The theoretical data rates were now in the hundreds of kilobits per second, though the actual data rates were still much lower. Phones running Android can be expected to have at least 2.5G data connectivity.

A second wave of data access improvement (sometimes referred to as 2.75G) further improved data rates, implemented by High Speed Packet Access (HSPA) for GSM and EV-DO (EVolution Data Optimized, or sometimes translated as EVolution Data Only) for CDMA. Theoretical data rates were now in the multimegabit-per-second range, and most Android phones can be expected to have these technologies, if not 3G.

The Rise of 3G

Also in the 1990s, the European telecom community started defining the next generation of mobile technology, first through ETSI and then through a new organization called 3rd Generation Partnership Program (3GPP). The standard developed by 3GPP is called Universal Mobile Telecommunications Standard (UMTS), and though based fundamentally on Wideband CDMA (WCDMA) technology, was carefully designed to allow both GSM and CDMA operators to evolve their networks efficiently from their installed infrastructure to the new standard. This would allow operators around the world to converge to a new common standard for 3G.*

In the early 2000s, operators spent huge sums of money to purchase spectrum for 3G wireless networks. 3G networks are now being deployed worldwide, and over the next few years, new smartphones (including Android-based phones) will all incorporate 3G technologies.

The Future: 4G

So what's next? The standards bodies are back at work defining the fourth generation of wireless network protocols, sometimes termed LTE (for Long Term Evolution). The apparent winner is a group of protocols called Orthogonal Frequency Division Multiplexing (OFDM), or sometimes OFDMA (the "A" is for Access). These protocols use

---

* Except for operators in the People's Republic of China, where the government mandated its own version of UMTS, called Time Division-Synchronous Code Division Multiple Access (TD-SCDMA). TD-SCDMA uses TDMA as well as CDMA to provide some unique advantages for data traffic. It also avoids the need for PRC handset makers to pay royalties for most WCDMA intellectual property.

radio frequency subcarriers to further improve the data rates achievable for wireless devices. Similar protocols are used in the WiMAX standards (the higher bandwidth, longer-range follow-on to WiFi), but it is not clear how WiMAX and LTE will relate to one another.

Just as with 3G, a round of spectrum auctions is starting to take place for 4G, and operators are already investing large sums of money into getting ready for 4G services. Suffice to say that your applications built for Android will someday encounter phones running 4G protocols, and will be able to take advantage of the higher data rates and lower latencies that will come with these protocols.

To wrap up, Figure A-1 shows the evolution of protocols discussed in this chapter in relation to the decade in which they were first deployed and the effective bandwidth they achieve.

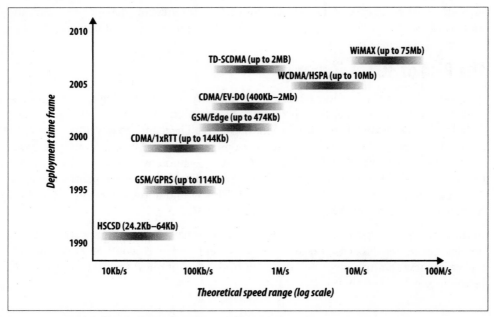

Figure A-1. Mobile protocols, bandwidth, and dates of deployment

Index

We'd like to hear your suggestions for improving our indexes. Send email to *index@oreilly.com*.

NOTES variable (NotePad), 120
NotesList class, 118
NOTES_ID variable (NotePad), 121
NOTES_TABLE_NAME variable (NotePad), 120

O

OFDM (Orthogonal Frequency Division Multiplexing), 307
onBind method, 10, 273
onCallStateChanged method, 289
OnClickListener method, 54, 167, 191
    checkboxes and, 197
onCreate method, 8
    ContentProvider method, extending, 119
    onStart method and, 10
    SQLiteOpenHelper class and, 102
onCreateOptionsMenu method, 146
onDestroy method, 9, 10
onDraw method, 227, 236
OnFocusChangeListener class, 180
onKey methods, 178
onKeyDown method, 177
onLayout method, 226
onMeasure method, 226
onPause method, 9, 10
onResume method, 9, 10
onStart method, 9
    onCreate method, 10
onStop method, 9, 10
onTouchEvent method, 177
onTransact method (AIDL), 271
onUpdate method, 104
onUpgrade method, 102
Open Handset Alliance, 3, 4
open source software, 4
OpenGL graphics, 252–255
Orthogonal Frequency Division Multiplexing (OFDM), 307
Outline pane (Debug perspective), 65
Outline view (Debug perspective), 34
Overview view (manifest file), 36

P

Package Explorer (Eclipse), 25, 59
Package Explorer (Java perspective), 33
package parameter (manifest), 44
Paint, 228, 246

parents of View trees, 208
PATH environment variables, setting up, 13, 16
PathEffect attribute (Paint), 246
PdpConnection class, 297
PDPContextState class, 297
performance of emulation versus device, 88
permissions, 45
Permissions view (manifest file), 38
persistent data storage, 101–136
perspectives (Eclipse), 33
    DDMS, 74
    Debug, 65
        Logcat, 67
Phone interface, 294
PhoneBase class, 294
PhoneFactory class, 294
PhoneNotifier interface, 294
PhoneNumberFormattingTextWatcher package (android.telephony), 288
PhoneNumberUtils package (android.telephony), 288
phones, connecting to, 277–286
PhoneStateIntentReceiver class, 294
PhoneStateListener package (android.telephony), 288
PhoneSubInfo class, 294
pixels (px) dimensions, 51
    positioning layouts, 215
Platform Porting Kit (Android), 5
PNG files, creating icons with, 89
points (pts) dimensions, 52
pound sign (#)
    adb shell prompt and, 73
    defining colors, 49
PppLink class, 297
preorder traversal, 159
private keys, 92
.project file, 31
projection parameter (managedQuery), 132
proprietary software stacks, developing mobile applications and, 4
<provider> tag, 128
providers, connecting to, 149
Proxy objects, 271
ps shell command, 73
pts (points) dimensions, 52
public keys, generating, 92
publishing applications, 87–97

pull remote local adb command, 74
push local remote adb command, 74
px (pixels) dimensions, 51
    positioning layouts, 215

Q

QEMU emulator, 39
query method, 110
    ContentProvider method, extending, 119

R

R.java file, 32, 36, 47
Radio Interface Layer (RIL), 291
RadioButtons, 193–198
relational databases, 101
RelativeLayout, 216
remote methods, 257
remote procedure calls (RPCs), 274
requestFocus method, 180
res (resources) subdirectory, 22, 31
    icon files and, 45
.res files, 20
resources subdirectory (see res subdirectory)
RIL (Radio Interface Layer), 291
RIL class, 297
RILConstants interface, 297
rm shell command, 73
rotate method, 248
rows (databases), 101
RPCs (Remote Procedure Calls), 274
runtime data collection, 75

S

Satellite View (MapView), 141
savedInstanceState bundle, 23
scaled pixels (sp) dimensions, 52
    positioning layouts, 215
Screen Capture pane (DDMS), 75
screen resolution/orientation of emulation
        versus device, 88
ScrollView, 204
SDK (Software Development Kit), 5, 13
    DDMS, 74
    debugging (see debugging)
    installing, 15
second generation (2G) digital cellulars, 305
SELECT statements, 102
selection parameter (managedQuery), 132

selectionArgs parameter (managedQuery),
    132
semiconductor companies, 5
Series 60 (Nokia), 4
server (adb), 71
services, 7, 273
ServiceState package (android.telephony), 288
ServiceStateTracker class, 298
setClickable map attribute, 143
setEnabled map attribute, 143
setMatrix method, 236
setMeasuredDimensions method, 224
setOnClickListener method, 167
setSatellite map attribute, 143
setStreetView map attribute, 143
setTraffic map attribute, 143
Shader (Paint), 246
ShadowLayer (Paint), 246
shadows, 246
shell adb command, 73
signing applications, 87–97
SimCard interface, 294
SimConstants interface, 298
SimException class, 298
SIMFileHandler class, 298
SimFileNotFound class, 298
SimPhoneBookInterfaceManager class, 298
SimProvider class, 298
SIMRecords class, 298
SimSmsInterfaceManager class, 298
SimTlv class, 298
SimUtils class, 298
SMSDispatcher class, 298
SmsHeader class, 298
SmsRawData class, 298
SmsResponse class, 299
sNotesProjectionMap variable (NotePad), 120
social networking, 27–30
Software Development Kit (see SDK)
software, writing for mobile applications, 5
sortOrder parameter (managedQuery), 132
Source Editor (Java perspective), 33
source files, 20
Source View (Debug perspective), 34
sources (src) subdirectory, 20, 30
sp (scaled pixels) dimensions, 52
    positioning layouts, 215
Spinner View, 50, 193–198
SQL (see databases)

SQLite, 53, 101–136
 adb shell and, 73
 as a database engine, 102
 updating data, 127
sqlite3 adb command, 73
SQLiteDatabase class
 modifying databases, 110
SQLiteOpenHelper class, 102
src (sources) subdirectory, 20, 30
.src files, 20
stack backtraces, 285
startActivity method, 139, 258
startActivityForResult method, 258, 264
startAnimation method (View), 247
startMethodTracing, 76
Step Over button (Debug toolbar), 66
stopMethodTracing, 76
Street View (MapView), 141
Stub interface, implementing, 271
subdirectories, building applications and, 20
super function, 103
SuppServiceNotification class, 299
surface view animation, 252
surfaceCreated method, 252
surfaceDestroyed method, 252
SurfaceHolder.Callback interface, 252
sUriMatcher variable (NotePad), 120
synchronized blocks, 161, 183

T

T-Mobile phones, running applications, 39–41
Tabbed Views (Java perspective), 33
TabContentFactory, 205
TabHost, 205–208
TableLayout, 213–215
tag:priority filter specs, 73
TDMA (Time Division Multiple Access), 306
Telephony, 75, 285, 287–303
 internals, 291–302
TelephonyIntents class, 295
TelephonyManager package
 (android.telephony), 288
TelephonyProperties class, 295
text, drawing, 230
TextView, 24, 188–191
 element (XML), 50
threads, 179–183

Threads/Heap/File Explorer pane (DDMS), 35, 74
Time Division Multiple Access (see TDMA)
TitleEditor Activity, 116
TitleEditor class, 118
toolkit, 12
tools (debugging), 57
touch events, listening for, 173
touch focus, 180
touchscreen operation of emulation versus device, 88
trace analysis, 75
Traceview, 58, 75–80
Traffic View (MapView), 141
transition animation, 247–250
translate method, 248
triangulation, 138

U

Ubuntu Linux
 Dapper Drake, 14
 USB drivers, loading for ADB, 40
UI component objects, 160
UMTS (Universal Mobile Telecommunications Standard), 307
uniform resource identifier (URI), 115
uninstall adb command, 74
Universal Mobile Telecommunications Standard (UMTS), 307
unmarshalled data, 266
unsigned versions of applications, 95
update method, 110
 ContentProvider method, extending, 119
UPDATE statements, 102, 127
uri parameter (managedQuery), 132
URIs (uniform resource identifiers), 115
<uses-permission android:name=...> element, 45
USP drivers, debugging on phones, 39

V

values folder, 33
Variables and Breakpoints pane (Debug perspective), 65
Variables, Breakpoints and Expressions view (Debug perspective), 34
versions, for applications, 90
vi editor, 16

View class, 158
view-model, 227
ViewGroups, 162, 198–208
    container views and, 222
    widgets and, 222
Views, 33, 188–198
    building, 157–185
    widgets and, 221
VoiceMailConstants class, 299
VoIP (Voice over IP), 302

W

WCDMA (Wideband CDMA), 307
Web Standard Tools (WST), 15
WHERE clause, 127
Wideband CDMA (WCDMA), 307
widgets, 187–218
    2D and 3D graphics and, 221–243
    Button, 51
Windows, 13, 14
    environment variables, setting up, 16
    USB drivers, loading for ADB, 39
Windows Mobile (Microsoft), 4
wireless protocols, 305–308
WST (Web Standard Tools), 15

X

x.trace file, 77
XML (eXtensible Markup Language), 23
    AndroidManifest.xml file and, 31
    initialization parameters in, 44–46
    Java code and, 43

Z

zoomIn method, 143
zoomInFixing( ) method, 144
zoomOut method, 144
zoomToSpan( ) method, 144

About the Authors

Rick Rogers has been developing and marketing embedded systems for more than 30 years. He has focused on software for mobile phones for the last nine years, working with Linux and other operating environments for companies such as Compaq, Intel, and Marvell Semiconductor. He is currently a mobile solutions architect at Wind River Systems.

John Lombardo has been working with Linux since version 0.9. His first book, *Embedded Linux* (Sams), was published in 2001. Since then, he's worked on several embedded products, including phones and routers. John holds a B.S. in computer science and is working on his M.B.A.

Zigurd Mednieks is chief user interface architect at D2 Technologies, a leading provider of IP communications technology, and is also a consultant and advisor to companies in the field of embedded user interfaces. He has held senior management positions at companies making mobile games, communications equipment, and computer telephony applications, and has written and contributed to books on programming and communications technology.

Blake Meike has more than 10 years of experience with Java. He has developed applications using most of the GUI toolkits and several of the Java mobile device platforms. He likes Android a lot.

Colophon

The animal on the cover of *Android Application Development* is an Eastern quoll (*Dasyurus viverrinus*), an endangered marsupial otherwise known as the Eastern native cat. Eastern quolls grow to about the same size as household cats, and their thick fur ranges in color from gray to brown and is dotted with white spots. However, unlike others of its kind (the Tiger quoll, for example), no spots cover its long, hairy tail.

No longer widespread throughout mainland Australia, the Eastern quoll remains common in Tasmania. It lives in rain forests and alpine areas, though it prefers dry grasslands and forests bordered by pastoral agricultural fields. Within these habitats, the Eastern quoll hunts for small mammals and steals food from the much larger Tasmanian devil by night; by day, it slumbers in logs and in nests in underground burrows.

While female Eastern quolls can birth up to 30 babies, typically only 6 will survive, as the mother only has 6 teats in her pouch for her children. Male and female Eastern quolls reach sexual maturation less than a year after being born. Provided it survives infancy, the quoll will live an average life span of six years.

Although some farmers dislike the quoll because it occasionally feeds on chickens and other small mammals (quolls will feed on injured or ill farm animals), the quoll also benefits farmers by consuming crop pests, mice, and carrion.

The cover image is from Wood's *Animate Creation Vol. I*. The cover font is Adobe ITC Garamond. The text font is Linotype Birka; the heading font is Adobe Myriad Condensed; and the code font is LucasFont's TheSansMonoCondensed.